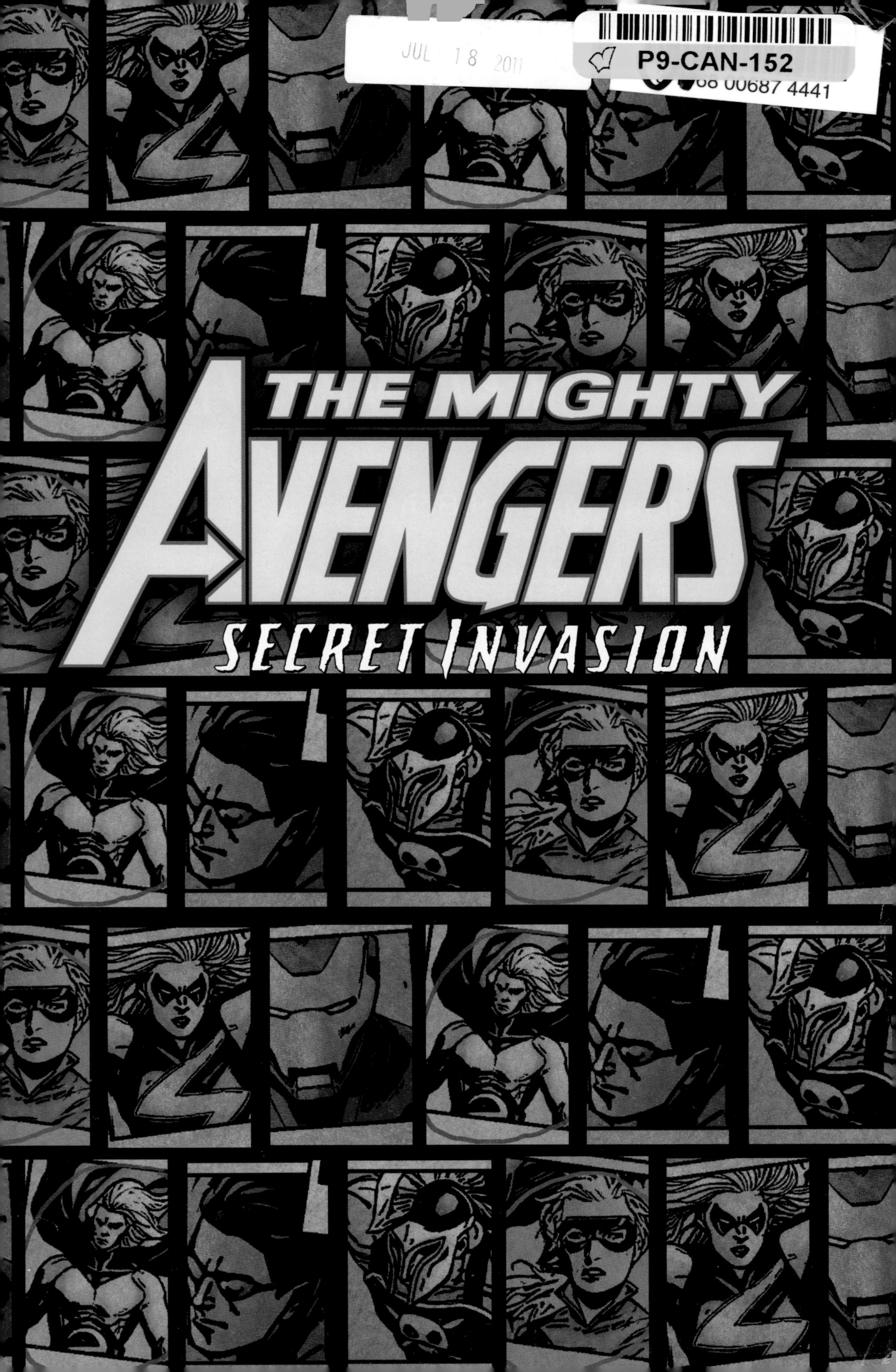

THE MIGHTY AVENGERS
SECRET INVASION

THE MIGHTY AVENGERS
SECRET INVASION

WRITER: Brian Michael Bendis

ISSUES #12-13
ARTIST: Alex Maleev
COLORIST: Matt Hollingsworth

ISSUE #14
PENCILER: Khoi Pham
INKER: Danny Miki
COLORIST: Dean White

ISSUE #15
BREAKDOWNS: John Romita Jr.
FINISHES: Klaus Janson & Tom Palmer
COLORISTS: Edgar Delgado with Guru eFX

LETTERER: Artmonkeys' Dave Lanphear
COVER ART: Marko Djurdjevic
ASSISTANT EDITOR: Thomas Brennan
ASSOCIATE EDITOR: Molly Lazer
EDITOR: Tom Brevoort

COLLECTION EDITOR: Jennifer Grünwald
ASSISTANT EDITORS: Cory Levine & John Denning
EDITOR, SPECIAL PROJECTS: Mark D. Beazley
SENIOR EDITOR, SPECIAL PROJECTS: Jeff Youngquist
SENIOR VICE PRESIDENT OF SALES: David Gabriel
PRODUCTION: Jerry Kalinowski
BOOK DESIGNER: Carrie Beadle

EDITOR IN CHIEF: Joe Quesada
PUBLISHER: Dan Buckley

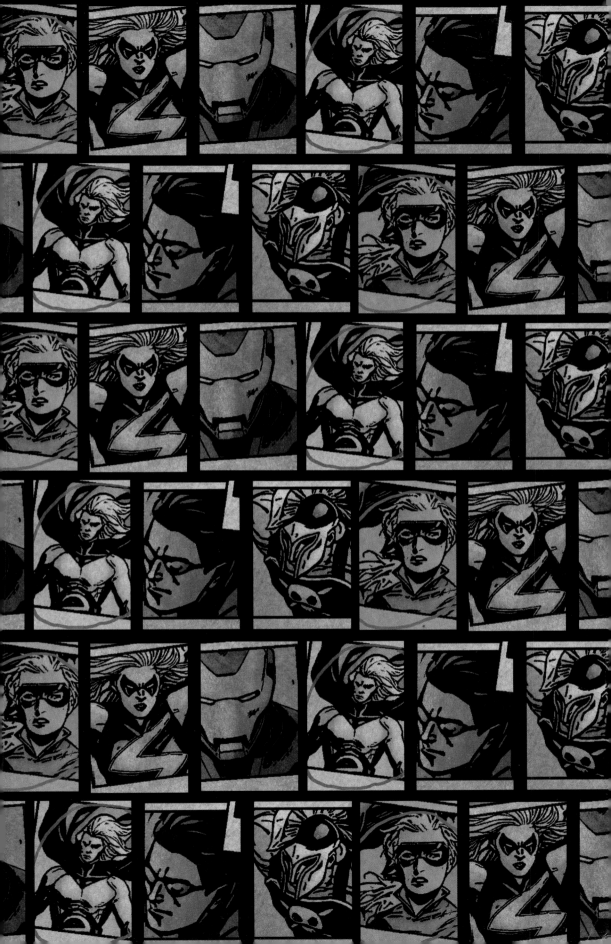

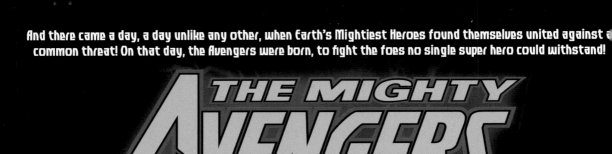

And there came a day, a day unlike any other, when Earth's Mightiest Heroes found themselves united against a common threat! On that day, the Avengers were born, to fight the foes no single super hero could withstand!

THE MIGHTY AVENGERS

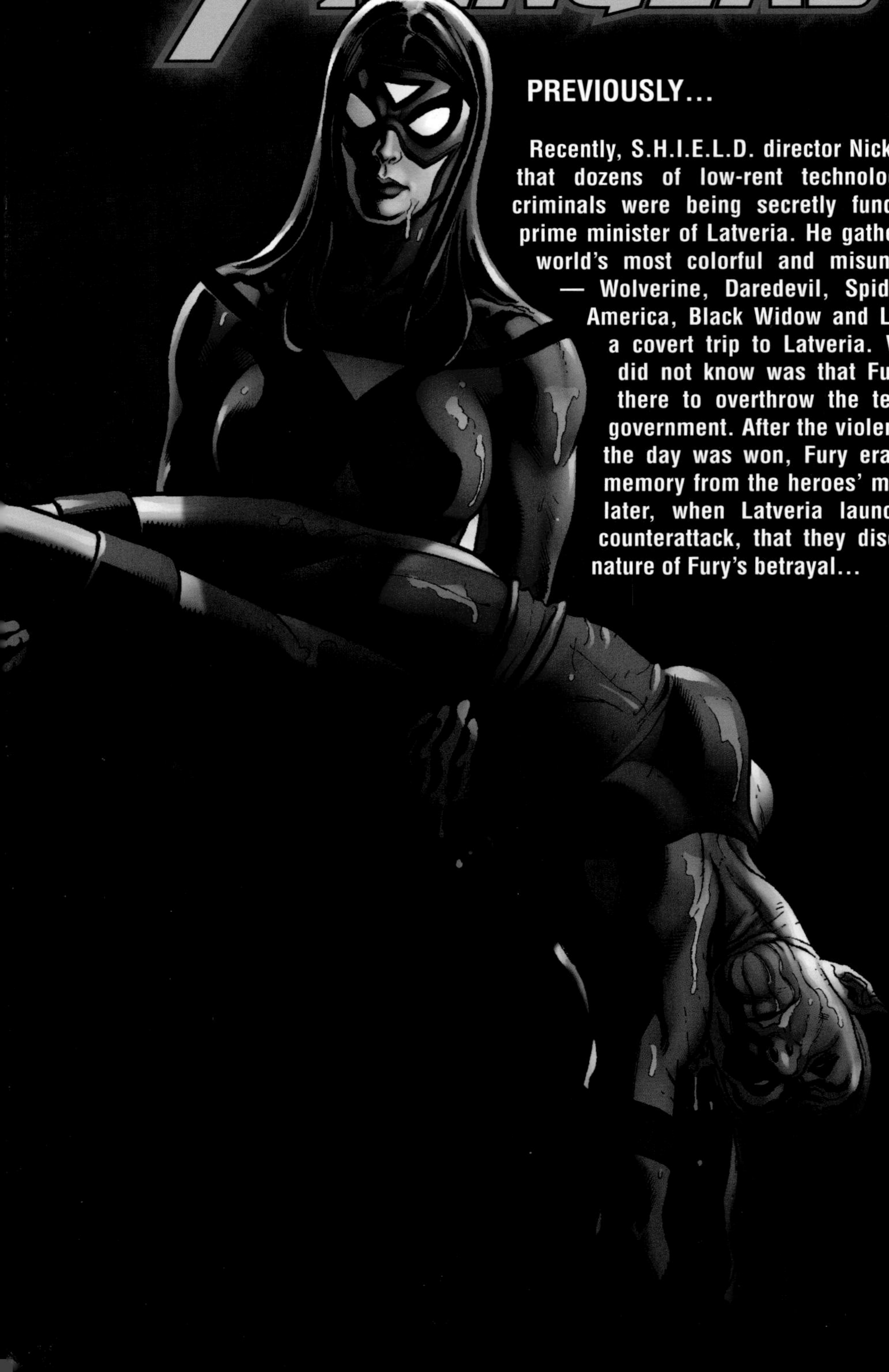

PREVIOUSLY...

Recently, S.H.I.E.L.D. director Nick Fury discovered that dozens of low-rent technology-based super-criminals were being secretly funded by the new prime minister of Latveria. He gathered some of the world's most colorful and misunderstood heroes — Wolverine, Daredevil, Spider-Man, Captain America, Black Widow and Luke Cage — for a covert trip to Latveria. What the heroes did not know was that Fury brought them there to overthrow the terrorist Latverian government. After the violence was over and the day was won, Fury erased the horrible memory from the heroes' minds. It was only later, when Latveria launched a vengeful counterattack, that they discovered the true nature of Fury's betrayal...

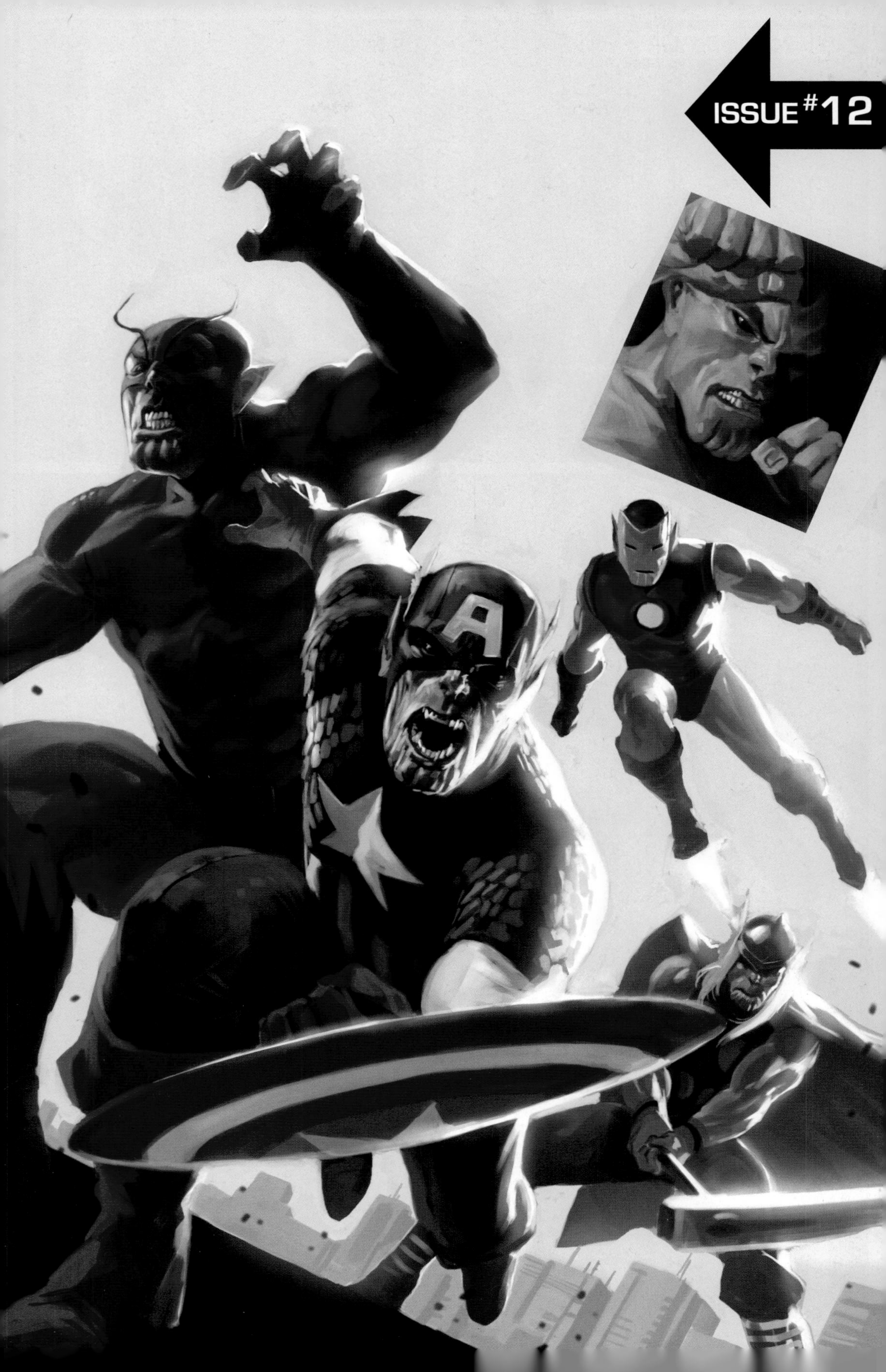
ISSUE #12

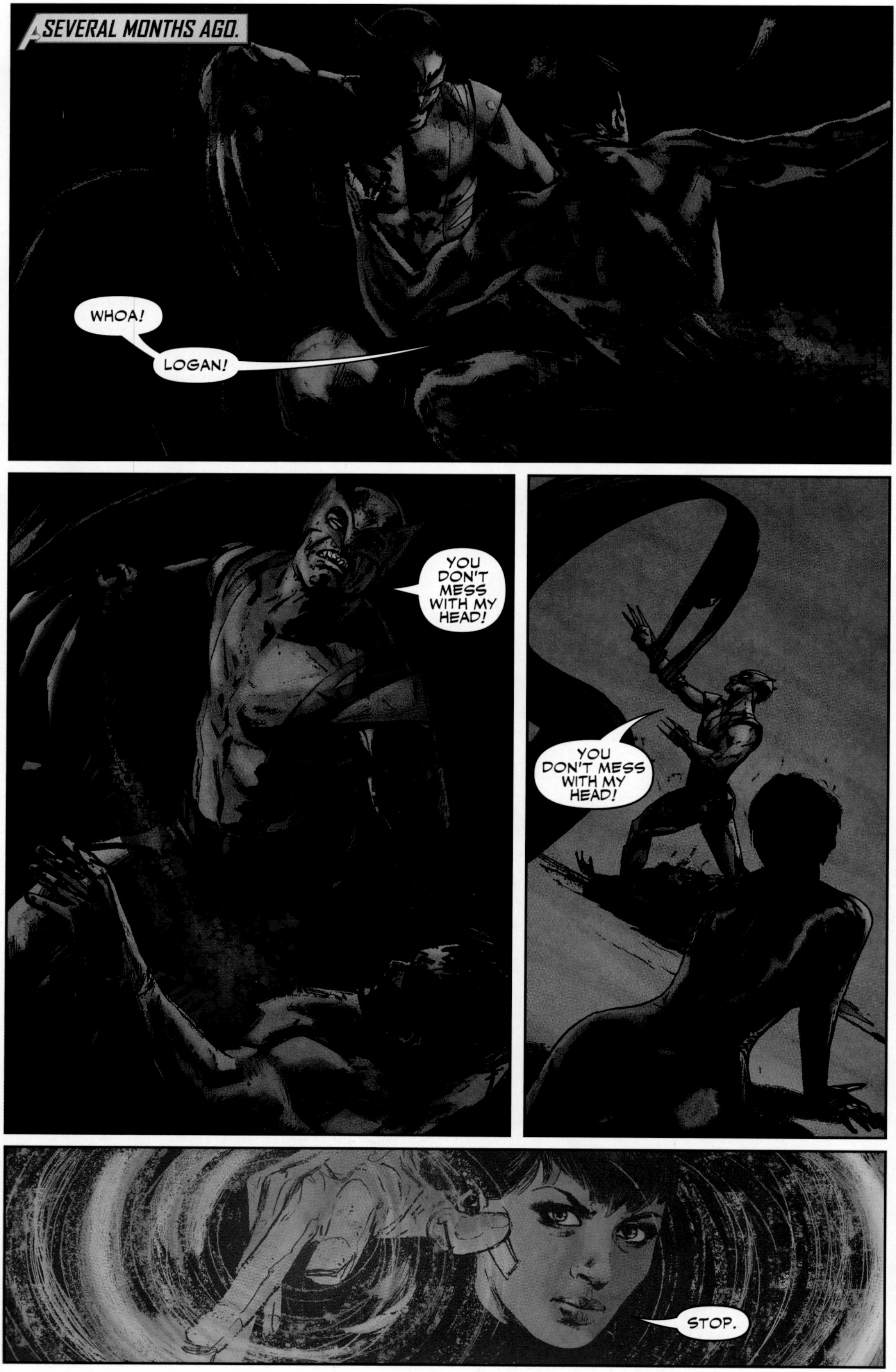
SEVERAL MONTHS AGO.
WHOA!
LOGAN!
YOU DON'T MESS WITH MY HEAD!
YOU DON'T MESS WITH MY HEAD!
STOP.

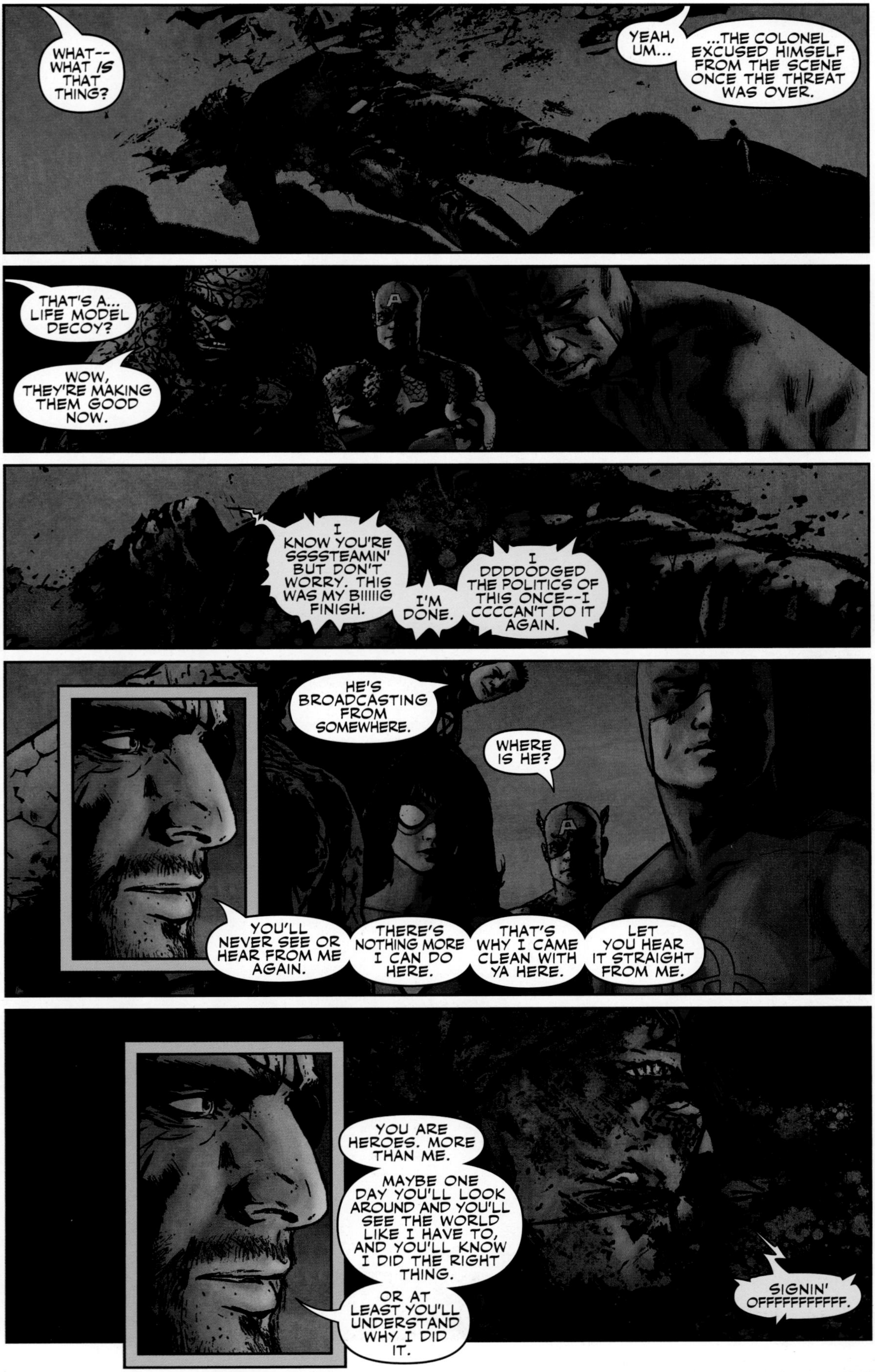
WHAT-- WHAT IS THAT THING?
YEAH, UM...
...THE COLONEL EXCUSED HIMSELF FROM THE SCENE ONCE THE THREAT WAS OVER.
THAT'S A... LIFE MODEL DECOY?
WOW, THEY'RE MAKING THEM GOOD NOW.
I KNOW YOU'RE SSSSTEAMIN' BUT DON'T WORRY. THIS WAS MY BIIIIIG FINISH.
I'M DONE.
I DDDDODGED THE POLITICS OF THIS ONCE--I CCCCAN'T DO IT AGAIN.
HE'S BROADCASTING FROM SOMEWHERE.
WHERE IS HE?
YOU'LL NEVER SEE OR HEAR FROM ME AGAIN.
THERE'S NOTHING MORE I CAN DO HERE.
THAT'S WHY I CAME CLEAN WITH YA HERE.
LET YOU HEAR IT STRAIGHT FROM ME.
YOU ARE HEROES. MORE THAN ME.
MAYBE ONE DAY YOU'LL LOOK AROUND AND YOU'LL SEE THE WORLD LIKE I HAVE TO, AND YOU'LL KNOW I DID THE RIGHT THING.
OR AT LEAST YOU'LL UNDERSTAND WHY I DID IT.
SIGNIN' OFFFFFFFFFFF.

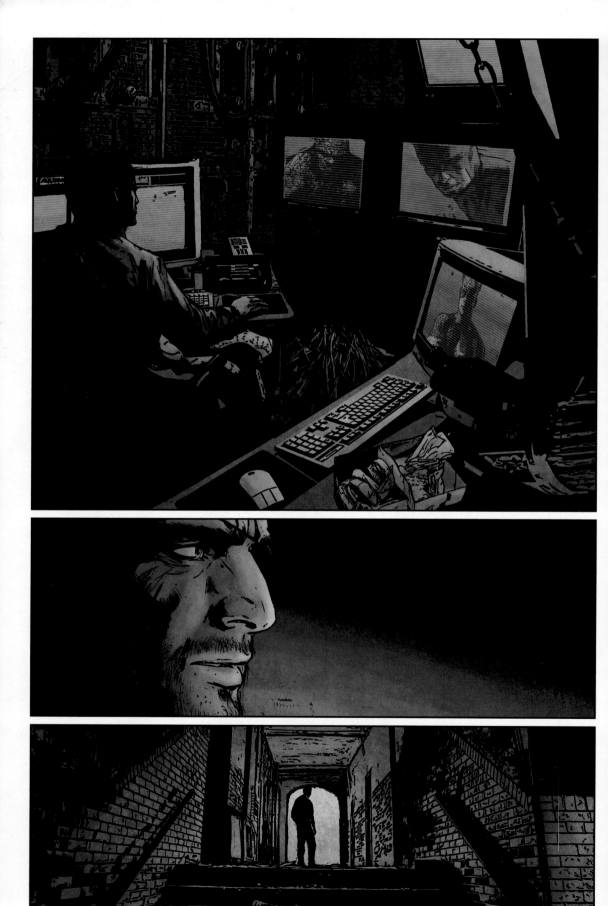

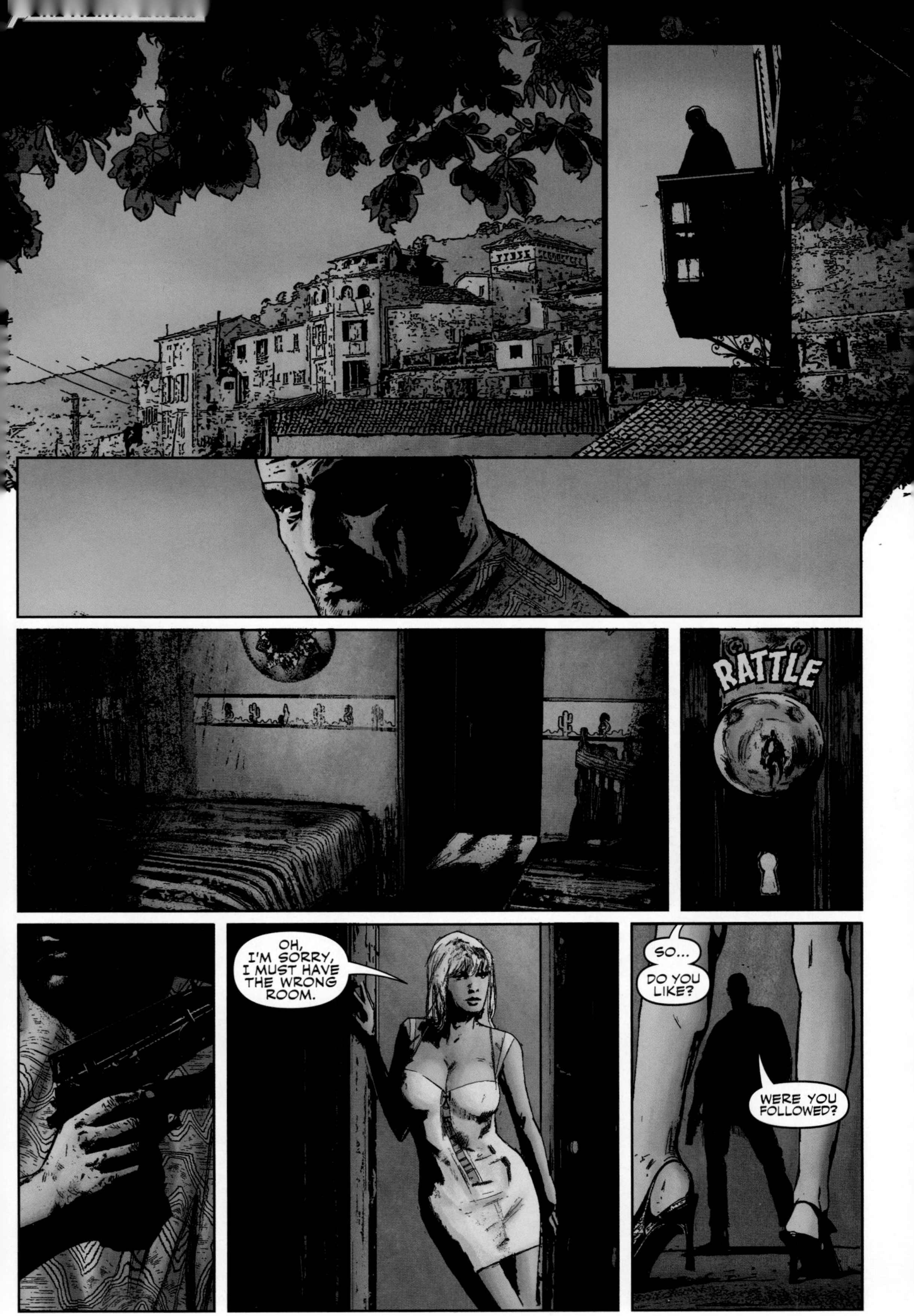
RATTLE
OH, I'M SORRY, I MUST HAVE THE WRONG ROOM.
SO...
DO YOU LIKE?
WERE YOU FOLLOWED?

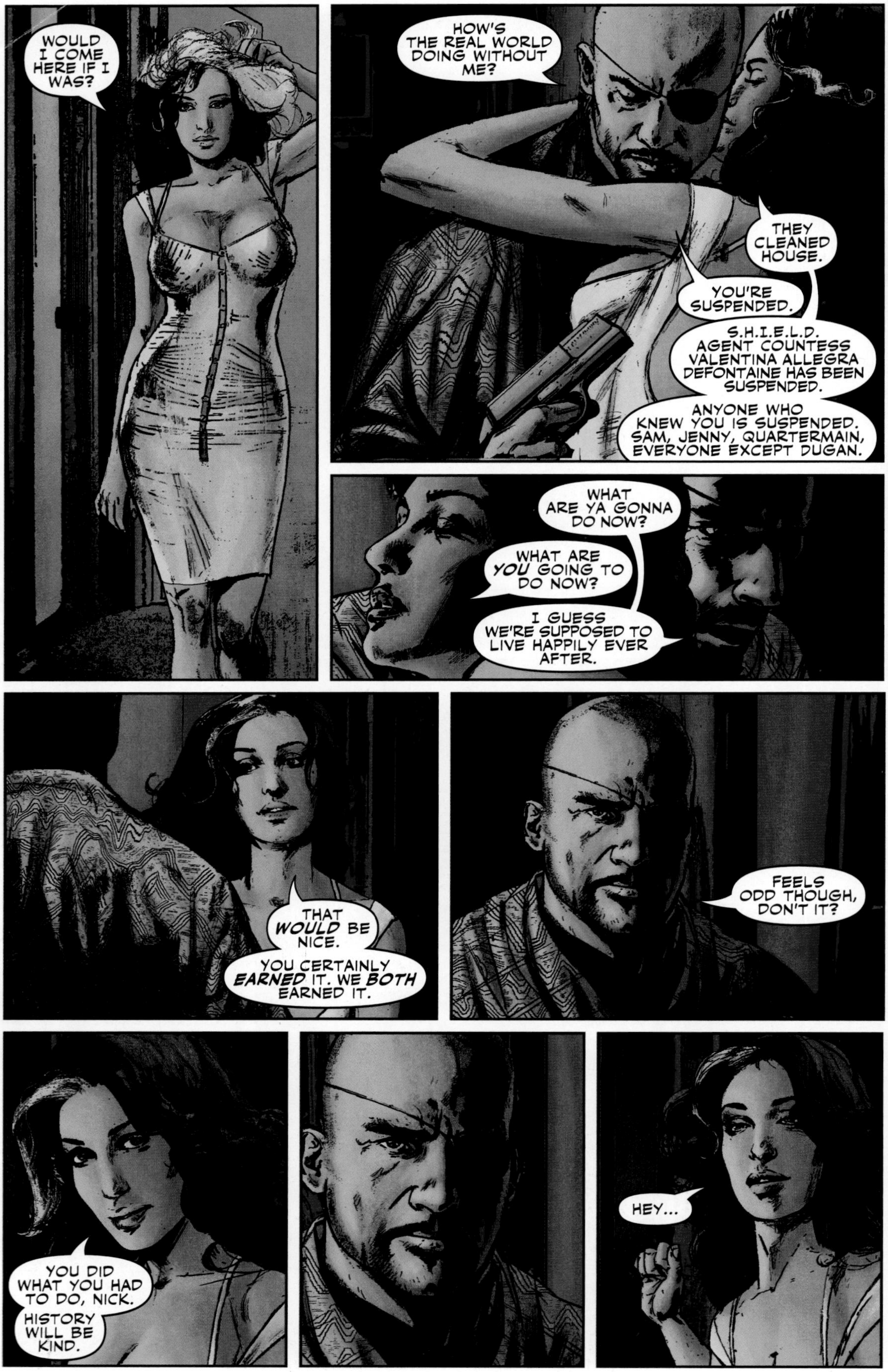
WOULD I COME HERE IF I WAS?
HOW'S THE REAL WORLD DOING WITHOUT ME?
THEY CLEANED HOUSE.
YOU'RE SUSPENDED.
S.H.I.E.L.D. AGENT COUNTESS VALENTINA ALLEGRA DEFONTAINE HAS BEEN SUSPENDED.
ANYONE WHO KNEW YOU IS SUSPENDED. SAM, JENNY, QUARTERMAIN, EVERYONE EXCEPT DUGAN.
WHAT ARE YA GONNA DO NOW?
WHAT ARE *YOU* GOING TO DO NOW?
I GUESS WE'RE SUPPOSED TO LIVE HAPPILY EVER AFTER.
THAT *WOULD* BE NICE.
YOU CERTAINLY *EARNED* IT. WE *BOTH* EARNED IT.
FEELS ODD THOUGH, DON'T IT?
YOU DID WHAT YOU HAD TO DO, NICK.
HISTORY WILL BE KIND.
HEY...

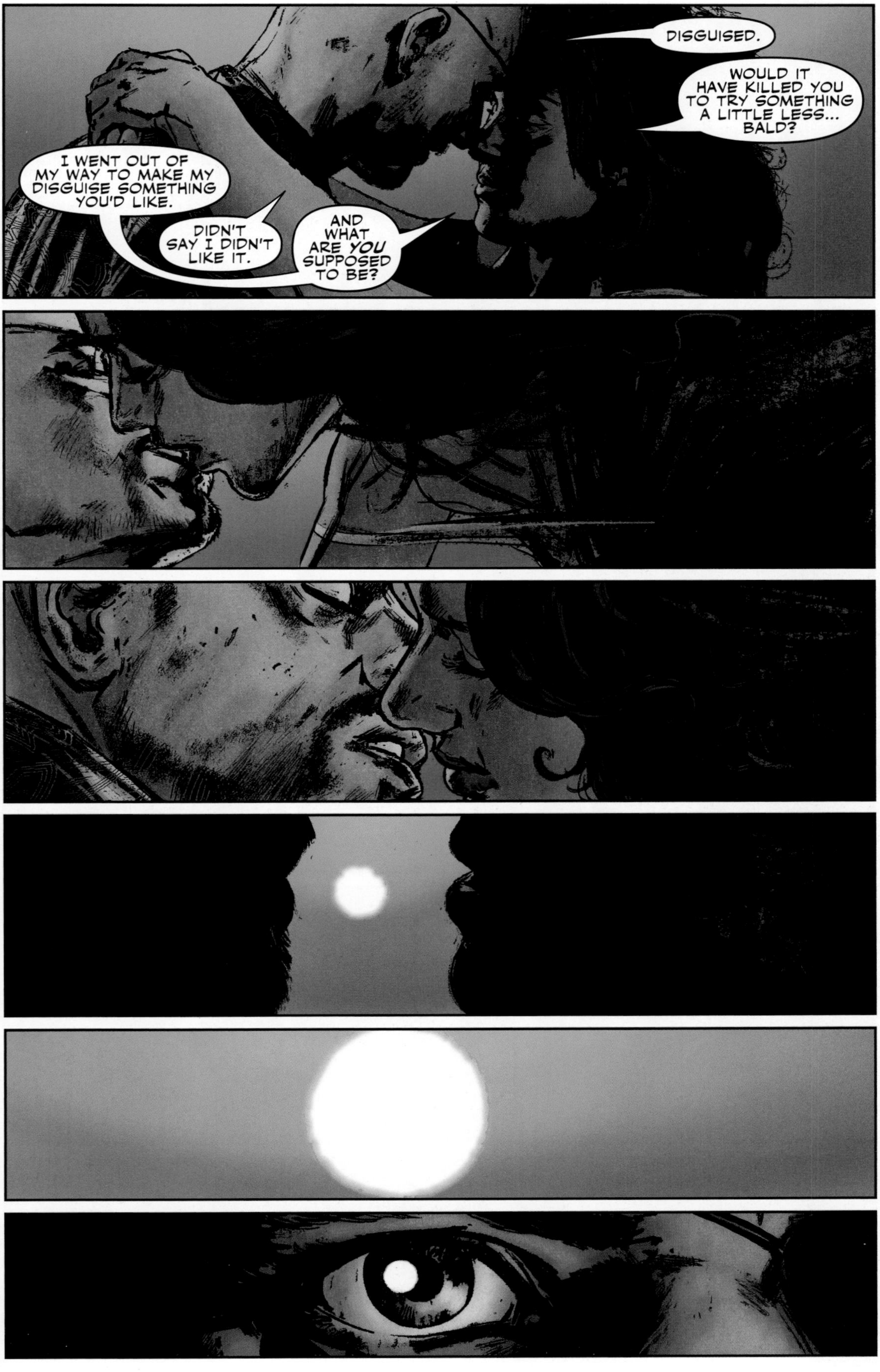
DISGUISED.
WOULD IT HAVE KILLED YOU TO TRY SOMETHING A LITTLE LESS... BALD?
I WENT OUT OF MY WAY TO MAKE MY DISGUISE SOMETHING YOU'D LIKE.
DIDN'T SAY I DIDN'T LIKE IT.
AND WHAT ARE *YOU* SUPPOSED TO BE?

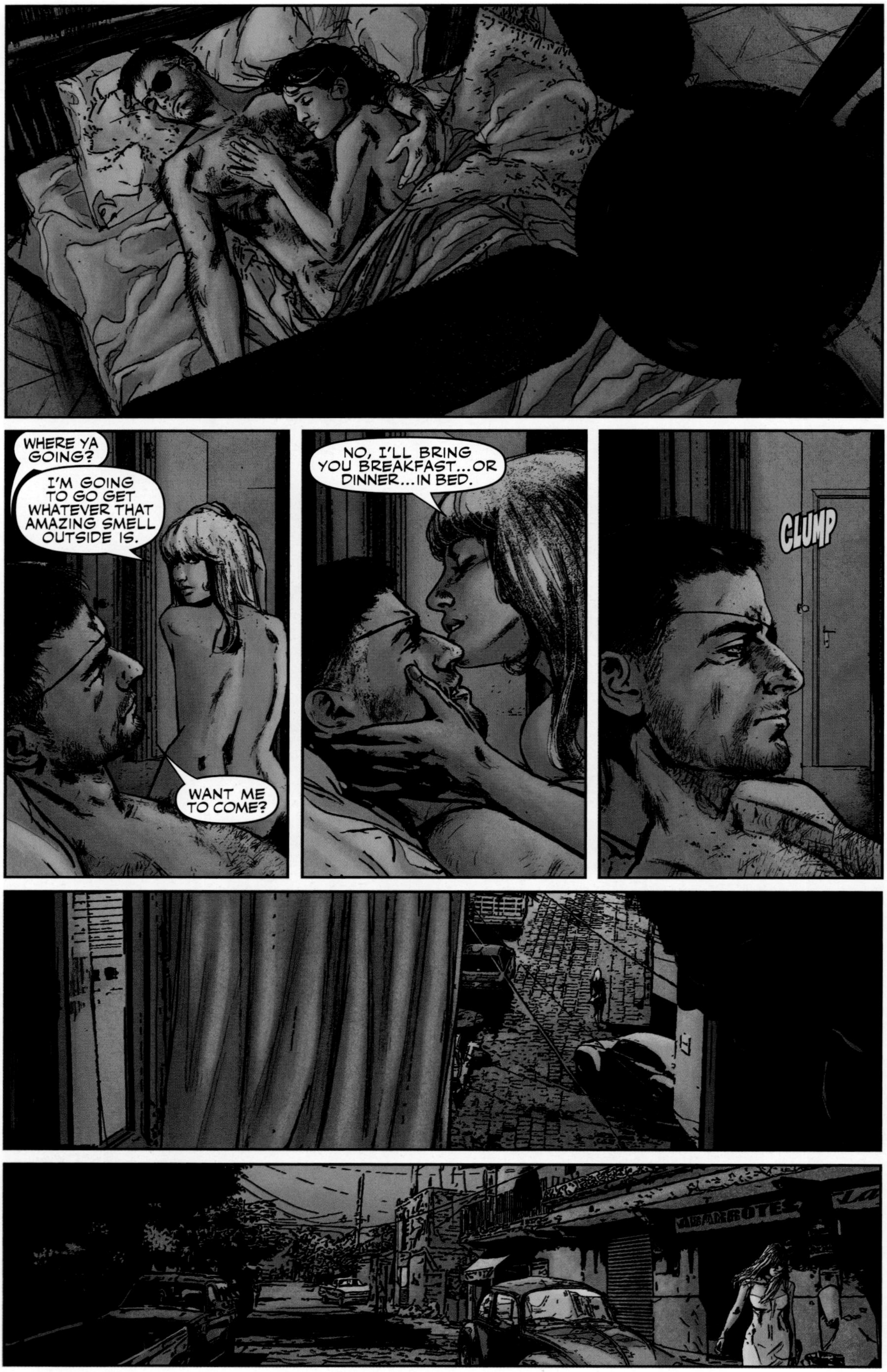
WHERE YA GOING?
I'M GOING TO GO GET WHATEVER THAT AMAZING SMELL OUTSIDE IS.
WANT ME TO COME?
NO, I'LL BRING YOU BREAKFAST...OR DINNER...IN BED.
CLUMP

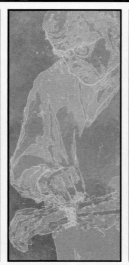

DID YOU GET THEM?

I GOT HIS CONFIDENCE. IT WILL TAKE A WEEK AT LEAST.

A WEEK?

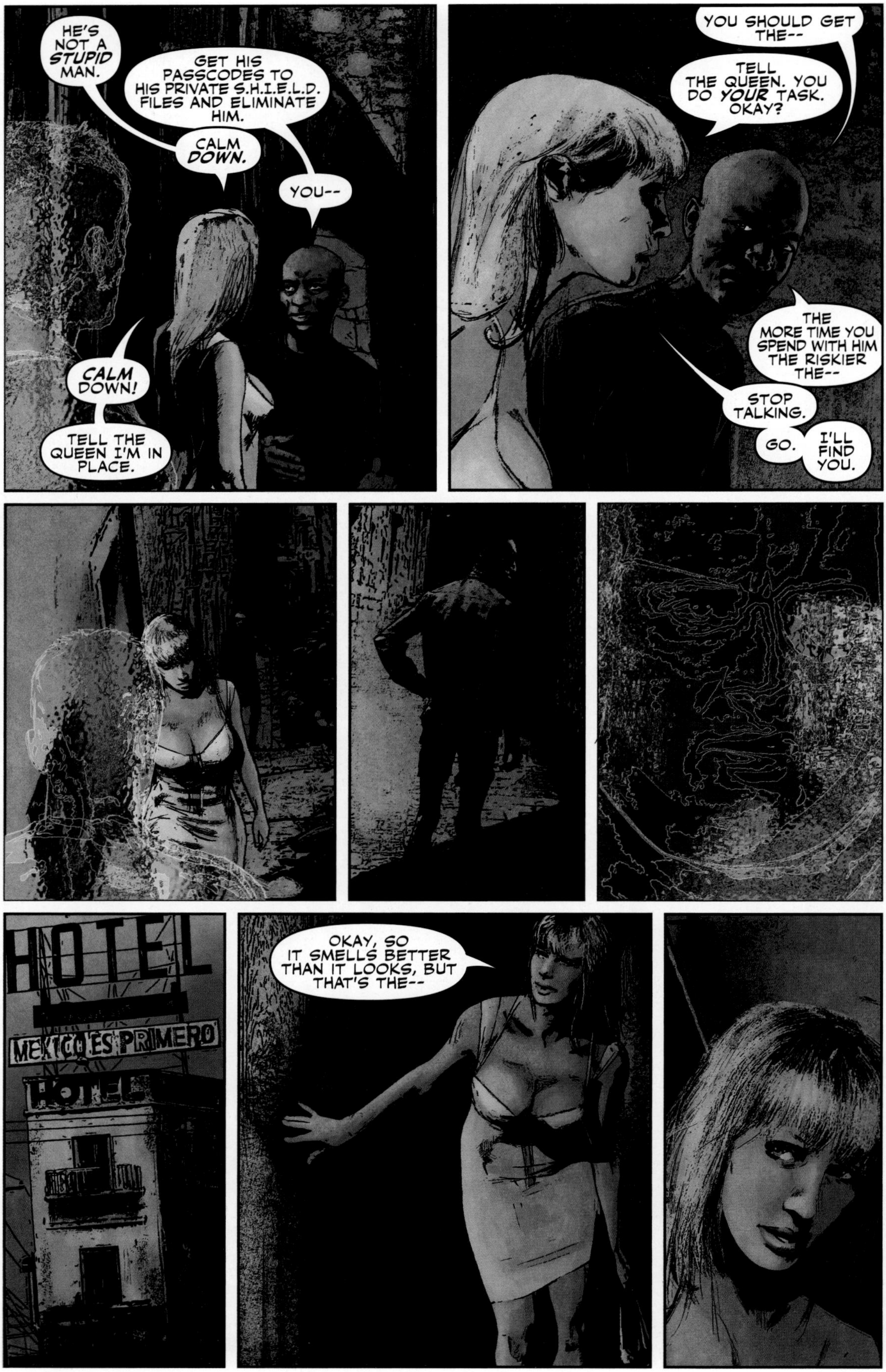

HE'S NOT A *STUPID* MAN.
GET HIS PASSCODES TO HIS PRIVATE S.H.I.E.L.D. FILES AND ELIMINATE HIM.
CALM *DOWN.*
YOU--
CALM DOWN!
TELL THE QUEEN I'M IN PLACE.
YOU SHOULD GET THE--
TELL THE QUEEN. YOU DO *YOUR* TASK. OKAY?
THE MORE TIME YOU SPEND WITH HIM THE RISKIER THE--
STOP TALKING.
GO.
I'LL FIND YOU.
HOTEL
MEXICO ES PRIMERO
HOTEL
OKAY, SO IT SMELLS BETTER THAN IT LOOKS, BUT THAT'S THE--

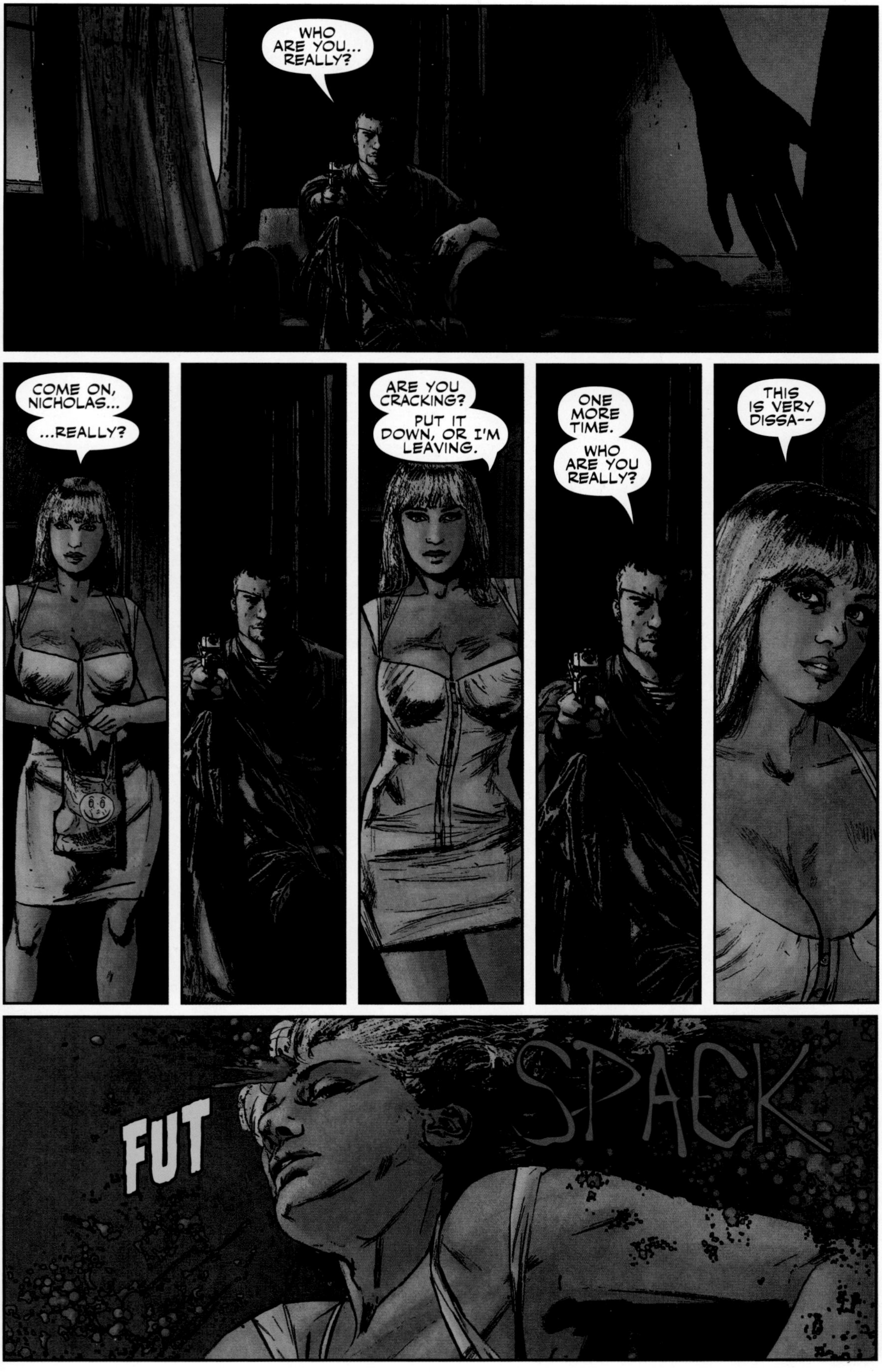
WHO ARE YOU... REALLY?
COME ON, NICHOLAS...
...REALLY?
ARE YOU CRACKING?
PUT IT DOWN, OR I'M LEAVING.
ONE MORE TIME.
WHO ARE YOU REALLY?
THIS IS VERY DISSA--
FUT
SPACK

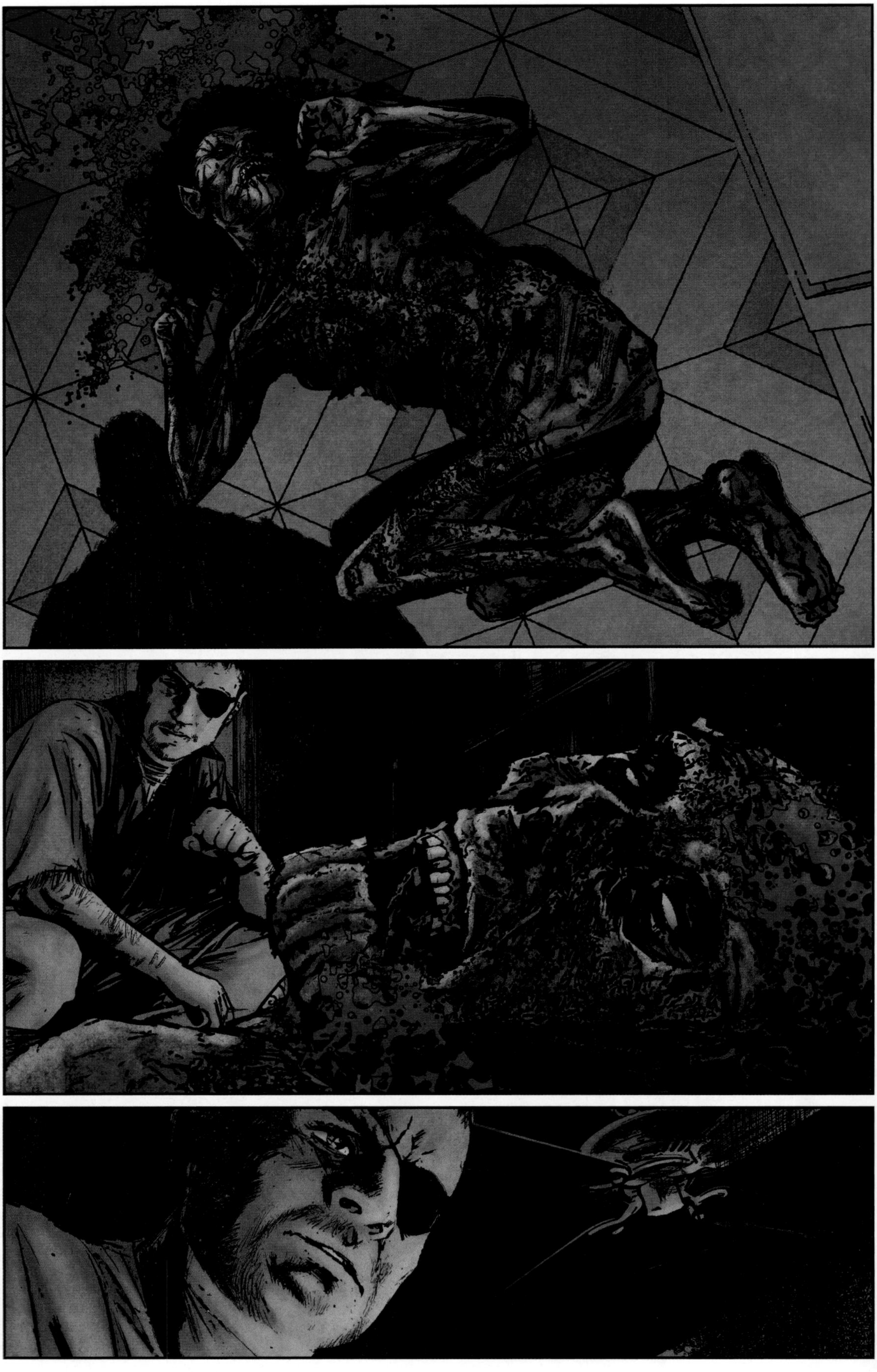

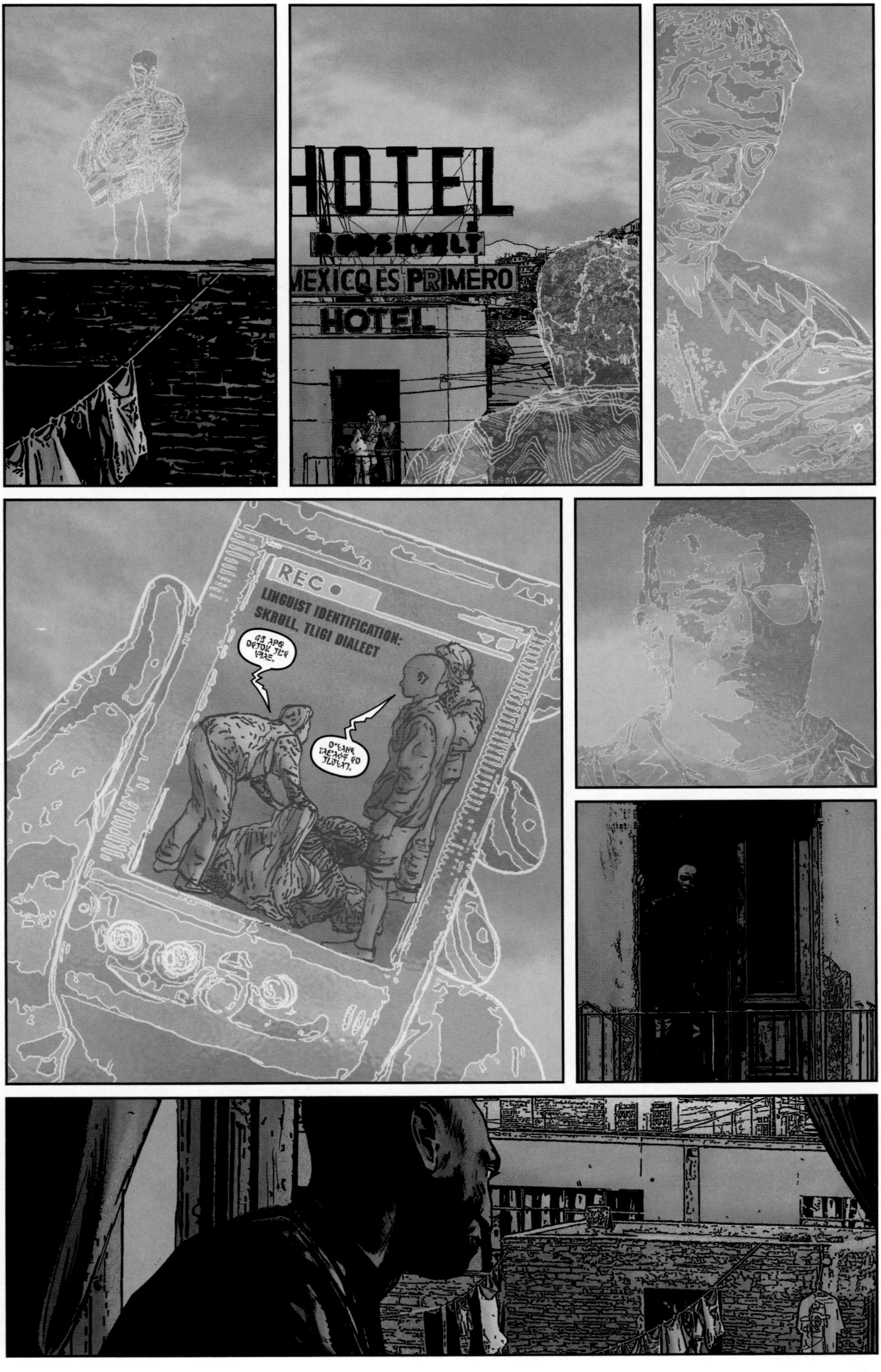
HOTEL
ROOSEVELT
MEXICO ES PRIMERO
HOTEL
REC
LINGUIST IDENTIFICATION:
SKRULL, TLIGI DIALECT

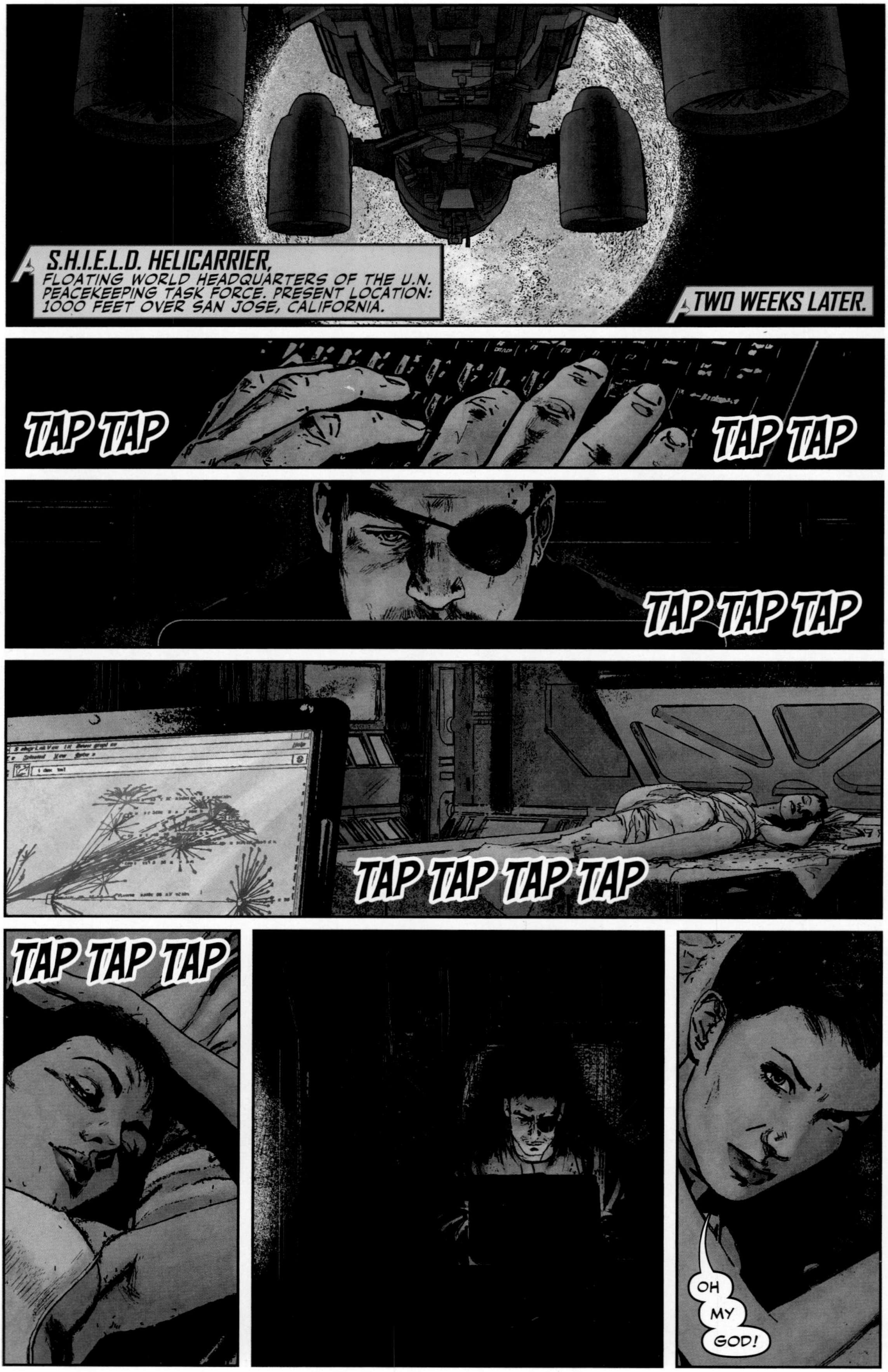
S.H.I.E.L.D. HELICARRIER,
FLOATING WORLD HEADQUARTERS OF THE U.N. PEACEKEEPING TASK FORCE. PRESENT LOCATION: 1000 FEET OVER SAN JOSE, CALIFORNIA.
TWO WEEKS LATER.
TAP TAP
TAP TAP
TAP TAP TAP
TAP TAP TAP TAP
TAP TAP TAP
OH MY GOD!

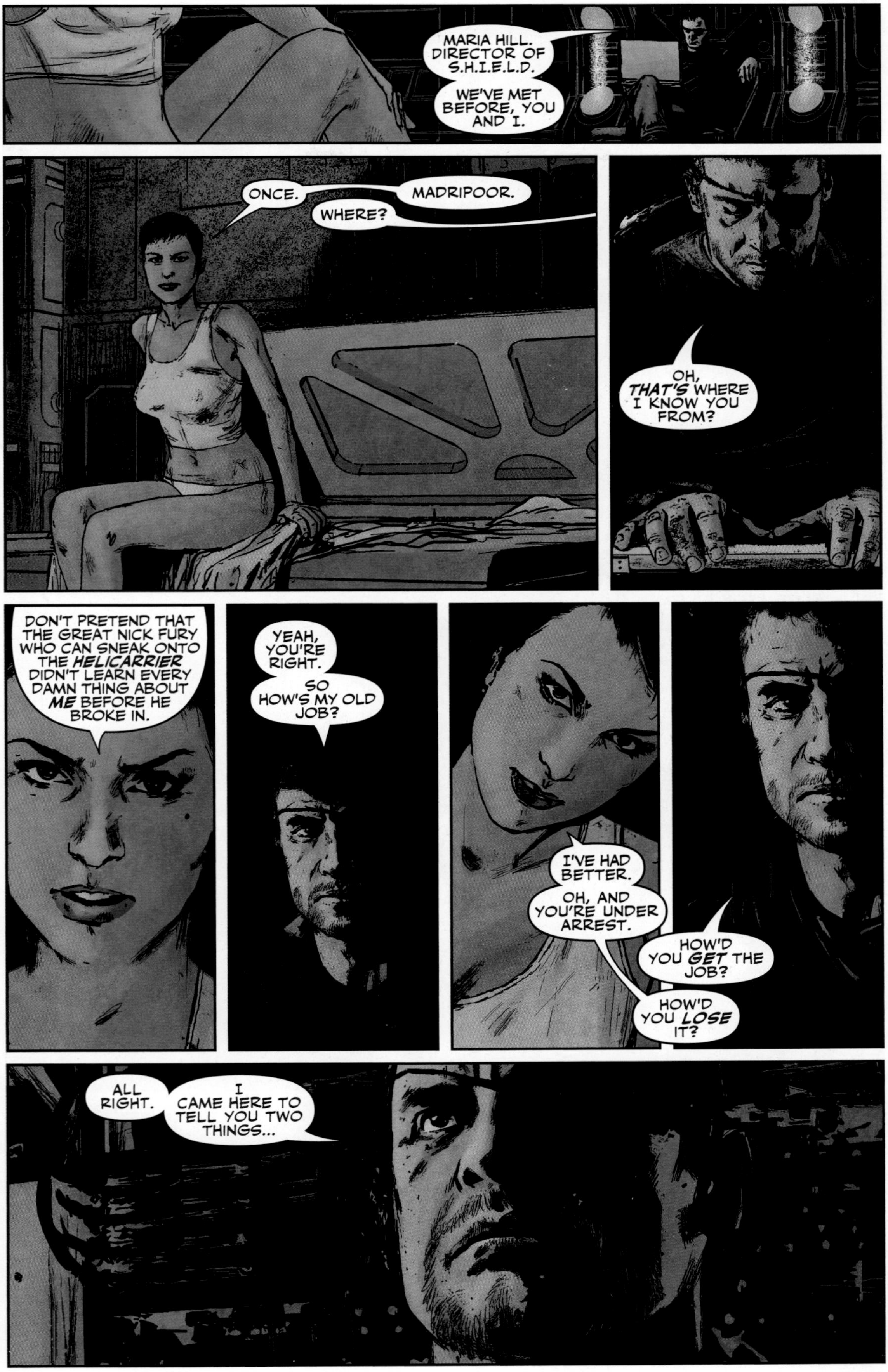
MARIA HILL. DIRECTOR OF S.H.I.E.L.D.
WE'VE MET BEFORE, YOU AND I.
ONCE.
WHERE?
MADRIPOOR.
OH, *THAT'S* WHERE I KNOW YOU FROM?
DON'T PRETEND THAT THE GREAT NICK FURY WHO CAN SNEAK ONTO THE *HELICARRIER* DIDN'T LEARN EVERY DAMN THING ABOUT *ME* BEFORE HE BROKE IN.
YEAH, YOU'RE RIGHT.
SO HOW'S MY OLD JOB?
I'VE HAD BETTER.
OH, AND YOU'RE UNDER ARREST.
HOW'D YOU *GET* THE JOB?
HOW'D YOU *LOSE* IT?
ALL RIGHT.
I CAME HERE TO TELL YOU TWO THINGS...

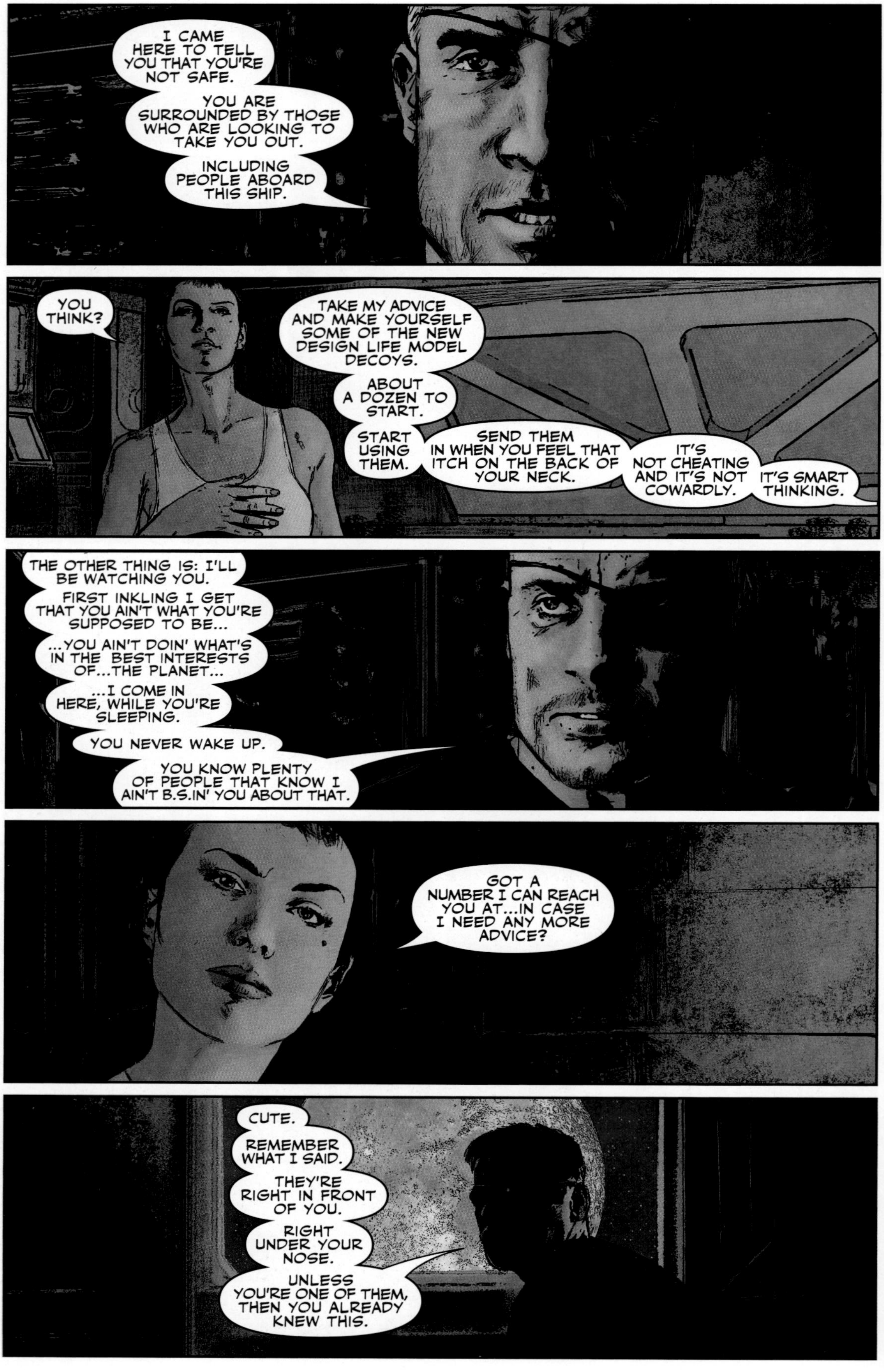
I CAME HERE TO TELL YOU THAT YOU'RE NOT SAFE.
YOU ARE SURROUNDED BY THOSE WHO ARE LOOKING TO TAKE YOU OUT.
INCLUDING PEOPLE ABOARD THIS SHIP.
YOU THINK?
TAKE MY ADVICE AND MAKE YOURSELF SOME OF THE NEW DESIGN LIFE MODEL DECOYS.
ABOUT A DOZEN TO START.
START USING THEM.
SEND THEM IN WHEN YOU FEEL THAT ITCH ON THE BACK OF YOUR NECK.
IT'S NOT CHEATING AND IT'S NOT COWARDLY.
IT'S SMART THINKING.
THE OTHER THING IS: I'LL BE WATCHING YOU.
FIRST INKLING I GET THAT YOU AIN'T WHAT YOU'RE SUPPOSED TO BE...
...YOU AIN'T DOIN' WHAT'S IN THE BEST INTERESTS OF...THE PLANET...
...I COME IN HERE, WHILE YOU'RE SLEEPING.
YOU NEVER WAKE UP.
YOU KNOW PLENTY OF PEOPLE THAT KNOW I AIN'T B.S.IN' YOU ABOUT THAT.
GOT A NUMBER I CAN REACH YOU AT...IN CASE I NEED ANY MORE ADVICE?
CUTE.
REMEMBER WHAT I SAID.
THEY'RE RIGHT IN FRONT OF YOU.
RIGHT UNDER YOUR NOSE.
UNLESS YOU'RE ONE OF THEM, THEN YOU ALREADY KNEW THIS.

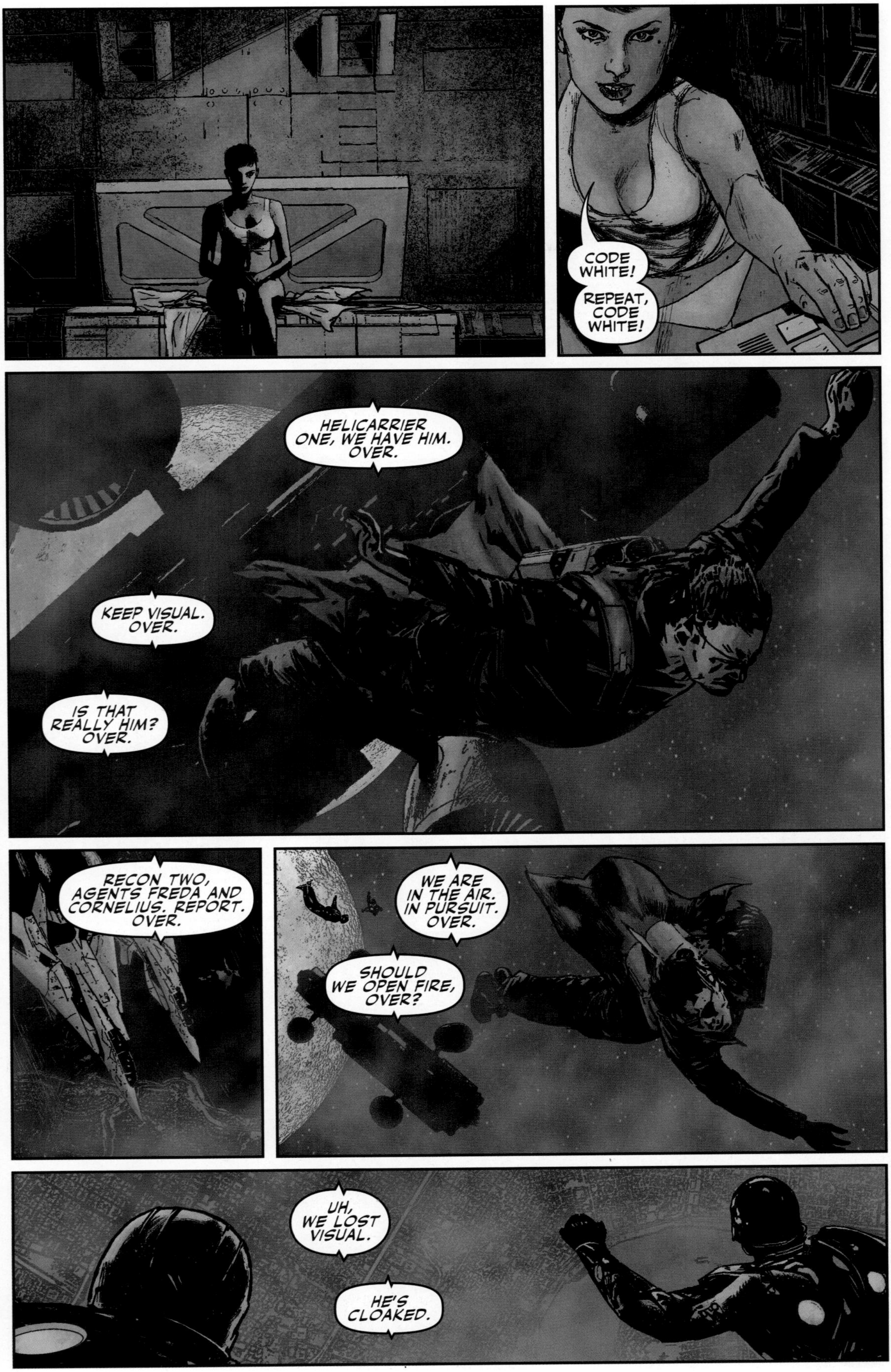
CODE WHITE!
REPEAT, CODE WHITE!
HELICARRIER ONE, WE HAVE HIM. OVER.
KEEP VISUAL. OVER.
IS THAT REALLY HIM? OVER.
RECON TWO, AGENTS FREDA AND CORNELIUS. REPORT. OVER.
WE ARE IN THE AIR. IN PURSUIT. OVER.
SHOULD WE OPEN FIRE, OVER?
UH, WE LOST VISUAL.
HE'S CLOAKED.

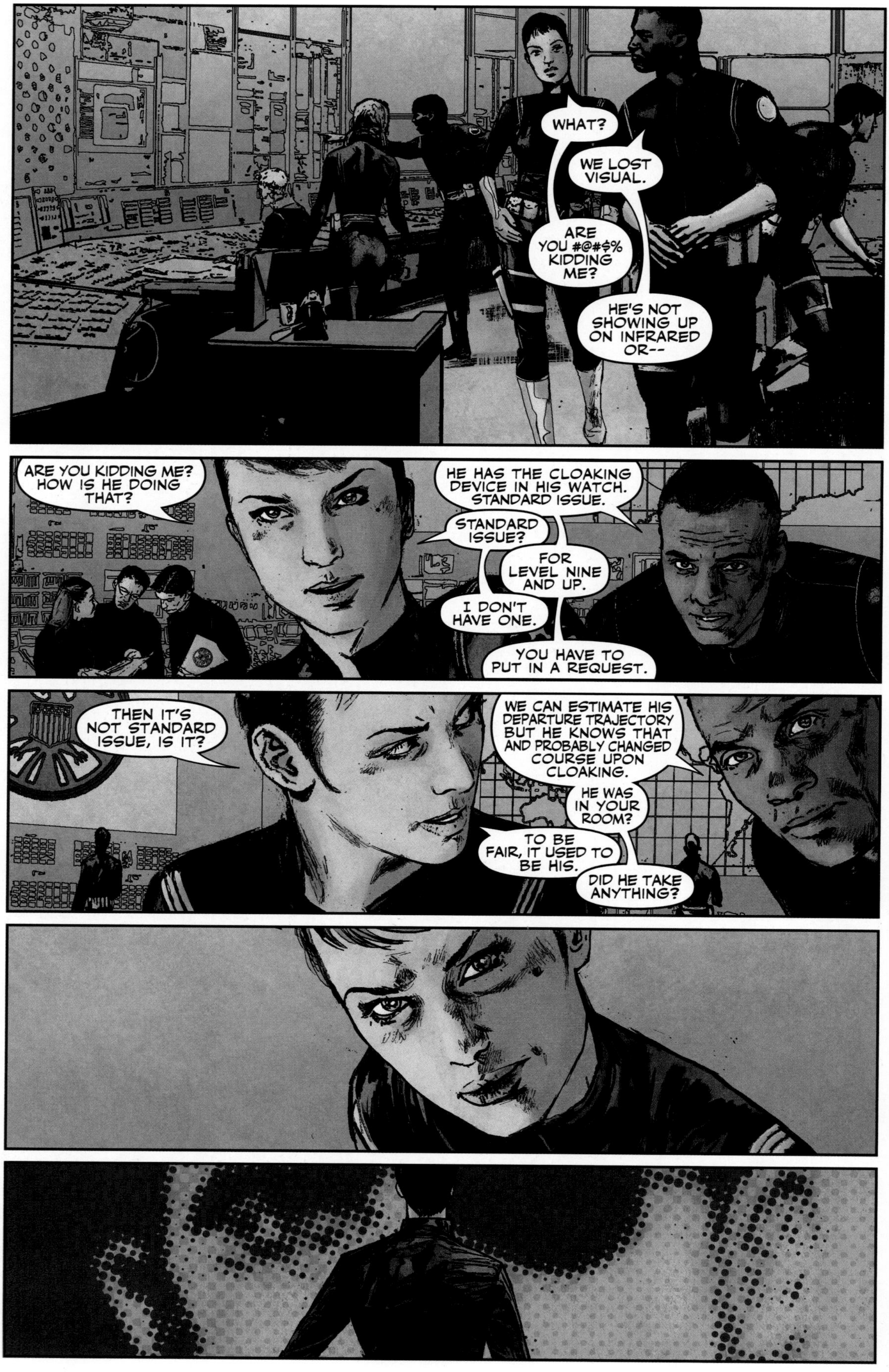
WHAT?
WE LOST VISUAL.
ARE YOU #@#$% KIDDING ME?
HE'S NOT SHOWING UP ON INFRARED OR--
ARE YOU KIDDING ME? HOW IS HE DOING THAT?
HE HAS THE CLOAKING DEVICE IN HIS WATCH. STANDARD ISSUE.
STANDARD ISSUE?
FOR LEVEL NINE AND UP.
I DON'T HAVE ONE.
YOU HAVE TO PUT IN A REQUEST.
THEN IT'S NOT STANDARD ISSUE, IS IT?
WE CAN ESTIMATE HIS DEPARTURE TRAJECTORY BUT HE KNOWS THAT AND PROBABLY CHANGED COURSE UPON CLOAKING.
HE WAS IN YOUR ROOM?
TO BE FAIR, IT USED TO BE HIS.
DID HE TAKE ANYTHING?

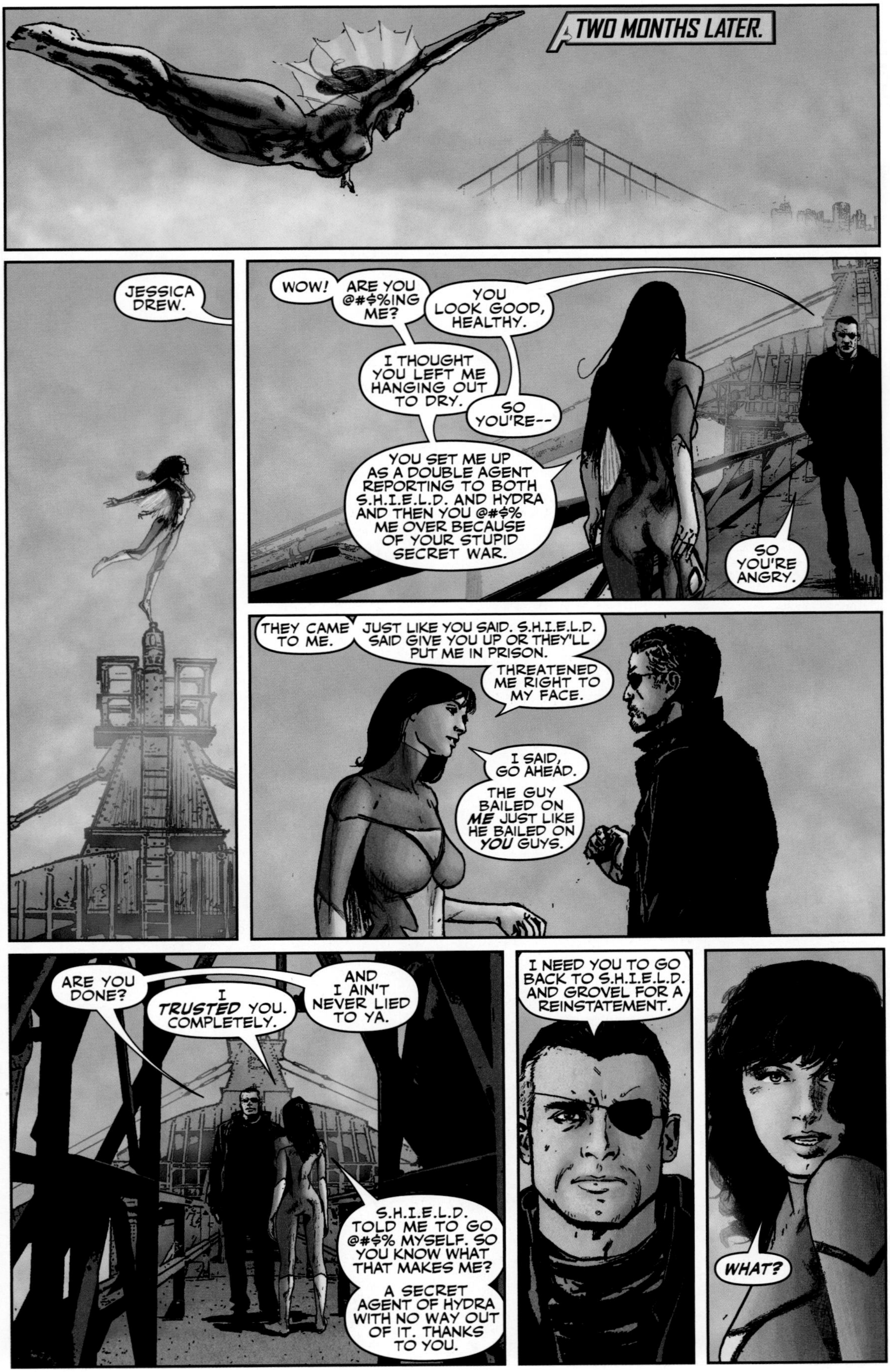
TWO MONTHS LATER.
JESSICA DREW.
WOW!
ARE YOU @#$%ING ME?
YOU LOOK GOOD, HEALTHY.
I THOUGHT YOU LEFT ME HANGING OUT TO DRY.
SO YOU'RE--
YOU SET ME UP AS A DOUBLE AGENT REPORTING TO BOTH S.H.I.E.L.D. AND HYDRA AND THEN YOU @#$% ME OVER BECAUSE OF YOUR STUPID SECRET WAR.
SO YOU'RE ANGRY.
THEY CAME TO ME.
JUST LIKE YOU SAID. S.H.I.E.L.D. SAID GIVE YOU UP OR THEY'LL PUT ME IN PRISON.
THREATENED ME RIGHT TO MY FACE.
I SAID, GO AHEAD.
THE GUY BAILED ON *ME* JUST LIKE HE BAILED ON *YOU* GUYS.
ARE YOU DONE?
I *TRUSTED* YOU. COMPLETELY.
AND I AIN'T NEVER LIED TO YA.
S.H.I.E.L.D. TOLD ME TO GO @#$% MYSELF. SO YOU KNOW WHAT THAT MAKES ME?
A SECRET AGENT OF HYDRA WITH NO WAY OUT OF IT. THANKS TO YOU.
I NEED YOU TO GO BACK TO S.H.I.E.L.D. AND GROVEL FOR A REINSTATEMENT.
WHAT?

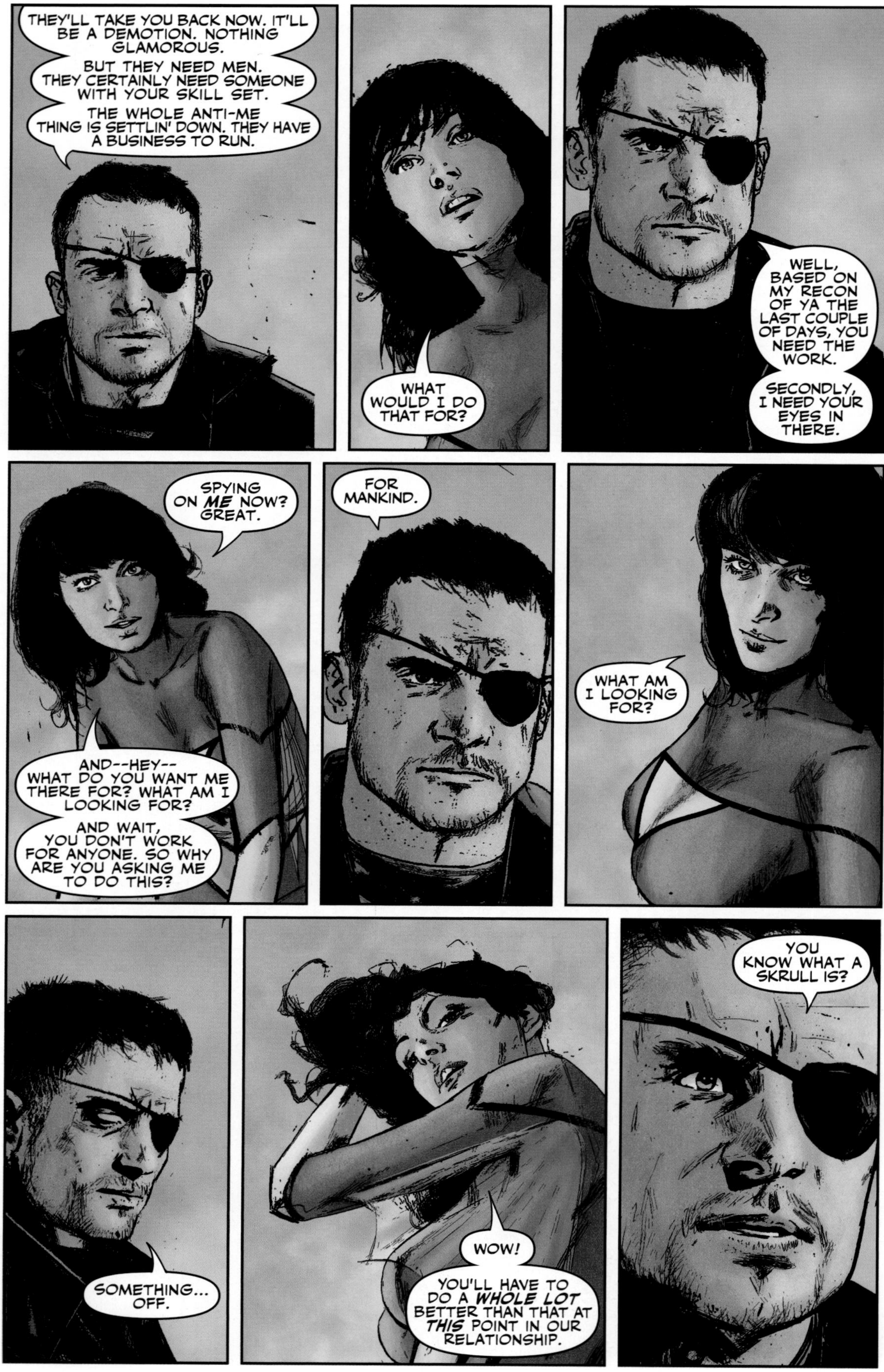

THEY'LL TAKE YOU BACK NOW. IT'LL BE A DEMOTION. NOTHING GLAMOROUS.
BUT THEY NEED MEN. THEY CERTAINLY NEED SOMEONE WITH YOUR SKILL SET.
THE WHOLE ANTI-ME THING IS SETTLIN' DOWN. THEY HAVE A BUSINESS TO RUN.
WHAT WOULD I DO THAT FOR?
WELL, BASED ON MY RECON OF YA THE LAST COUPLE OF DAYS, YOU NEED THE WORK.
SECONDLY, I NEED YOUR EYES IN THERE.
SPYING ON *ME* NOW? GREAT.
AND--HEY-- WHAT DO YOU WANT ME THERE FOR? WHAT AM I LOOKING FOR?
AND WAIT, YOU DON'T WORK FOR ANYONE. SO WHY ARE YOU ASKING ME TO DO THIS?
FOR MANKIND.
WHAT AM I LOOKING FOR?
SOMETHING... OFF.
WOW!
YOU'LL HAVE TO DO A ***WHOLE LOT*** BETTER THAN THAT AT ***THIS*** POINT IN OUR RELATIONSHIP.
YOU KNOW WHAT A SKRULL IS?

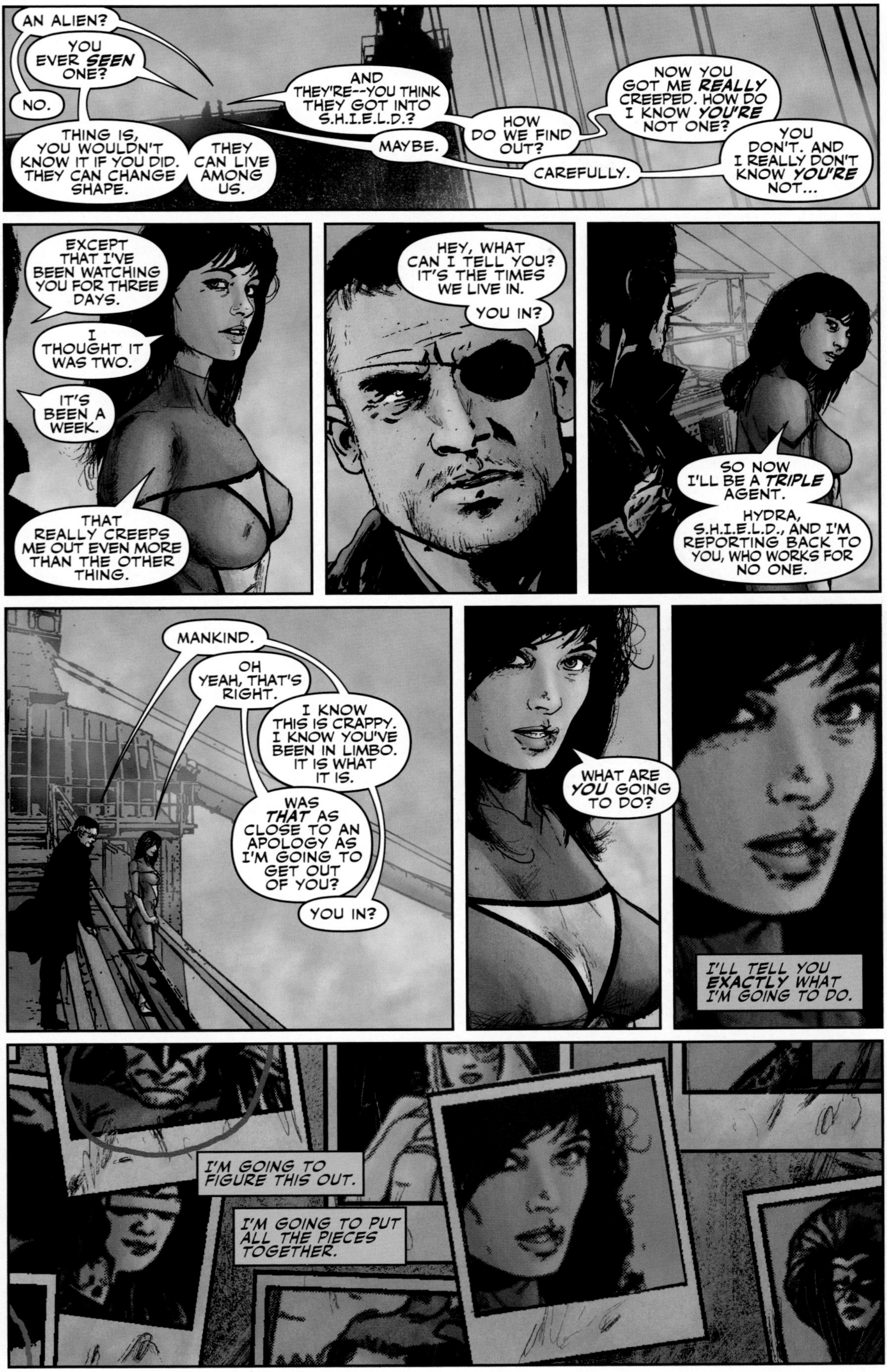

AN ALIEN?
YOU EVER SEEN ONE?
NO.
THING IS, YOU WOULDN'T KNOW IT IF YOU DID. THEY CAN CHANGE SHAPE.
THEY CAN LIVE AMONG US.
AND THEY'RE--YOU THINK THEY GOT INTO S.H.I.E.L.D.?
MAYBE.
HOW DO WE FIND OUT?
CAREFULLY.
NOW YOU GOT ME REALLY CREEPED. HOW DO I KNOW YOU'RE NOT ONE?
YOU DON'T. AND I REALLY DON'T KNOW YOU'RE NOT...
EXCEPT THAT I'VE BEEN WATCHING YOU FOR THREE DAYS.
I THOUGHT IT WAS TWO.
IT'S BEEN A WEEK.
THAT REALLY CREEPS ME OUT EVEN MORE THAN THE OTHER THING.
HEY, WHAT CAN I TELL YOU? IT'S THE TIMES WE LIVE IN.
YOU IN?
SO NOW I'LL BE A TRIPLE AGENT.
HYDRA, S.H.I.E.L.D., AND I'M REPORTING BACK TO YOU, WHO WORKS FOR NO ONE.
MANKIND.
OH YEAH, THAT'S RIGHT.
I KNOW THIS IS CRAPPY. I KNOW YOU'VE BEEN IN LIMBO. IT IS WHAT IT IS.
WAS THAT AS CLOSE TO AN APOLOGY AS I'M GOING TO GET OUT OF YOU?
YOU IN?
WHAT ARE YOU GOING TO DO?
I'LL TELL YOU EXACTLY WHAT I'M GOING TO DO.
I'M GOING TO FIGURE THIS OUT.
I'M GOING TO PUT ALL THE PIECES TOGETHER.

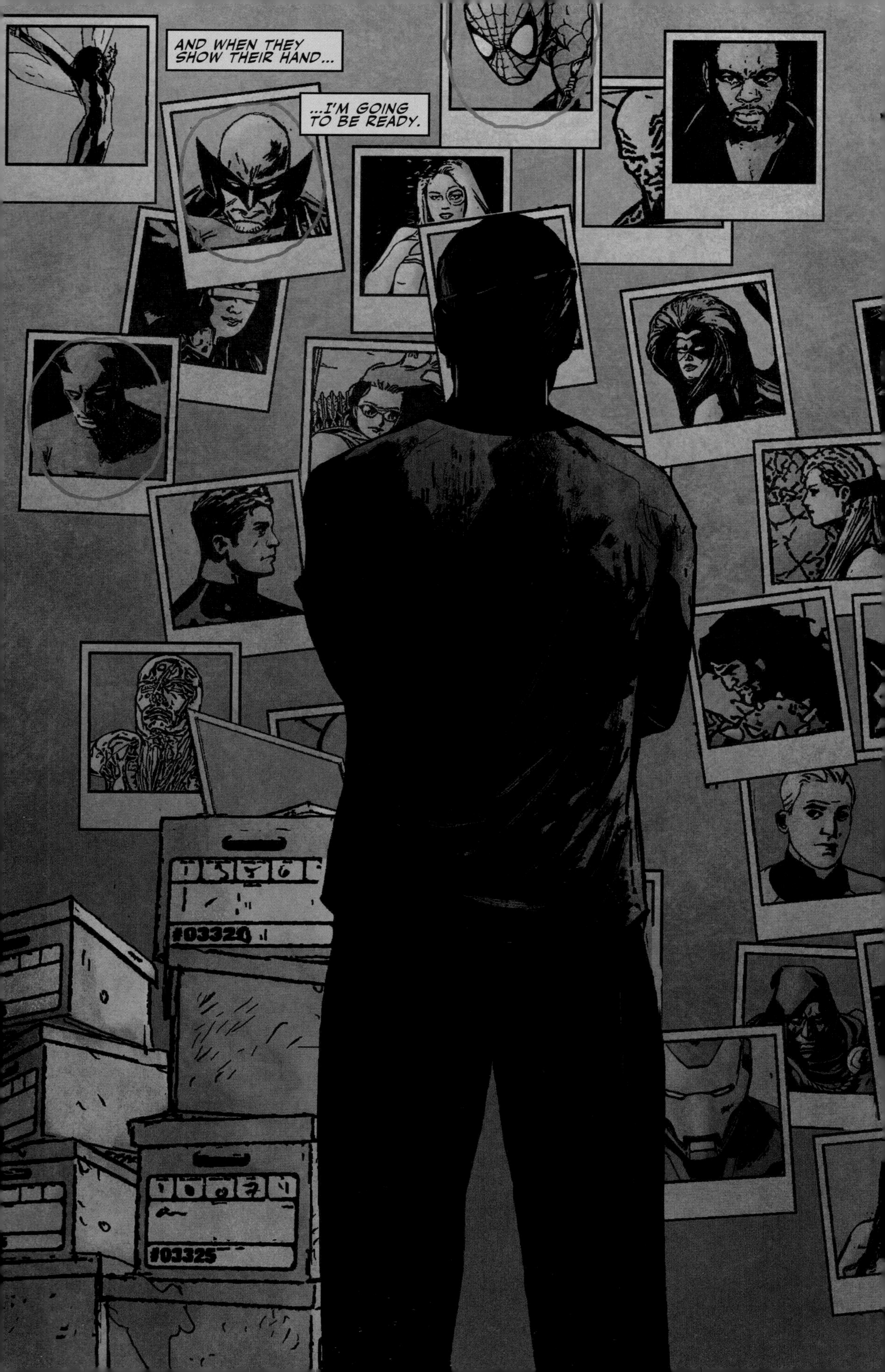
AND WHEN THEY SHOW THEIR HAND...
...I'M GOING TO BE READY.
#03320
#03325

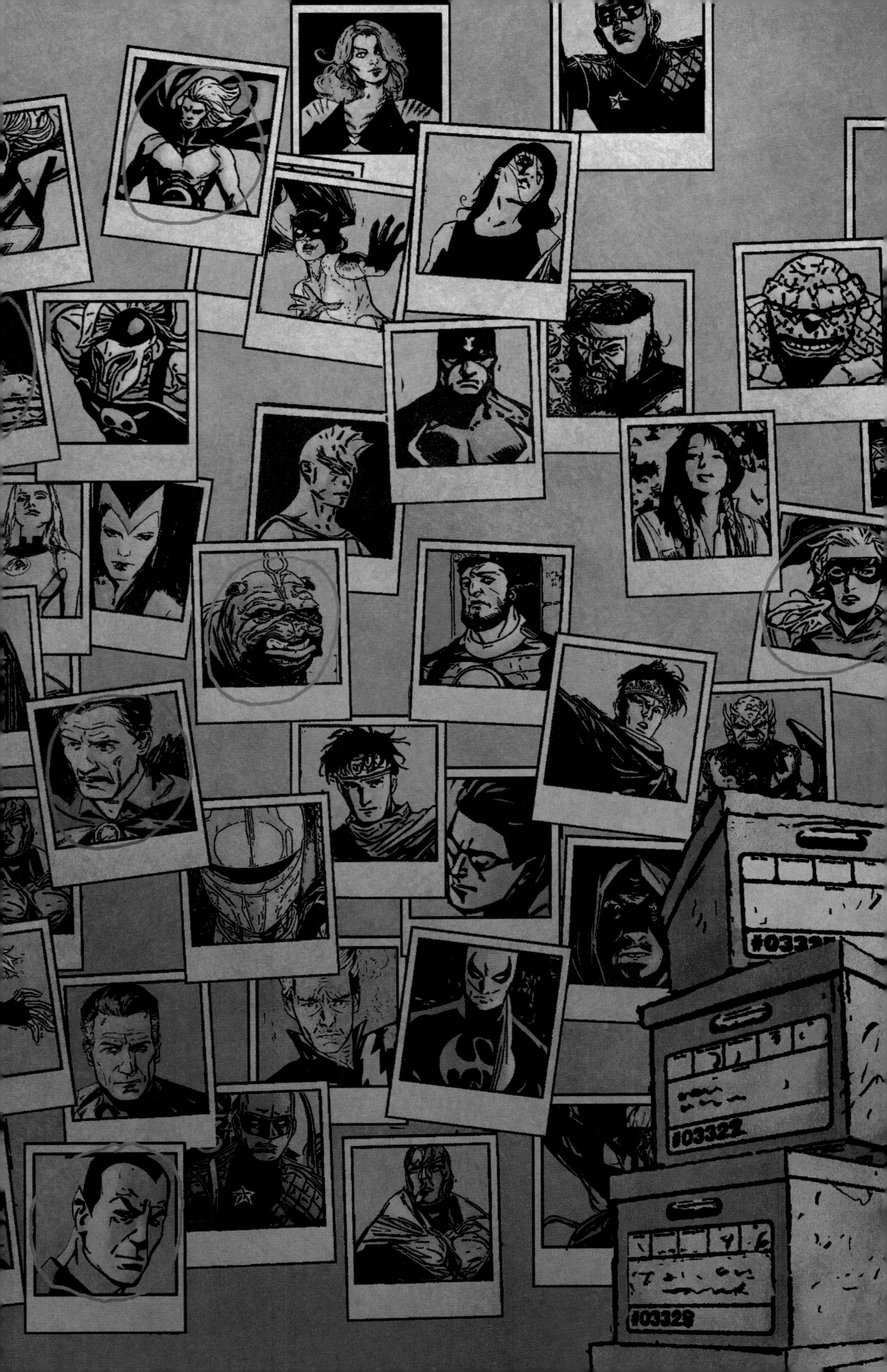

#03322
#03328

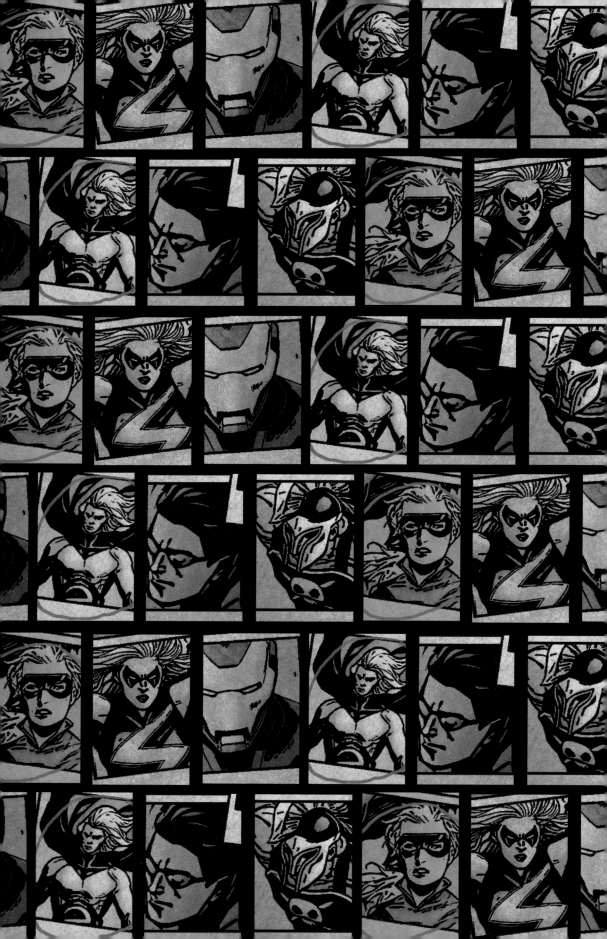

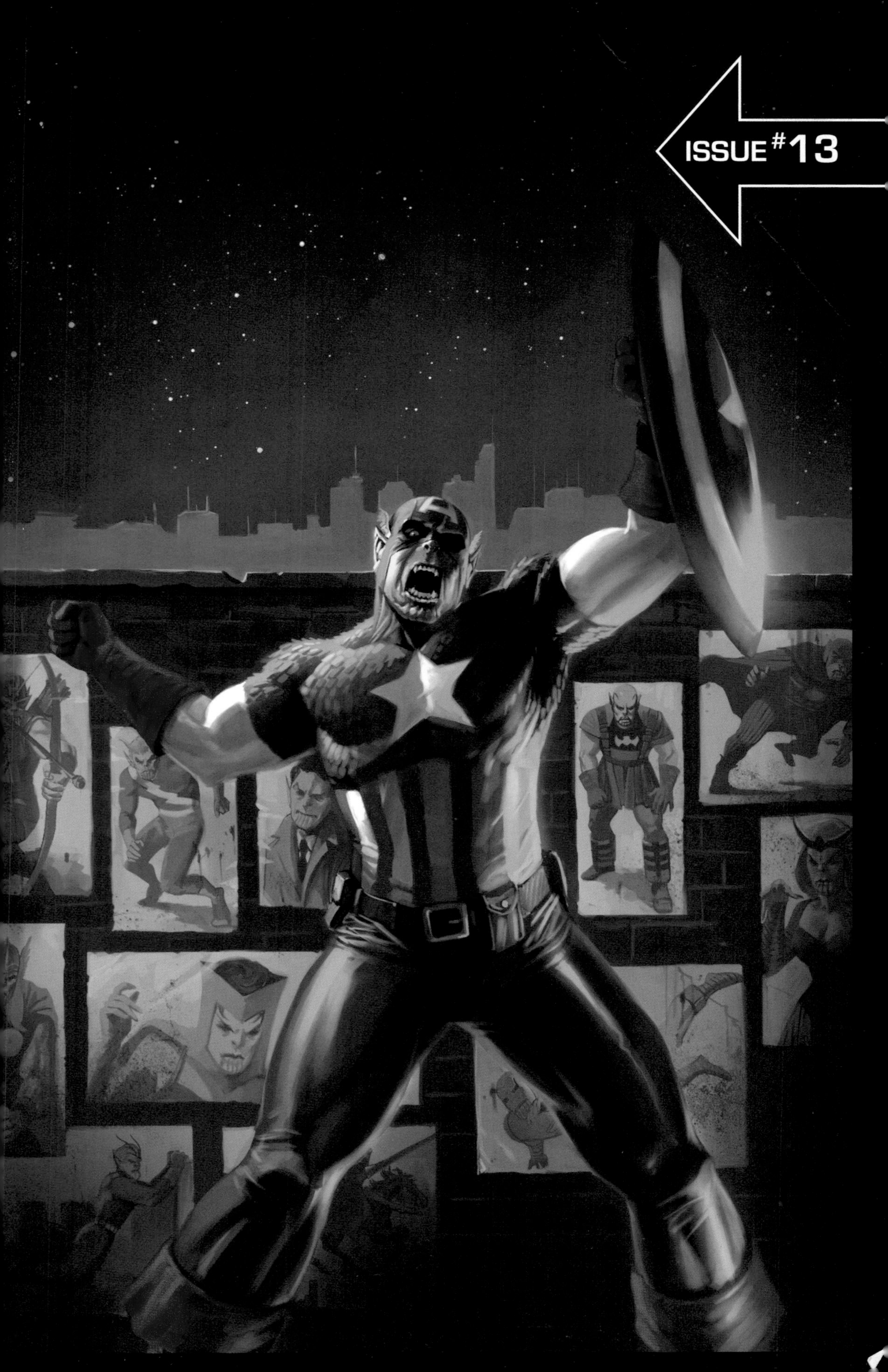
ISSUE #13

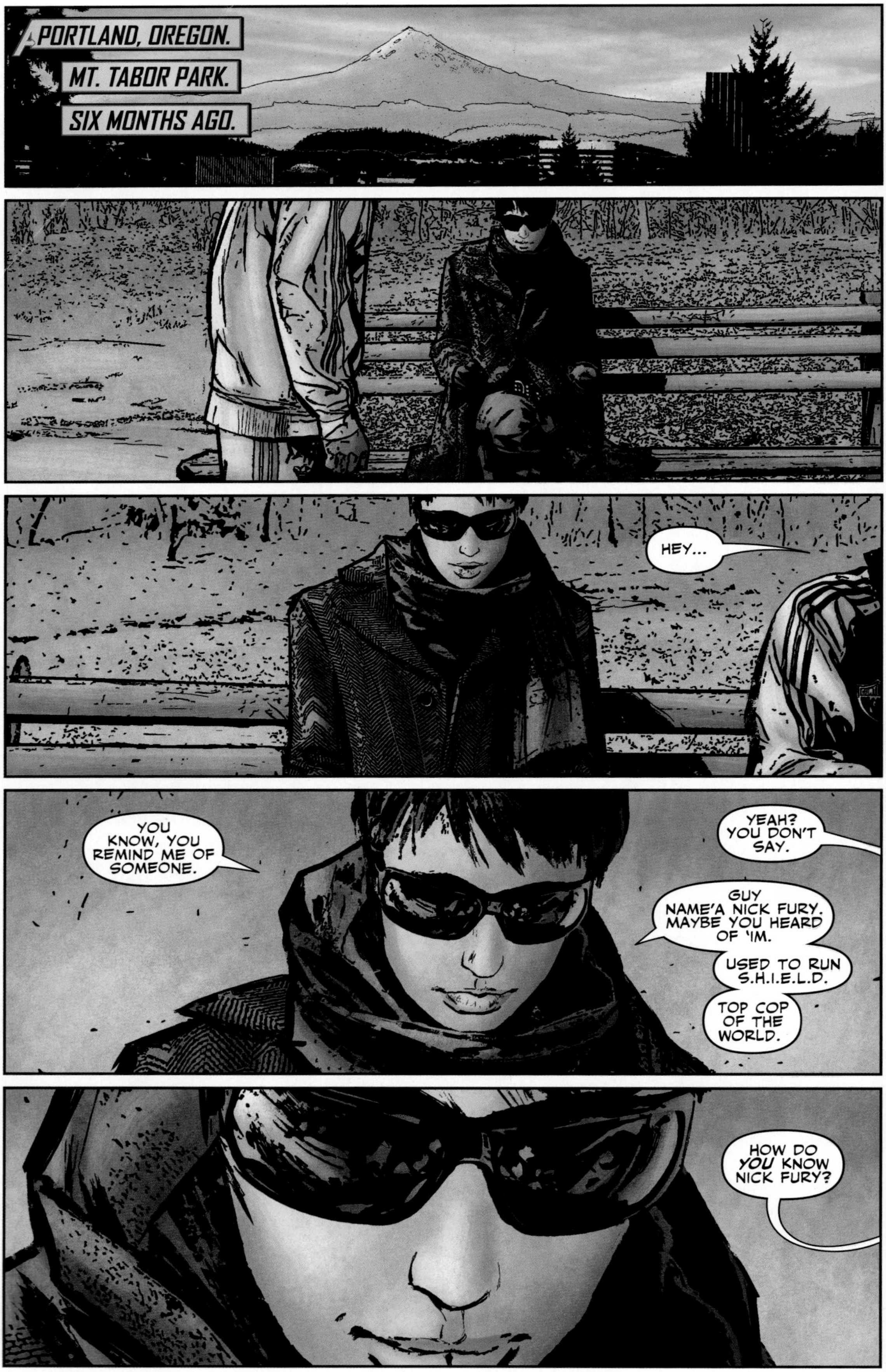
PORTLAND, OREGON.
MT. TABOR PARK.
SIX MONTHS AGO.
HEY...
YOU KNOW, YOU REMIND ME OF SOMEONE.
YEAH? YOU DON'T SAY.
GUY NAME'A NICK FURY. MAYBE YOU HEARD OF 'IM.
USED TO RUN S.H.I.E.L.D.
TOP COP OF THE WORLD.
HOW DO YOU KNOW NICK FURY?

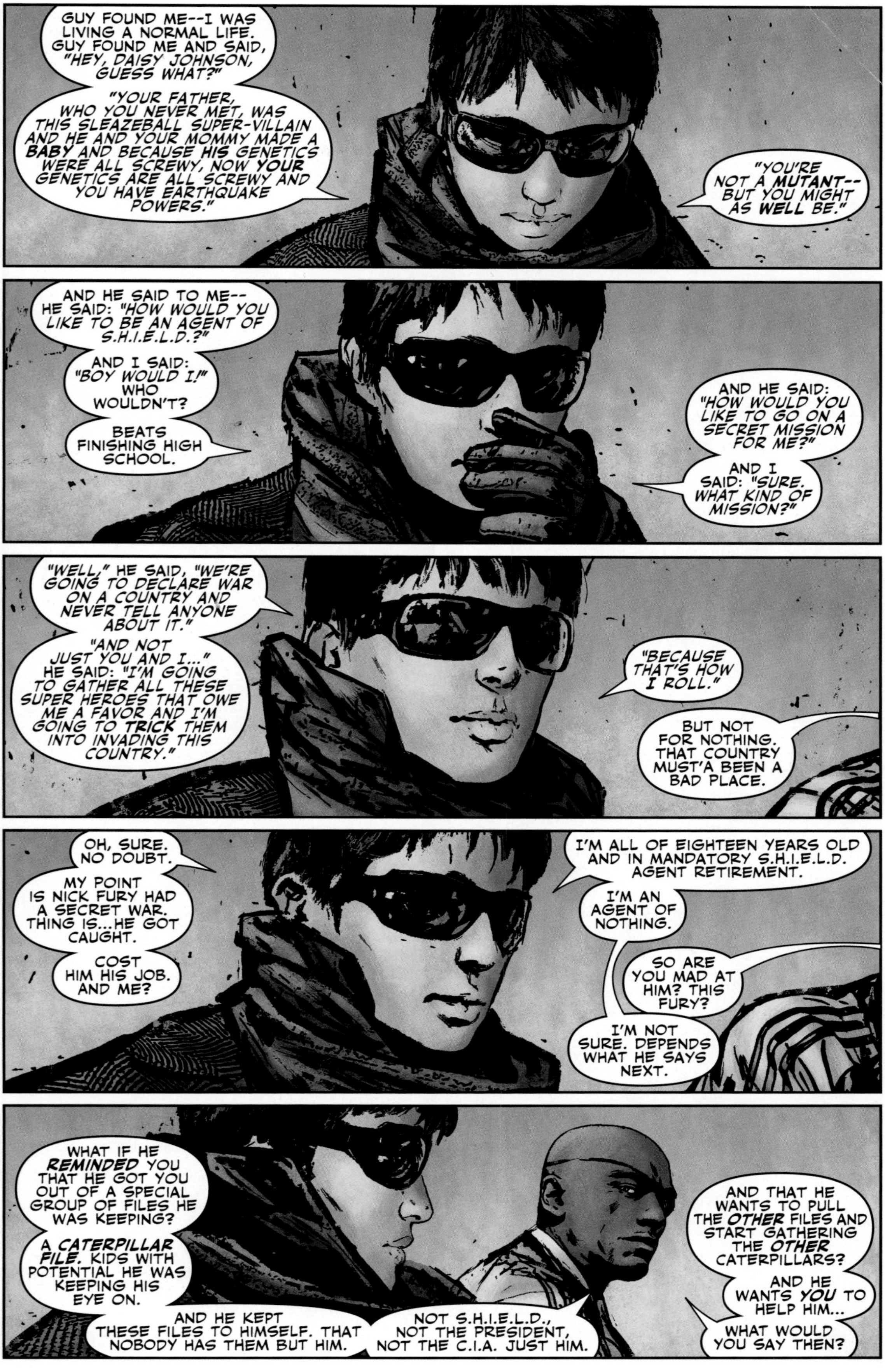
GUY FOUND ME--I WAS LIVING A NORMAL LIFE. GUY FOUND ME AND SAID, "HEY, DAISY JOHNSON, GUESS WHAT?"
"YOUR FATHER, WHO YOU NEVER MET, WAS THIS SLEAZEBALL SUPER-VILLAIN AND HE AND YOUR MOMMY MADE A BABY AND BECAUSE HIS GENETICS WERE ALL SCREWY, NOW YOUR GENETICS ARE ALL SCREWY AND YOU HAVE EARTHQUAKE POWERS."
"YOU'RE NOT A MUTANT--BUT YOU MIGHT AS WELL BE."
AND HE SAID TO ME--HE SAID: "HOW WOULD YOU LIKE TO BE AN AGENT OF S.H.I.E.L.D.?"
AND I SAID: "BOY WOULD I!" WHO WOULDN'T?
BEATS FINISHING HIGH SCHOOL.
AND HE SAID: "HOW WOULD YOU LIKE TO GO ON A SECRET MISSION FOR ME?"
AND I SAID: "SURE. WHAT KIND OF MISSION?"
"WELL," HE SAID, "WE'RE GOING TO DECLARE WAR ON A COUNTRY AND NEVER TELL ANYONE ABOUT IT."
"AND NOT JUST YOU AND I..." HE SAID: "I'M GOING TO GATHER ALL THESE SUPER HEROES THAT OWE ME A FAVOR AND I'M GOING TO TRICK THEM INTO INVADING THIS COUNTRY."
"BECAUSE THAT'S HOW I ROLL."
BUT NOT FOR NOTHING. THAT COUNTRY MUST'A BEEN A BAD PLACE.
OH, SURE. NO DOUBT.
MY POINT IS NICK FURY HAD A SECRET WAR. THING IS...HE GOT CAUGHT.
COST HIM HIS JOB. AND ME?
I'M ALL OF EIGHTEEN YEARS OLD AND IN MANDATORY S.H.I.E.L.D. AGENT RETIREMENT.
I'M AN AGENT OF NOTHING.
SO ARE YOU MAD AT HIM? THIS FURY?
I'M NOT SURE. DEPENDS WHAT HE SAYS NEXT.
WHAT IF HE REMINDED YOU THAT HE GOT YOU OUT OF A SPECIAL GROUP OF FILES HE WAS KEEPING?
A CATERPILLAR FILE. KIDS WITH POTENTIAL HE WAS KEEPING HIS EYE ON.
AND HE KEPT THESE FILES TO HIMSELF. THAT NOBODY HAS THEM BUT HIM.
NOT S.H.I.E.L.D., NOT THE PRESIDENT, NOT THE C.I.A. JUST HIM.
AND THAT HE WANTS TO PULL THE OTHER FILES AND START GATHERING THE OTHER CATERPILLARS?
AND HE WANTS YOU TO HELP HIM...
WHAT WOULD YOU SAY THEN?

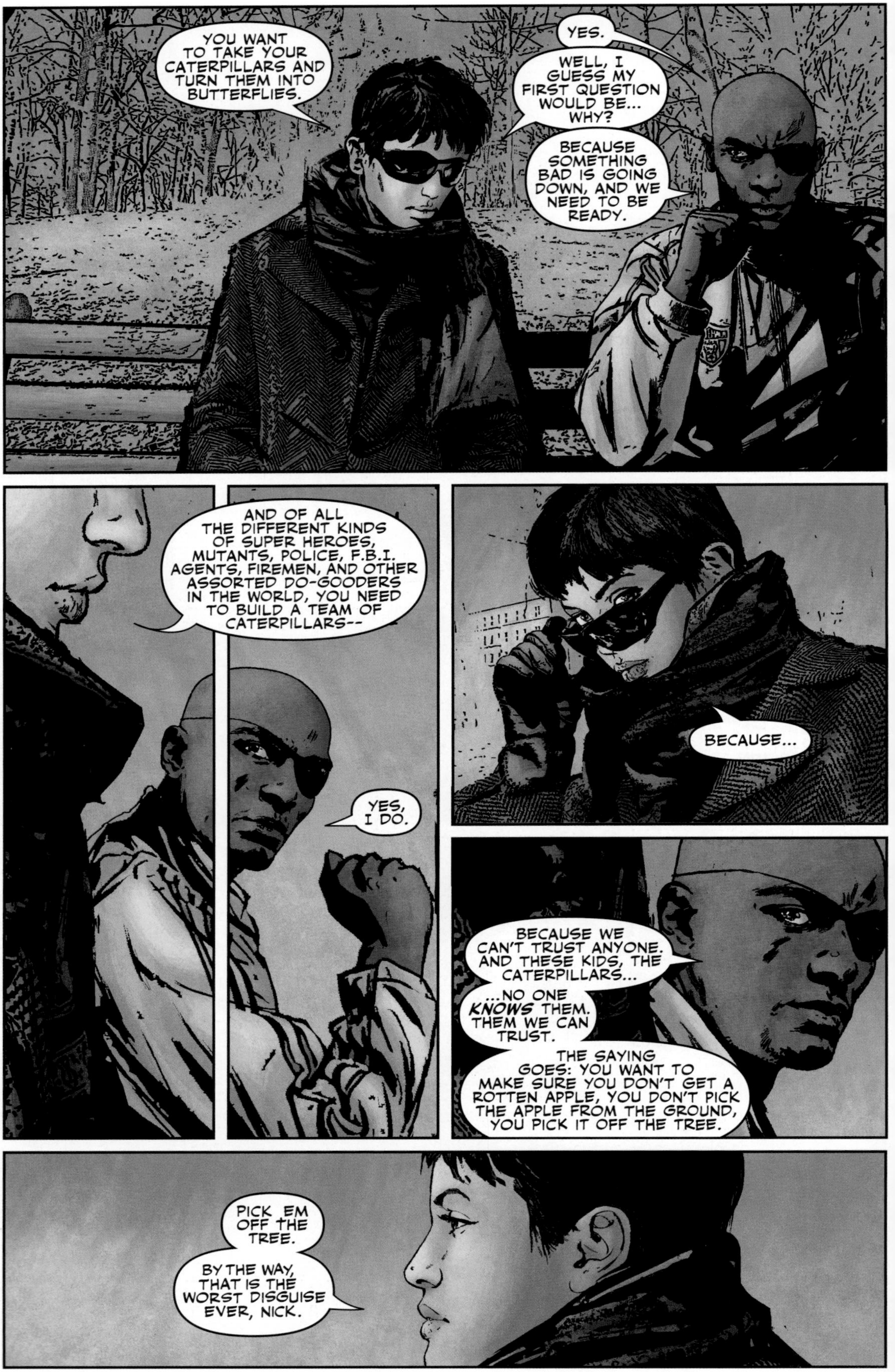
YOU WANT TO TAKE YOUR CATERPILLARS AND TURN THEM INTO BUTTERFLIES.
YES.
WELL, I GUESS MY FIRST QUESTION WOULD BE... WHY?
BECAUSE SOMETHING BAD IS GOING DOWN, AND WE NEED TO BE READY.
AND OF ALL THE DIFFERENT KINDS OF SUPER HEROES, MUTANTS, POLICE, F.B.I. AGENTS, FIREMEN, AND OTHER ASSORTED DO-GOODERS IN THE WORLD, YOU NEED TO BUILD A TEAM OF CATERPILLARS--
YES, I DO.
BECAUSE...
BECAUSE WE CAN'T TRUST ANYONE. AND THESE KIDS, THE CATERPILLARS...
...NO ONE *KNOWS* THEM. THEM WE CAN TRUST.
THE SAYING GOES: YOU WANT TO MAKE SURE YOU DON'T GET A ROTTEN APPLE, YOU DON'T PICK THE APPLE FROM THE GROUND, YOU PICK IT OFF THE TREE.
PICK EM OFF THE TREE.
BY THE WAY, THAT IS THE WORST DISGUISE EVER, NICK.

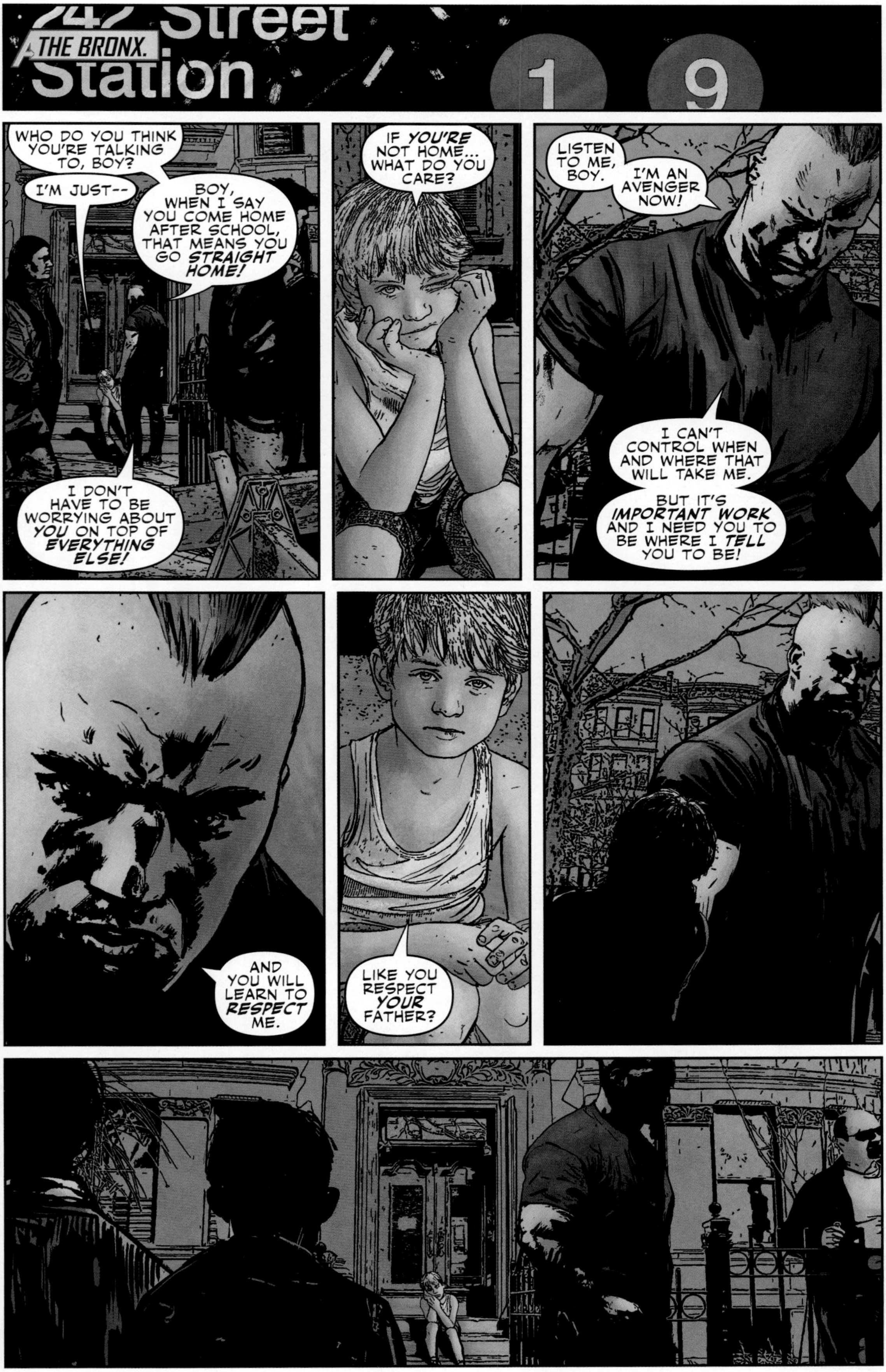
242 Street Station
THE BRONX.
1
9
WHO DO YOU THINK YOU'RE TALKING TO, BOY?
I'M JUST--
BOY, WHEN I SAY YOU COME HOME AFTER SCHOOL, THAT MEANS YOU GO STRAIGHT HOME!
I DON'T HAVE TO BE WORRYING ABOUT YOU ON TOP OF EVERYTHING ELSE!
IF YOU'RE NOT HOME... WHAT DO YOU CARE?
LISTEN TO ME, BOY.
I'M AN AVENGER NOW!
I CAN'T CONTROL WHEN AND WHERE THAT WILL TAKE ME.
BUT IT'S IMPORTANT WORK AND I NEED YOU TO BE WHERE I TELL YOU TO BE!
AND YOU WILL LEARN TO RESPECT ME.
LIKE YOU RESPECT YOUR FATHER?

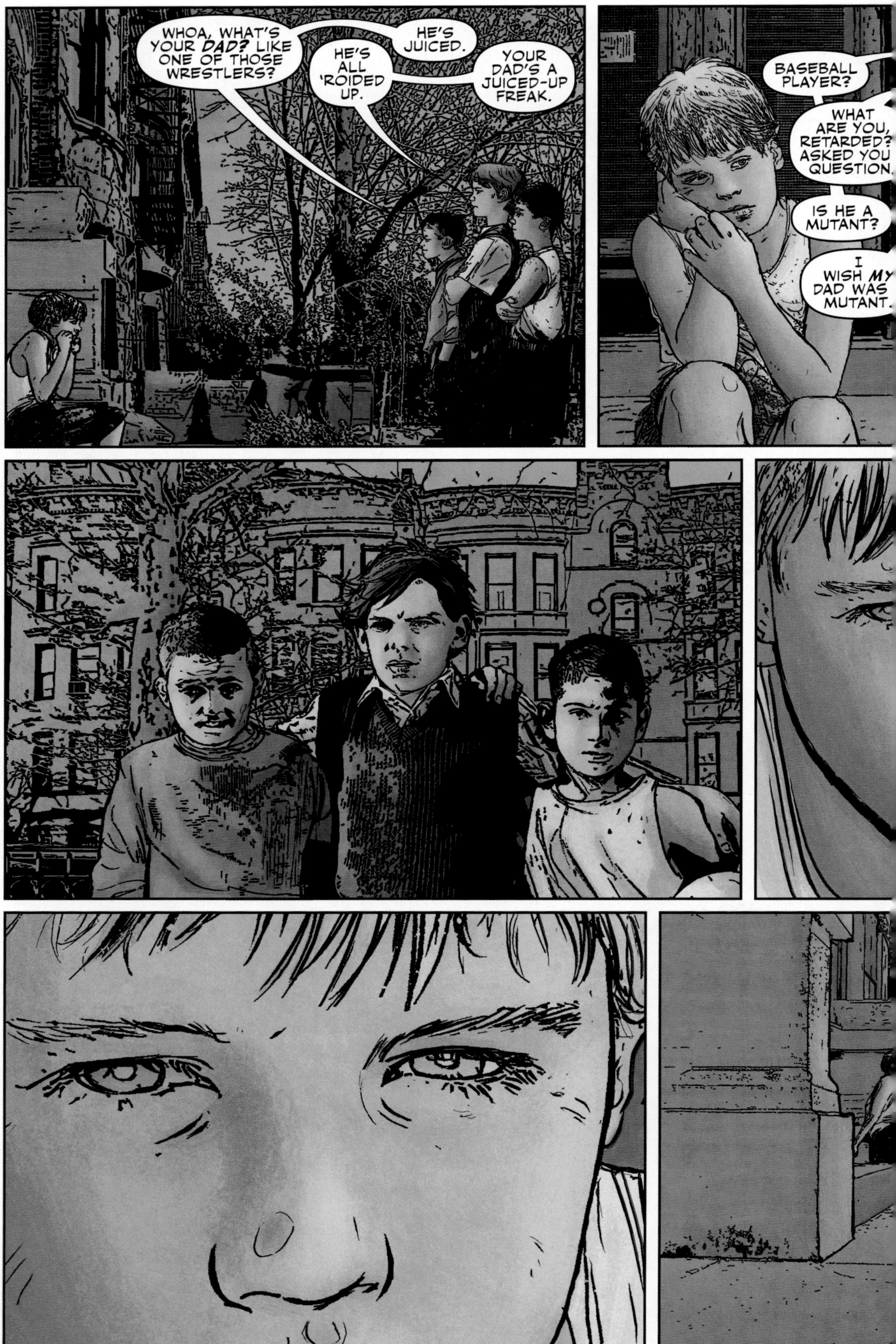
WHOA, WHAT'S YOUR DAD? LIKE ONE OF THOSE WRESTLERS?
HE'S JUICED.
HE'S ALL 'ROIDED UP.
YOUR DAD'S A JUICED-UP FREAK.
BASEBALL PLAYER?
WHAT ARE YOU, RETARDED? ASKED YOU QUESTION.
IS HE A MUTANT?
I WISH MY DAD WAS MUTANT.

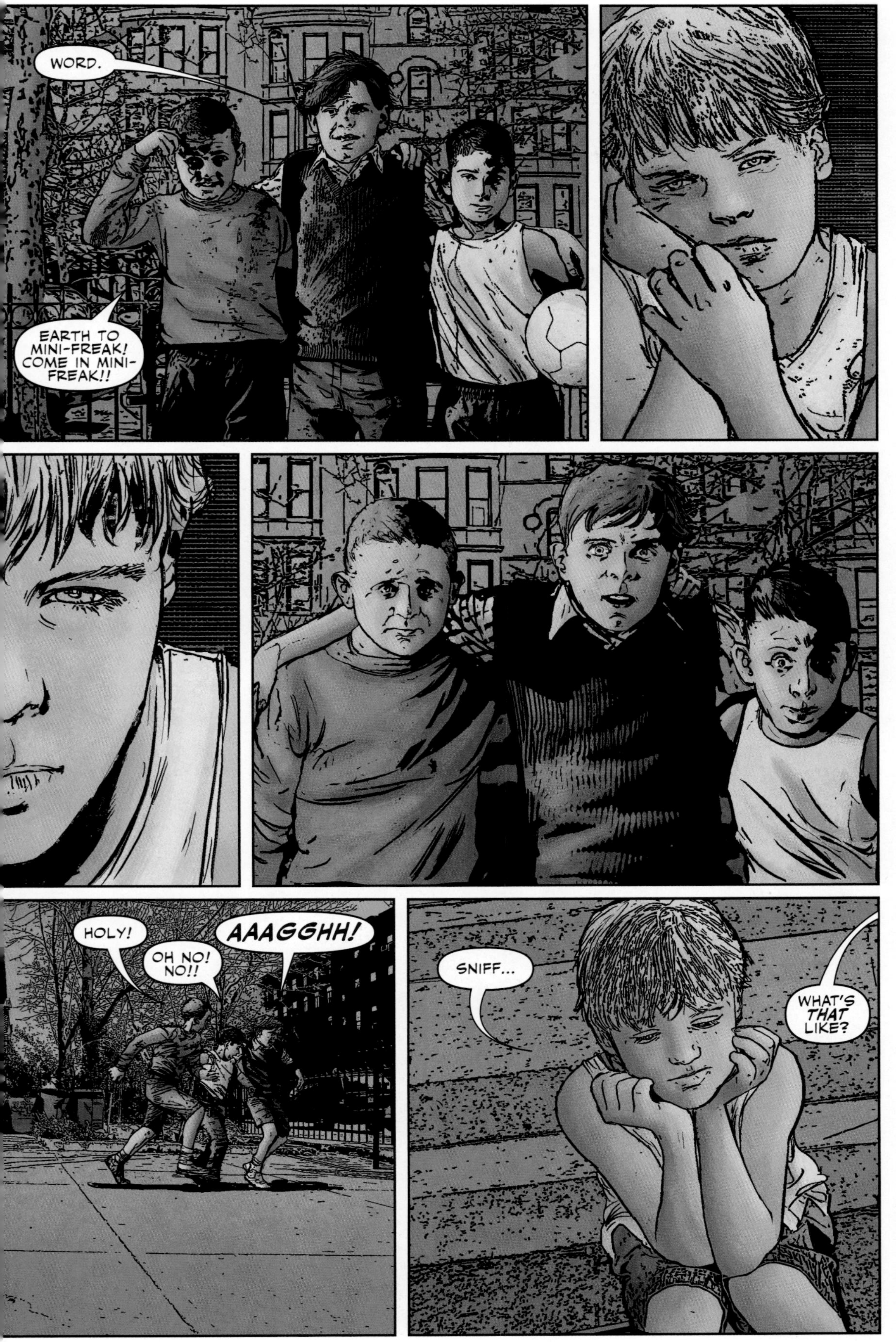
WORD.
EARTH TO MINI-FREAK! COME IN MINI-FREAK!!
HOLY!
OH NO! NO!!
AAAGGHH!
SNIFF...
WHAT'S THAT LIKE?

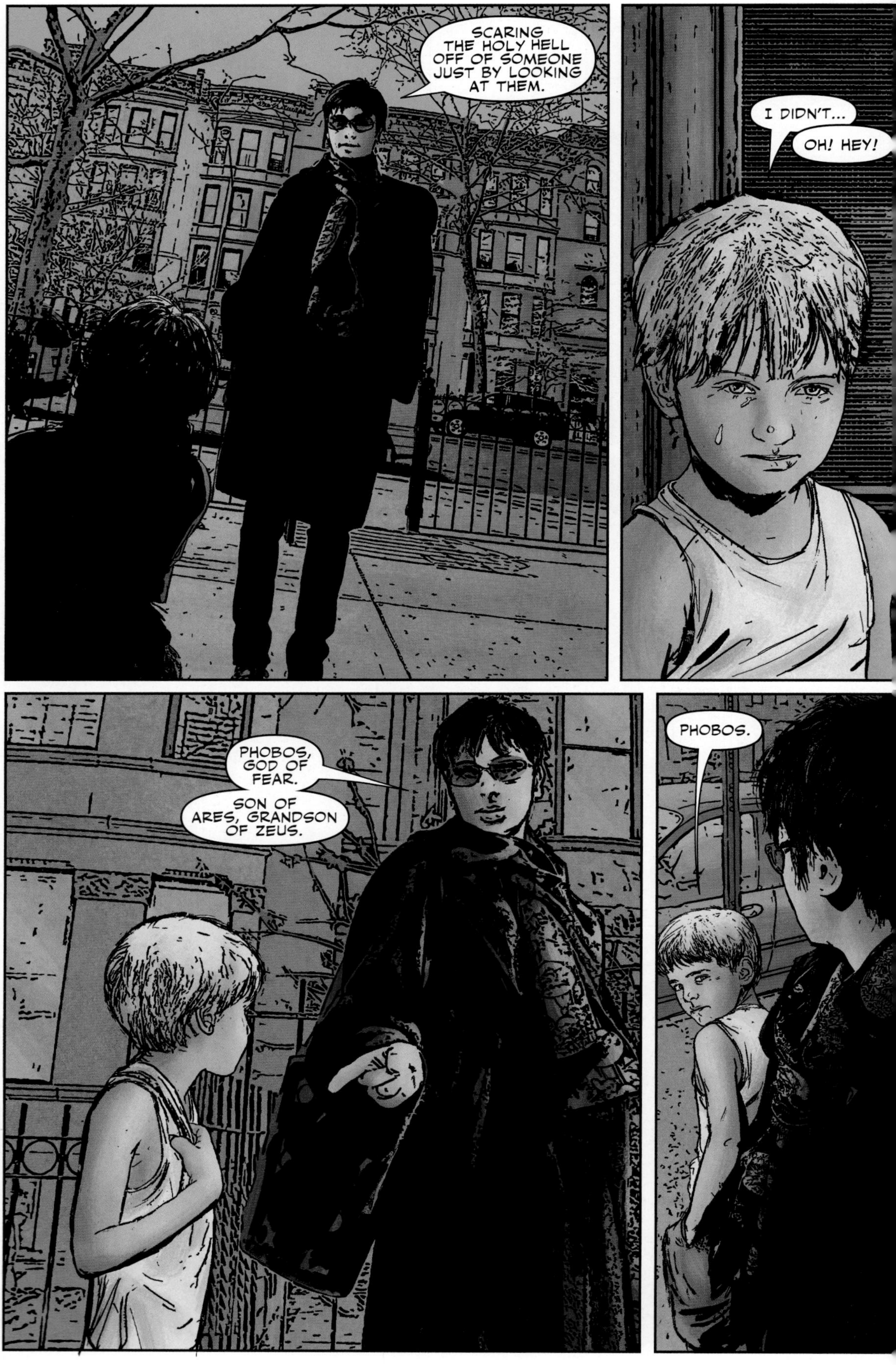
SCARING THE HOLY HELL OFF OF SOMEONE JUST BY LOOKING AT THEM.
I DIDN'T...
OH! HEY!
PHOBOS, GOD OF FEAR.
SON OF ARES, GRANDSON OF ZEUS.
PHOBOS.

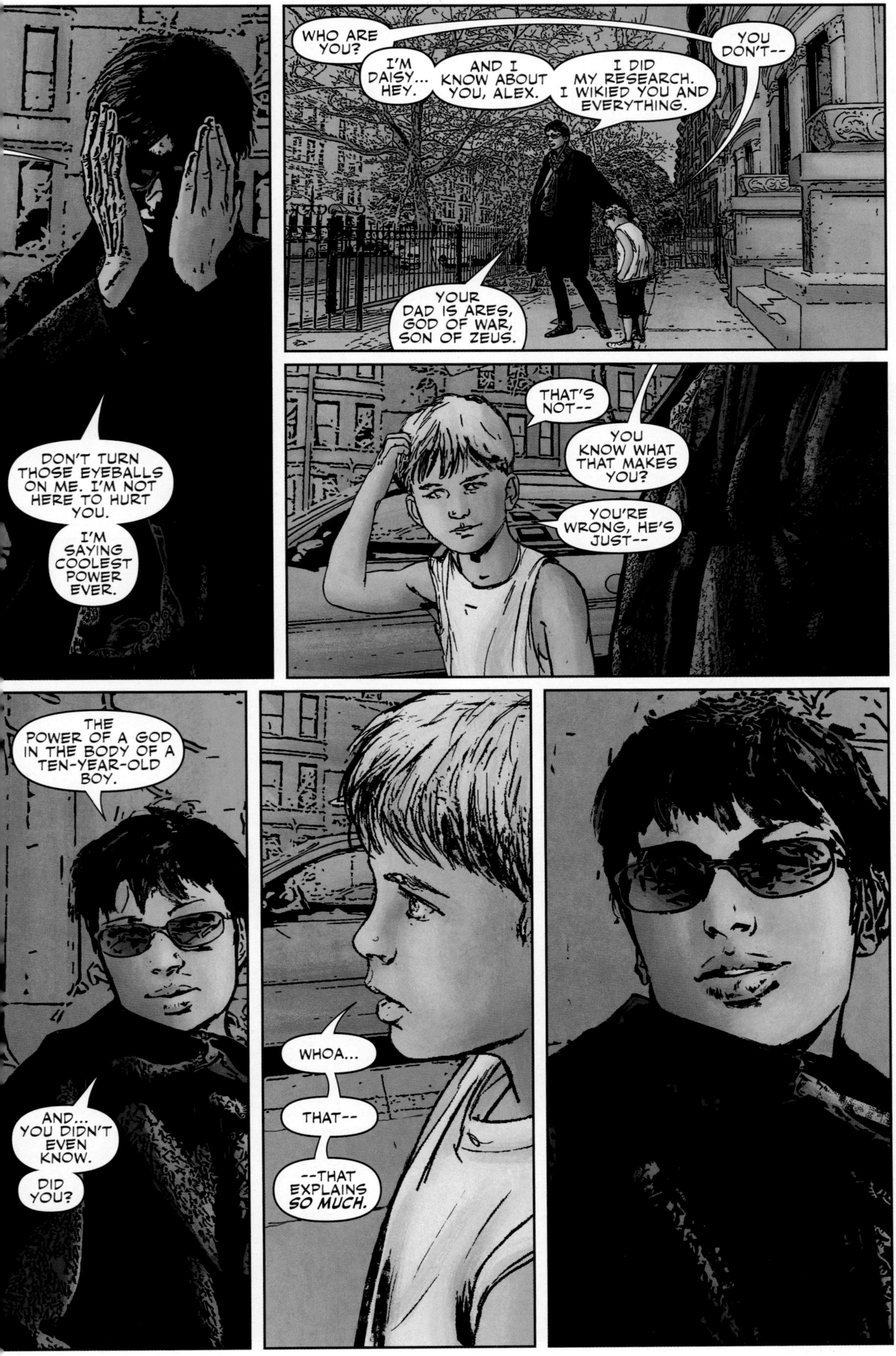
WHO ARE YOU?
I'M DAISY... HEY.
AND I KNOW ABOUT YOU, ALEX.
I DID MY RESEARCH. I WIKIED YOU AND EVERYTHING.
YOU DON'T--
YOUR DAD IS ARES, GOD OF WAR, SON OF ZEUS.
THAT'S NOT--
YOU KNOW WHAT THAT MAKES YOU?
YOU'RE WRONG, HE'S JUST--
DON'T TURN THOSE EYEBALLS ON ME. I'M NOT HERE TO HURT YOU.
I'M SAYING COOLEST POWER EVER.
THE POWER OF A GOD IN THE BODY OF A TEN-YEAR-OLD BOY.
AND... YOU DIDN'T EVEN KNOW.
DID YOU?
WHOA...
THAT--
--THAT EXPLAINS *SO MUCH.*

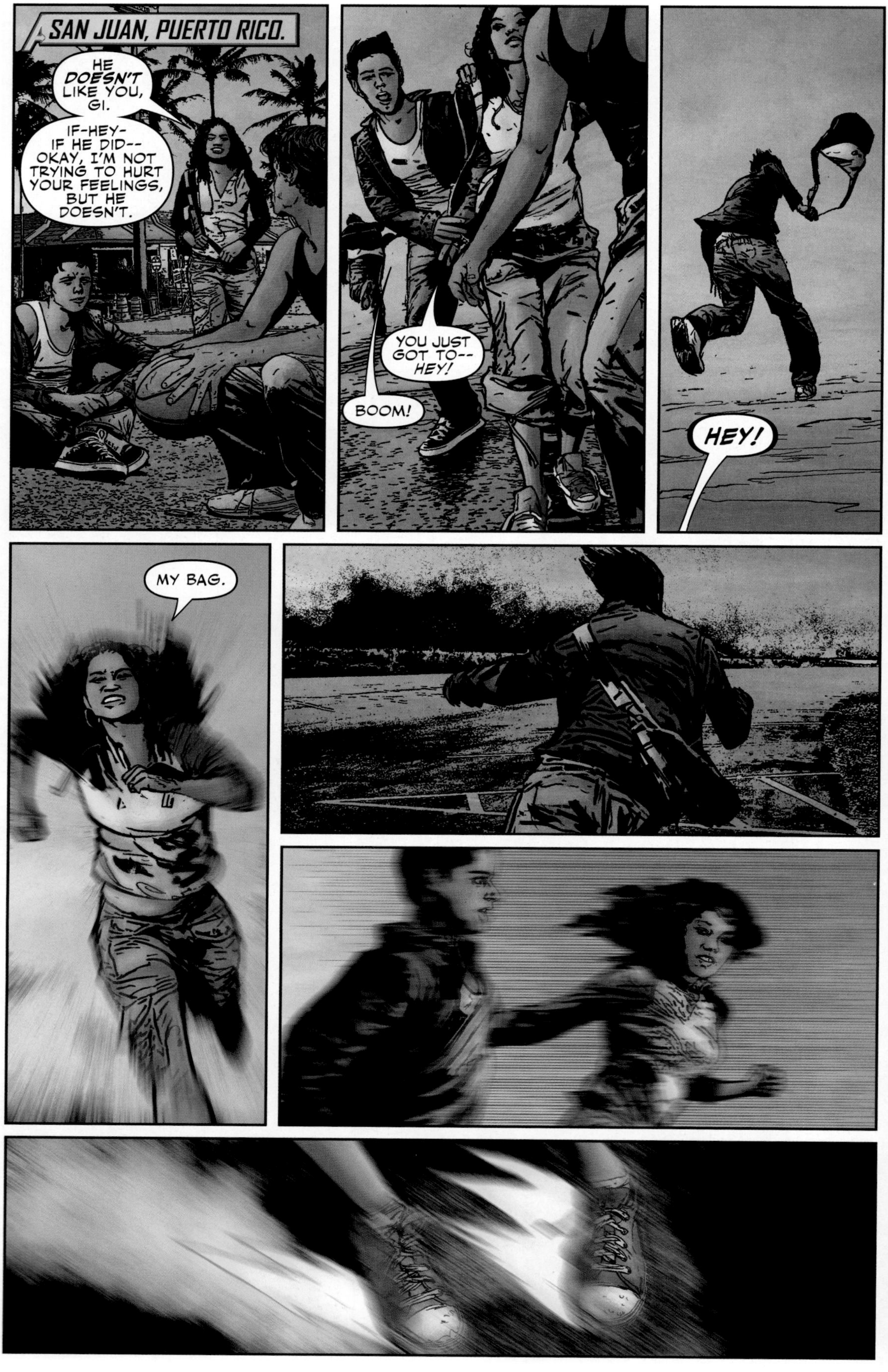
SAN JUAN, PUERTO RICO.
HE DOESN'T LIKE YOU, GI.
IF-HEY- IF HE DID-- OKAY, I'M NOT TRYING TO HURT YOUR FEELINGS, BUT HE DOESN'T.
YOU JUST GOT TO-- HEY!
BOOM!
HEY!
MY BAG.

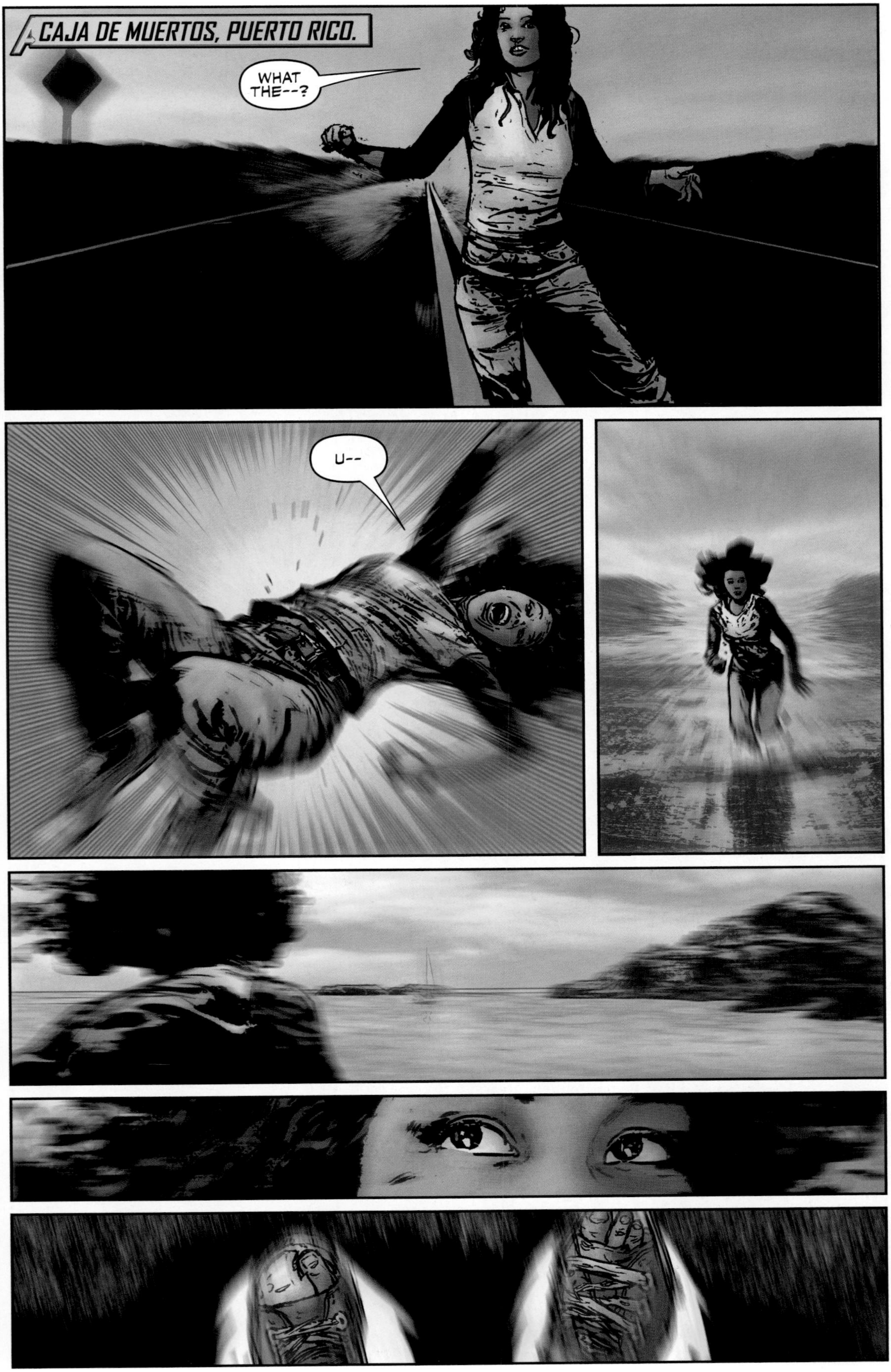
CAJA DE MUERTOS, PUERTO RICO.
WHAT THE--?
U--

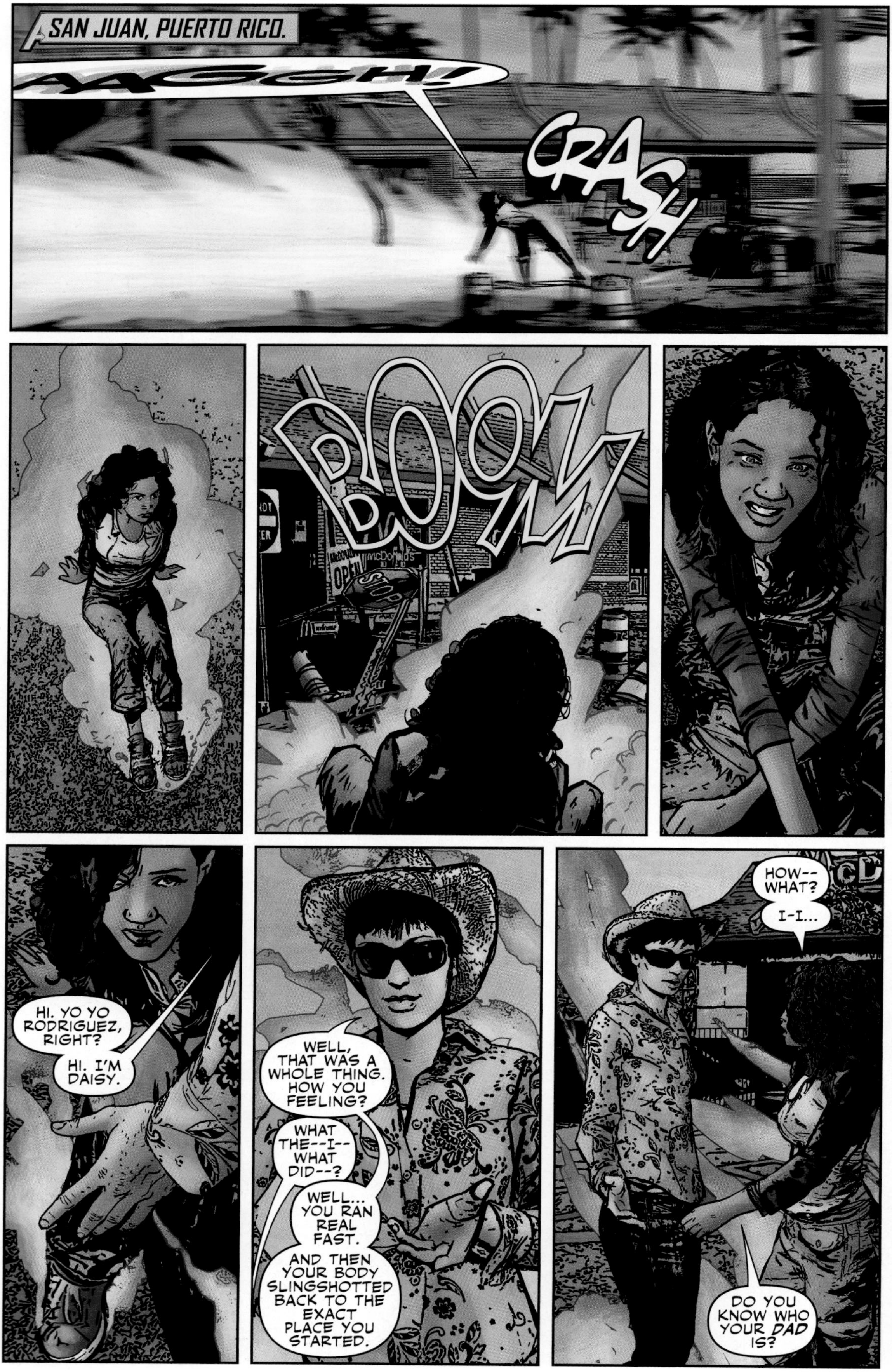
SAN JUAN, PUERTO RICO.
AAGGH!!
CRASH
BOOM
McDonald's
OPEN
STOP
HI. YO YO RODRIGUEZ, RIGHT?
HI. I'M DAISY.
WELL, THAT WAS A WHOLE THING. HOW YOU FEELING?
WHAT THE--I--WHAT DID--?
WELL... YOU RAN REAL FAST.
AND THEN YOUR BODY SLINGSHOTTED BACK TO THE EXACT PLACE YOU STARTED.
HOW--WHAT?
I-I...
DO YOU KNOW WHO YOUR *DAD* IS?

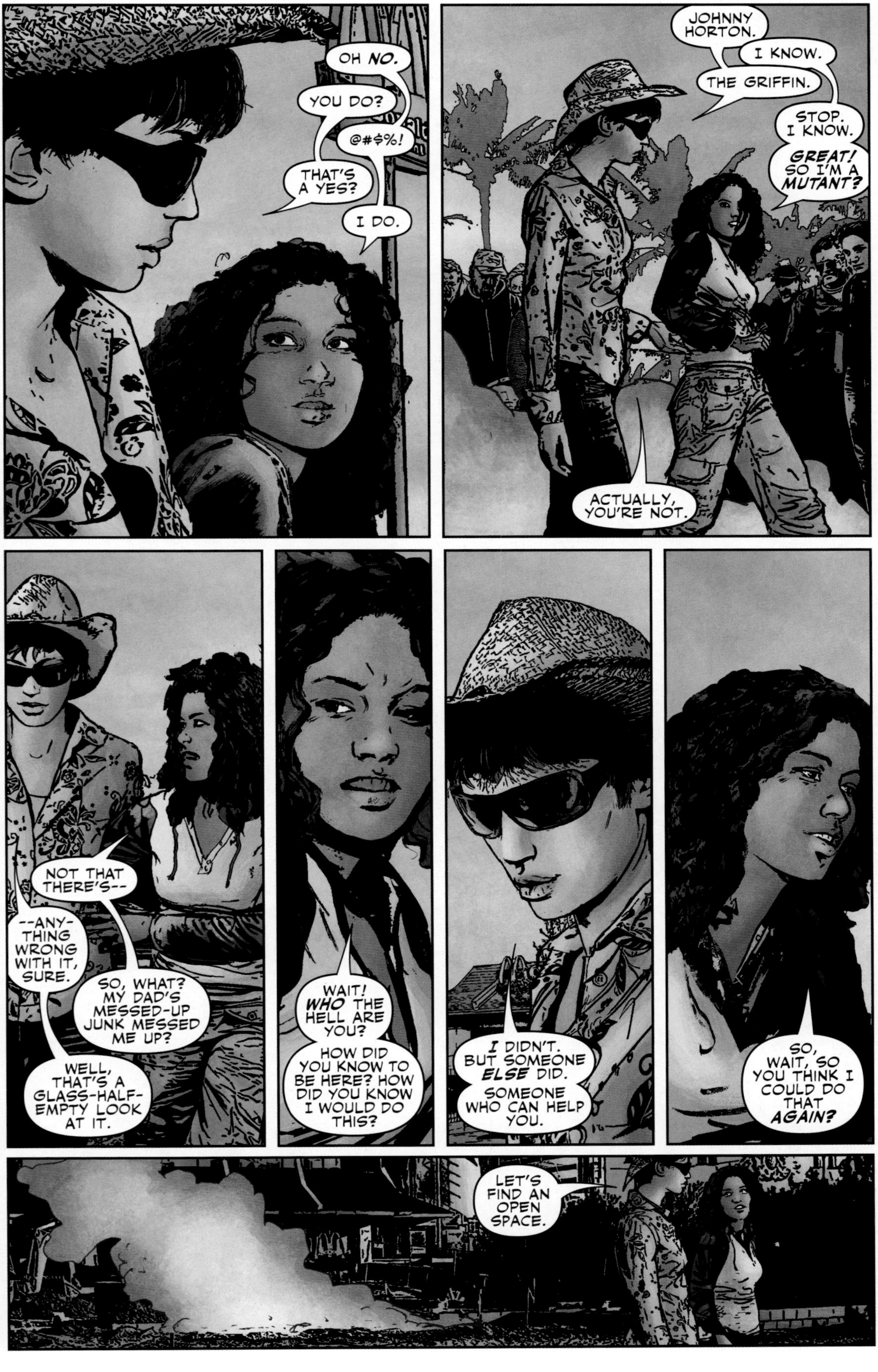
OH NO.
YOU DO?
@#$%!
THAT'S A YES?
I DO.
JOHNNY HORTON.
I KNOW.
THE GRIFFIN.
STOP. I KNOW.
GREAT! SO I'M A MUTANT?
ACTUALLY, YOU'RE NOT.
NOT THAT THERE'S--
--ANY-THING WRONG WITH IT, SURE.
SO, WHAT? MY DAD'S MESSED-UP JUNK MESSED ME UP?
WELL, THAT'S A GLASS-HALF-EMPTY LOOK AT IT.
WAIT! WHO THE HELL ARE YOU?
HOW DID YOU KNOW TO BE HERE? HOW DID YOU KNOW I WOULD DO THIS?
I DIDN'T. BUT SOMEONE ELSE DID.
SOMEONE WHO CAN HELP YOU.
SO, WAIT, SO YOU THINK I COULD DO THAT AGAIN?
LET'S FIND AN OPEN SPACE.

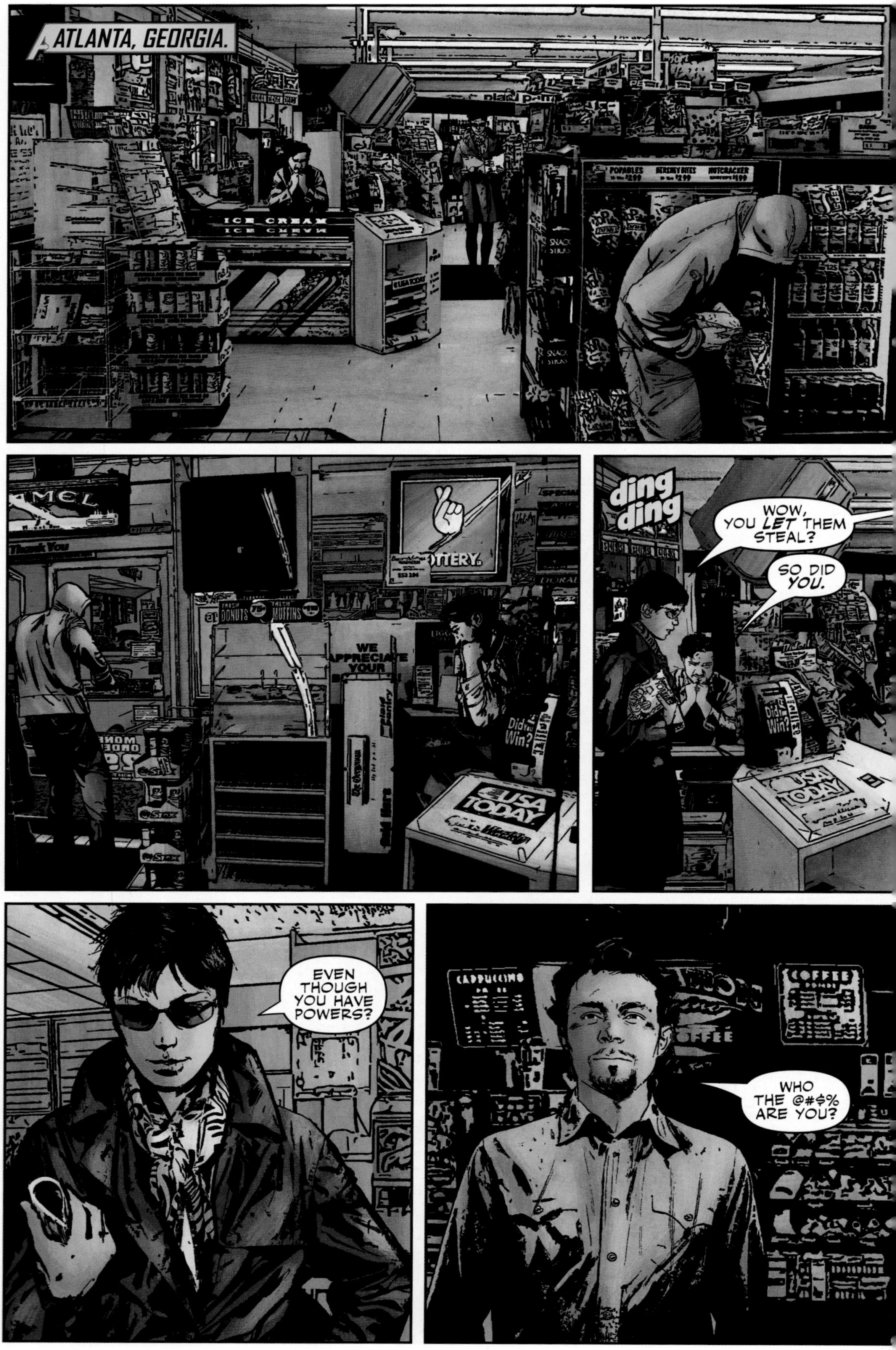
ATLANTA, GEORGIA.
POPABLES
HERSHEY BITES
NUTCRACKER
ICE CREAM
SNACK STICKS
Thank You
LOTTERY
DONUTS
MUFFINS
WE APPRECIATE YOUR
Did You Win?
USA TODAY
ding ding
WOW, YOU LET THEM STEAL?
SO DID YOU.
EVEN THOUGH YOU HAVE POWERS?
CAPPUCCINO
COFFEE
WHO THE @#$% ARE YOU?

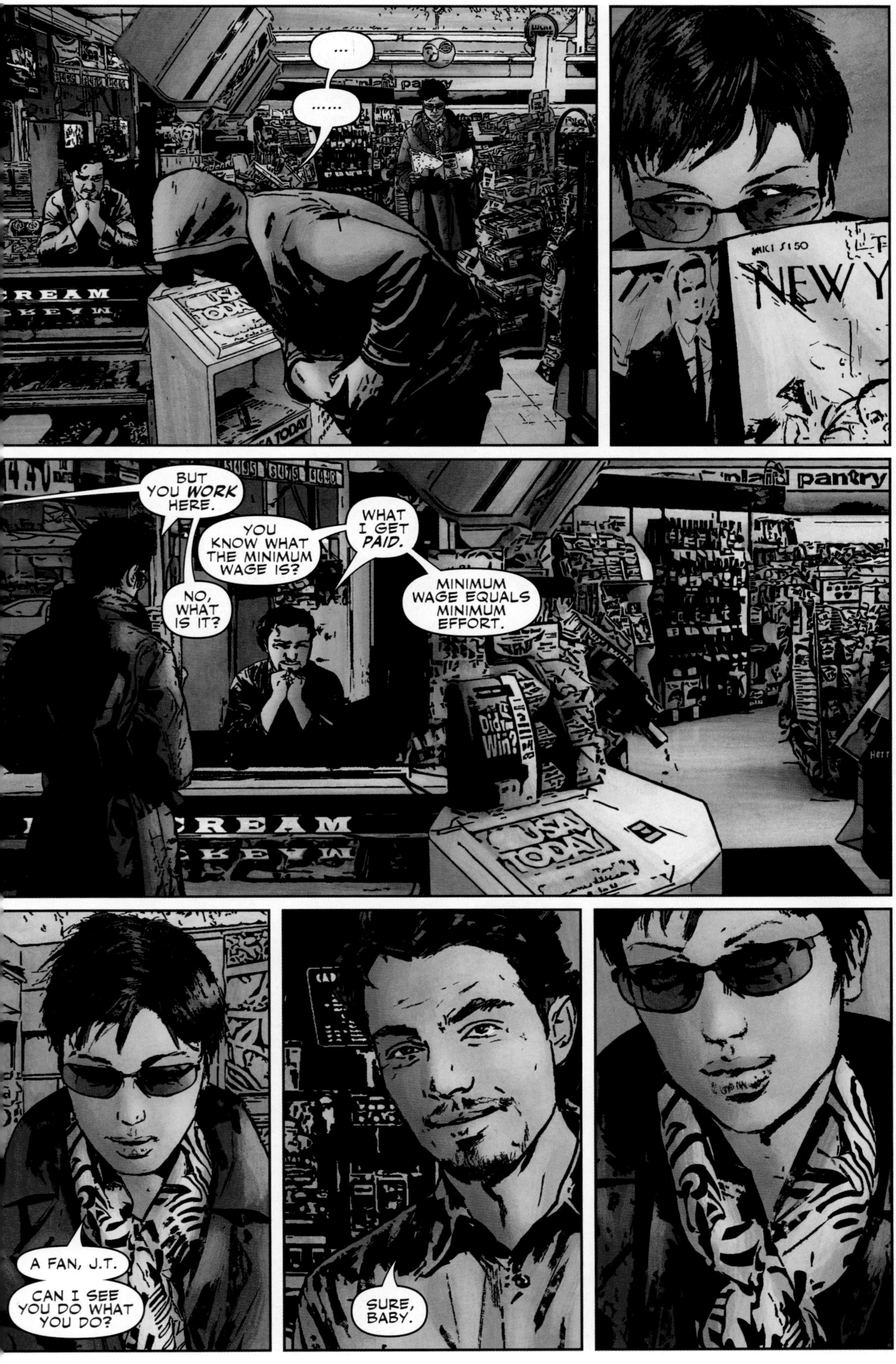
...
......
BUT YOU WORK HERE.
YOU KNOW WHAT THE MINIMUM WAGE IS?
NO, WHAT IS IT?
WHAT I GET PAID.
MINIMUM WAGE EQUALS MINIMUM EFFORT.
A FAN, J.T.
CAN I SEE YOU DO WHAT YOU DO?
SURE, BABY.

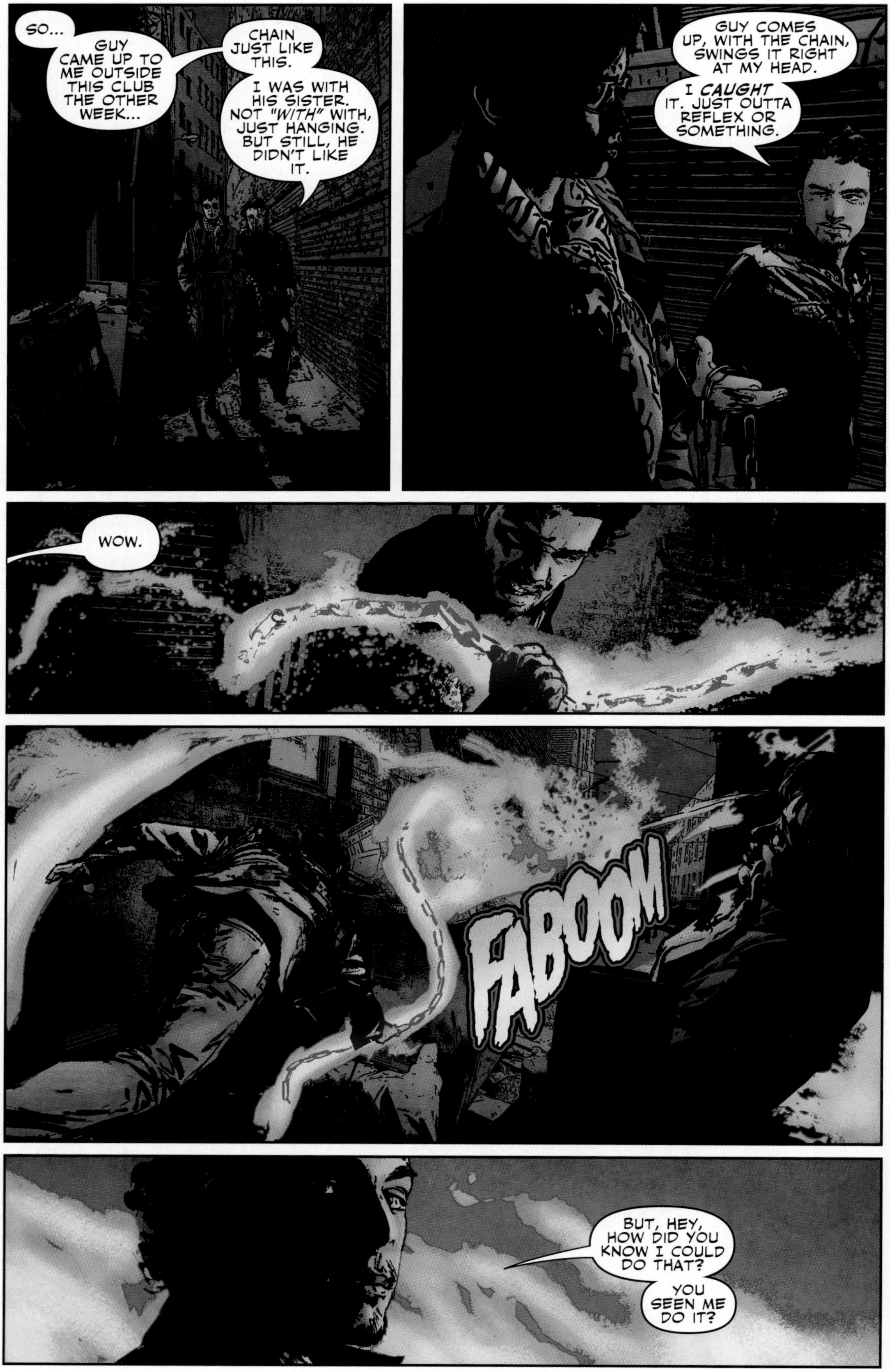
SO...
GUY CAME UP TO ME OUTSIDE THIS CLUB THE OTHER WEEK...
CHAIN JUST LIKE THIS.
I WAS WITH HIS SISTER. NOT "WITH" WITH, JUST HANGING. BUT STILL, HE DIDN'T LIKE IT.
GUY COMES UP, WITH THE CHAIN, SWINGS IT RIGHT AT MY HEAD.
I CAUGHT IT. JUST OUTTA REFLEX OR SOMETHING.
WOW.
FABOOM
BUT, HEY, HOW DID YOU KNOW I COULD DO THAT?
YOU SEEN ME DO IT?

NOPE.

NO?

NO, BUT I KNOW HOW YOU DO IT.

YOU DO?

YOU DON'T?

I, UH, I *DON'T*, ACTUALLY.

YOU KNOW WHO YOUR GRANDFATHER WAS?

NO.

REALLY?

REALLY.

THE ORIGINAL GHOST RIDER.

WHAT?

THE PHANTOM RIDER.

NO @#$%.

AND YOU GOT THE HAND-ME-DOWN POWERS OF A--

THAT IS *TOTALLY BALLS, MAN!* 'TIS KICK ASS!

THAT'S *AWESOME.*

AND I'M HERE TO TAKE YOU AWAY FROM *ALL THIS.*

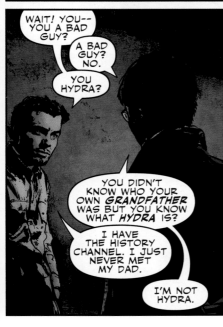

WAIT! YOU-- YOU A BAD GUY?

A BAD GUY? NO.

YOU HYDRA?

YOU DIDN'T KNOW WHO YOUR OWN *GRANDFATHER* WAS BUT YOU KNOW WHAT *HYDRA* IS?

I HAVE THE HISTORY CHANNEL. I JUST NEVER MET MY DAD.

I'M NOT HYDRA.

YOU S.H.I.E.L.D.? BECAUSE IF YOU'RE S.H.I.E.L.D., IN MY BOOK YOU MIGHT AS *WELL* BE HYDRA. ONE SIDE OF THE SAME BULL--

YES, WELL, THIS ISN'T S.H.I.E.L.D.

A.I.M.?

HOW ABOUT YOU COME WITH ME AND MAKE SOMETHING OF YOURSELF INSTEAD OF SITTING BEHIND THE COUNTER OF LIFE.

"THE COUNTER OF LIFE?"

DID YOU ACTUALLY SAY THAT OUT LOUD?

AND ABOUT THIS *"MAKING SOMETHING OF MYSELF."*

THERE *MONEY* IN MAKING SOMETHING OF MYSELF?

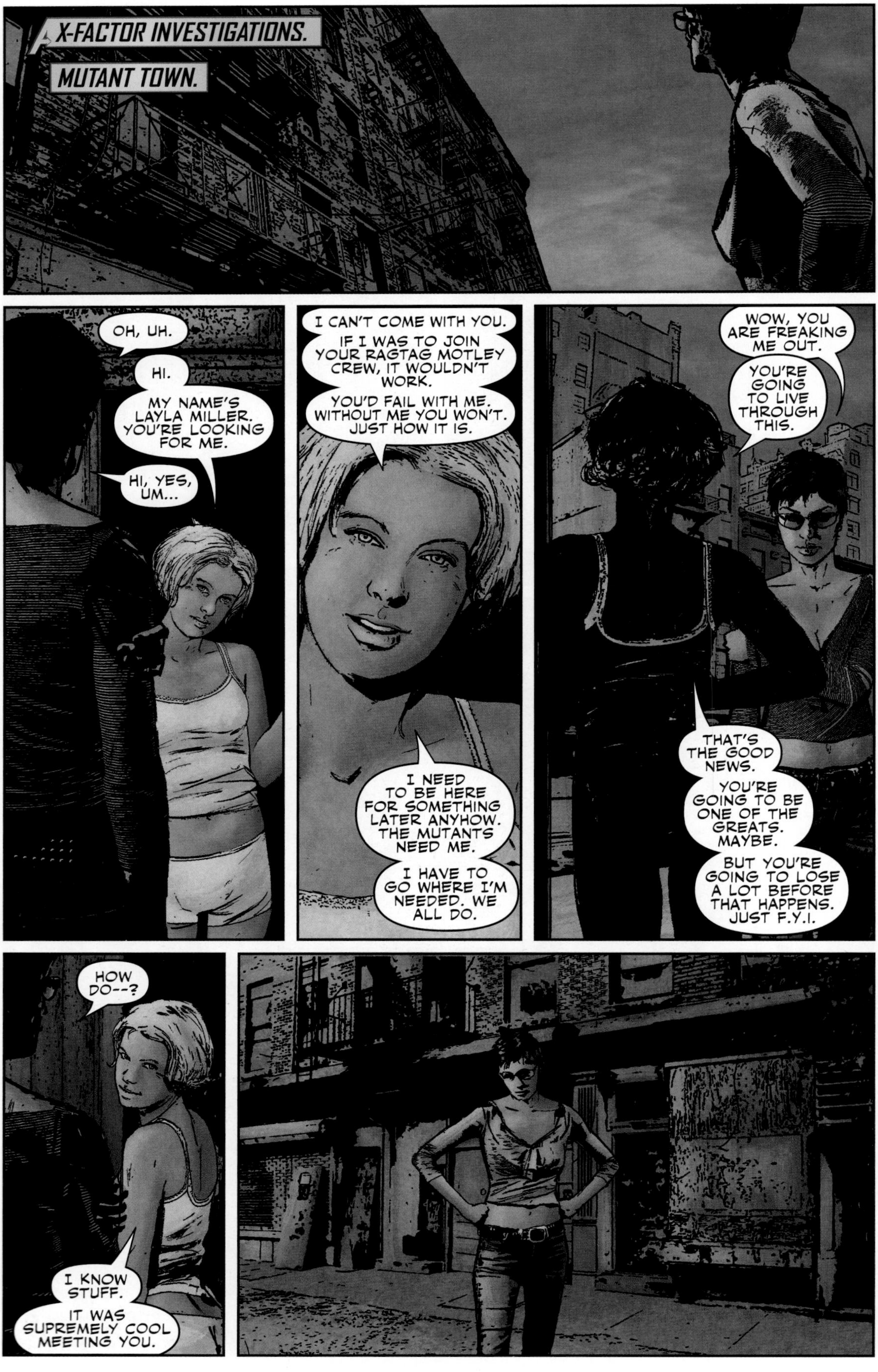
X-FACTOR INVESTIGATIONS.
MUTANT TOWN.
OH, UH.
HI.
MY NAME'S LAYLA MILLER. YOU'RE LOOKING FOR ME.
HI, YES, UM...
I CAN'T COME WITH YOU.
IF I WAS TO JOIN YOUR RAGTAG MOTLEY CREW, IT WOULDN'T WORK.
YOU'D FAIL WITH ME. WITHOUT ME YOU WON'T. JUST HOW IT IS.
I NEED TO BE HERE FOR SOMETHING LATER ANYHOW. THE MUTANTS NEED ME.
I HAVE TO GO WHERE I'M NEEDED. WE ALL DO.
WOW, YOU ARE FREAKING ME OUT.
YOU'RE GOING TO LIVE THROUGH THIS.
THAT'S THE GOOD NEWS.
YOU'RE GOING TO BE ONE OF THE GREATS. MAYBE.
BUT YOU'RE GOING TO LOSE A LOT BEFORE THAT HAPPENS. JUST F.Y.I.
HOW DO--?
I KNOW STUFF.
IT WAS SUPREMELY COOL MEETING YOU.

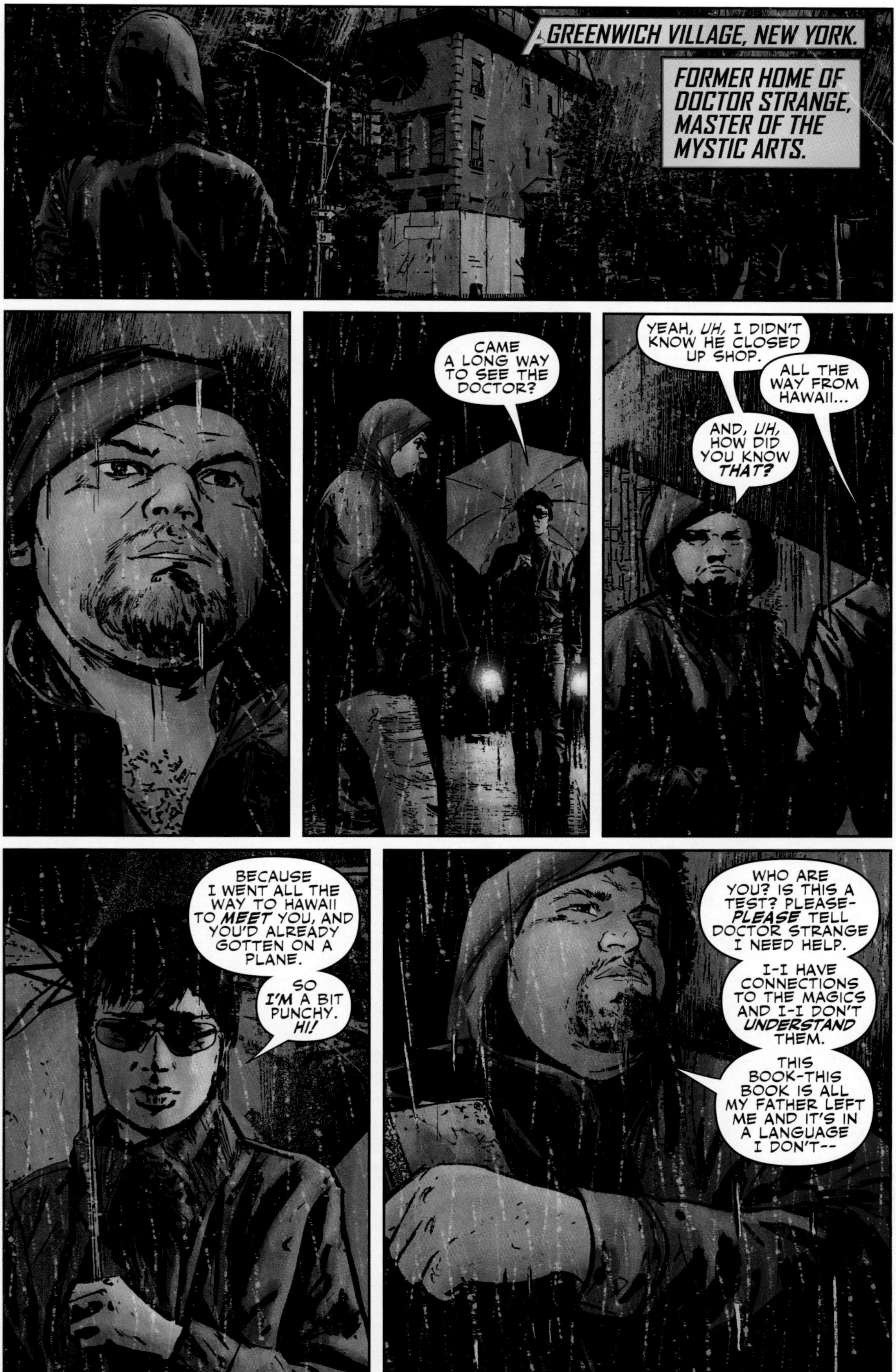
GREENWICH VILLAGE, NEW YORK.
FORMER HOME OF DOCTOR STRANGE, MASTER OF THE MYSTIC ARTS.
CAME A LONG WAY TO SEE THE DOCTOR?
YEAH, *UH,* I DIDN'T KNOW HE CLOSED UP SHOP.
ALL THE WAY FROM HAWAII...
AND, *UH,* HOW DID YOU KNOW ***THAT?***
BECAUSE I WENT ALL THE WAY TO HAWAII TO ***MEET*** YOU, AND YOU'D ALREADY GOTTEN ON A PLANE.
SO ***I'M*** A BIT PUNCHY. ***HI!***
WHO ARE YOU? IS THIS A TEST? PLEASE- ***PLEASE*** TELL DOCTOR STRANGE I NEED HELP.
I-I HAVE CONNECTIONS TO THE MAGICS AND I-I DON'T ***UNDERSTAND*** THEM.
THIS BOOK-THIS BOOK IS ALL MY FATHER LEFT ME AND IT'S IN A LANGUAGE I DON'T--

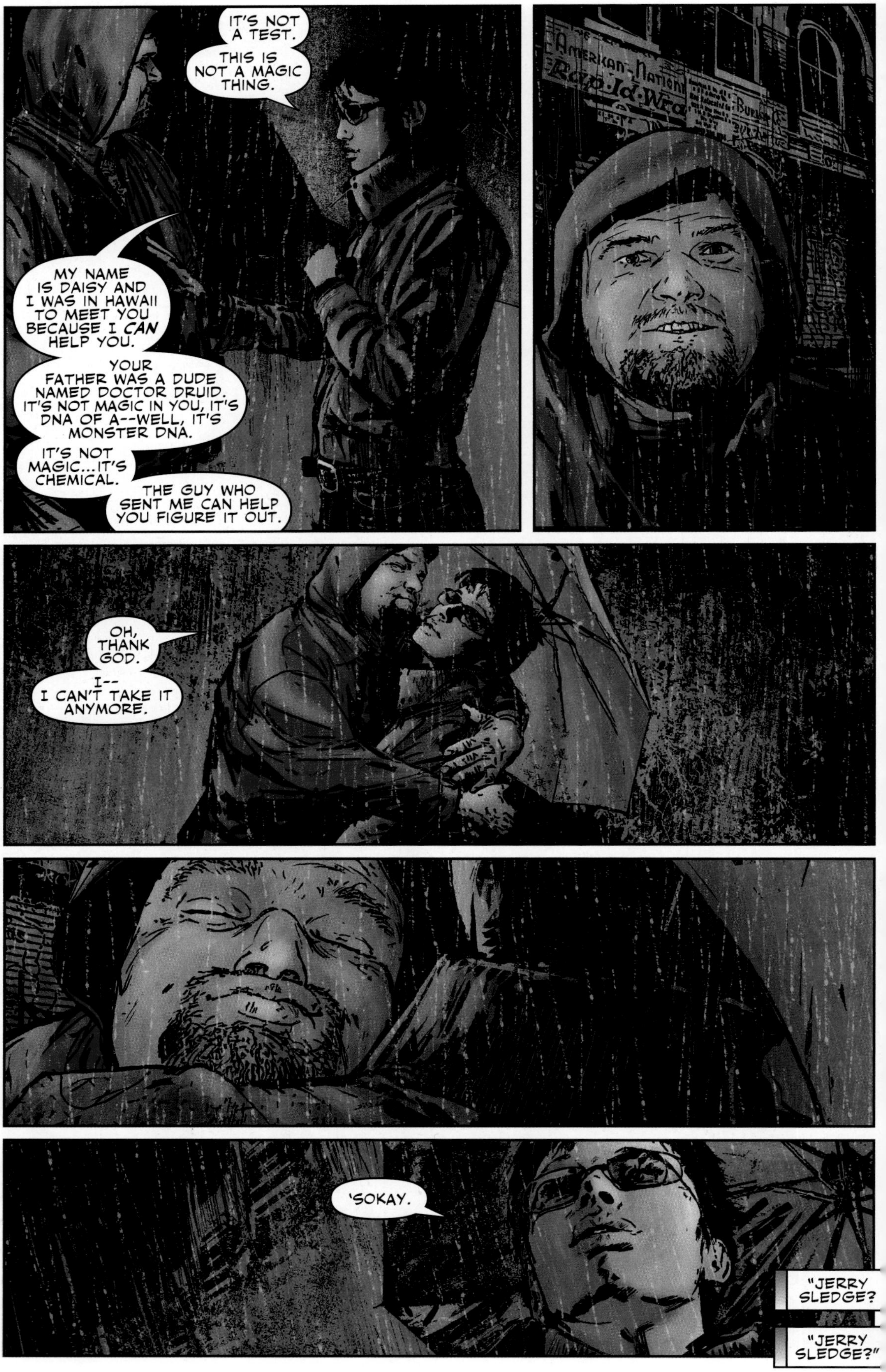
IT'S NOT A TEST.
THIS IS NOT A MAGIC THING.
MY NAME IS DAISY AND I WAS IN HAWAII TO MEET YOU BECAUSE I CAN HELP YOU.
YOUR FATHER WAS A DUDE NAMED DOCTOR DRUID. IT'S NOT MAGIC IN YOU, IT'S DNA OF A--WELL, IT'S MONSTER DNA.
IT'S NOT MAGIC...IT'S CHEMICAL.
THE GUY WHO SENT ME CAN HELP YOU FIGURE IT OUT.
OH, THANK GOD.
I-- I CAN'T TAKE IT ANYMORE.
'SOKAY.
"JERRY SLEDGE?
"JERRY SLEDGE?"

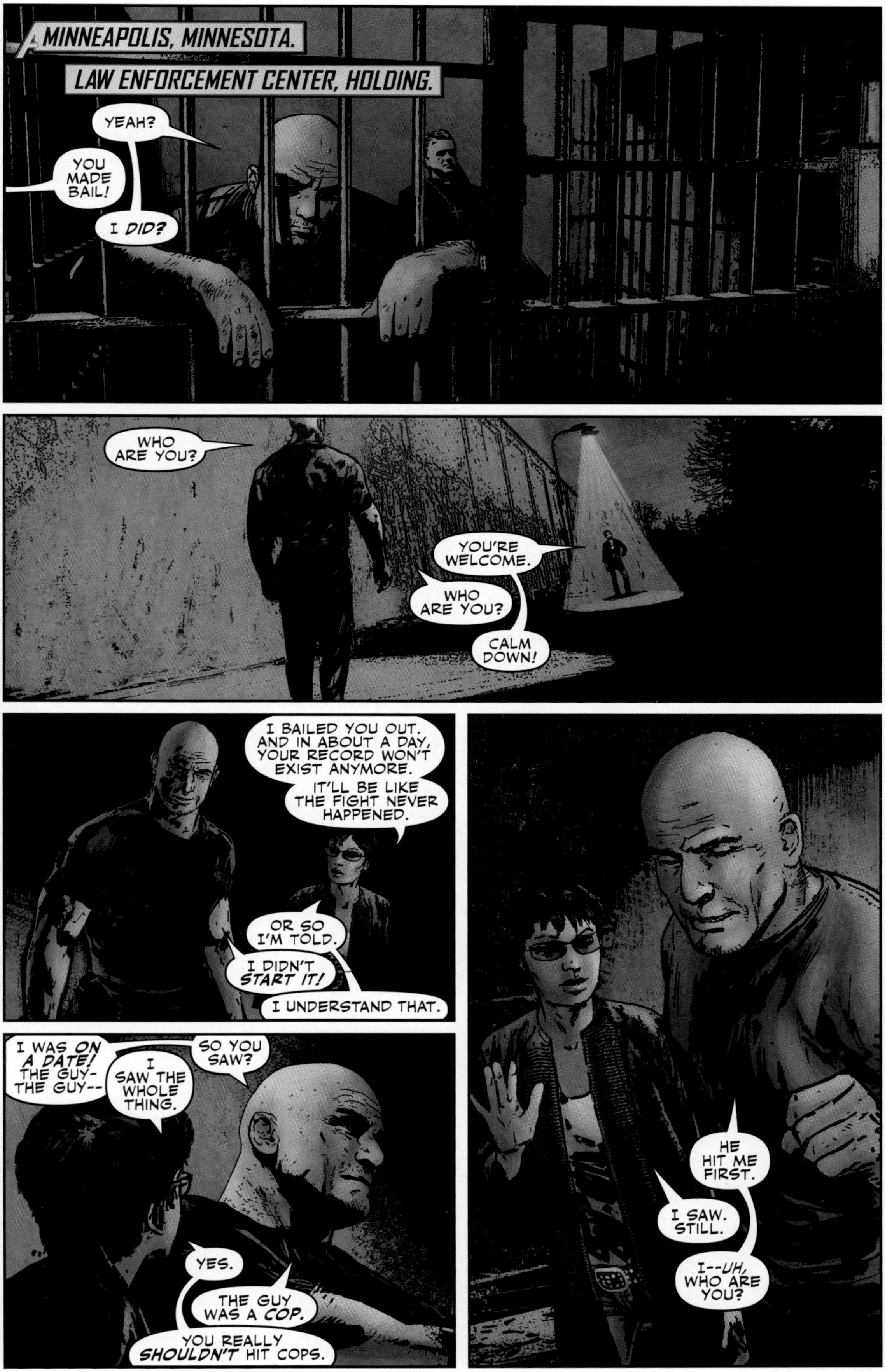
MINNEAPOLIS, MINNESOTA.
LAW ENFORCEMENT CENTER, HOLDING.
YEAH?
YOU MADE BAIL!
I DID?
WHO ARE YOU?
YOU'RE WELCOME.
WHO ARE YOU?
CALM DOWN!
I BAILED YOU OUT. AND IN ABOUT A DAY, YOUR RECORD WON'T EXIST ANYMORE.
IT'LL BE LIKE THE FIGHT NEVER HAPPENED.
OR SO I'M TOLD.
I DIDN'T START IT!
I UNDERSTAND THAT.
I WAS ON A DATE! THE GUY- THE GUY--
I SAW THE WHOLE THING.
SO YOU SAW?
YES.
THE GUY WAS A COP.
YOU REALLY SHOULDN'T HIT COPS.
HE HIT ME FIRST.
I SAW. STILL.
I--UH, WHO ARE YOU?

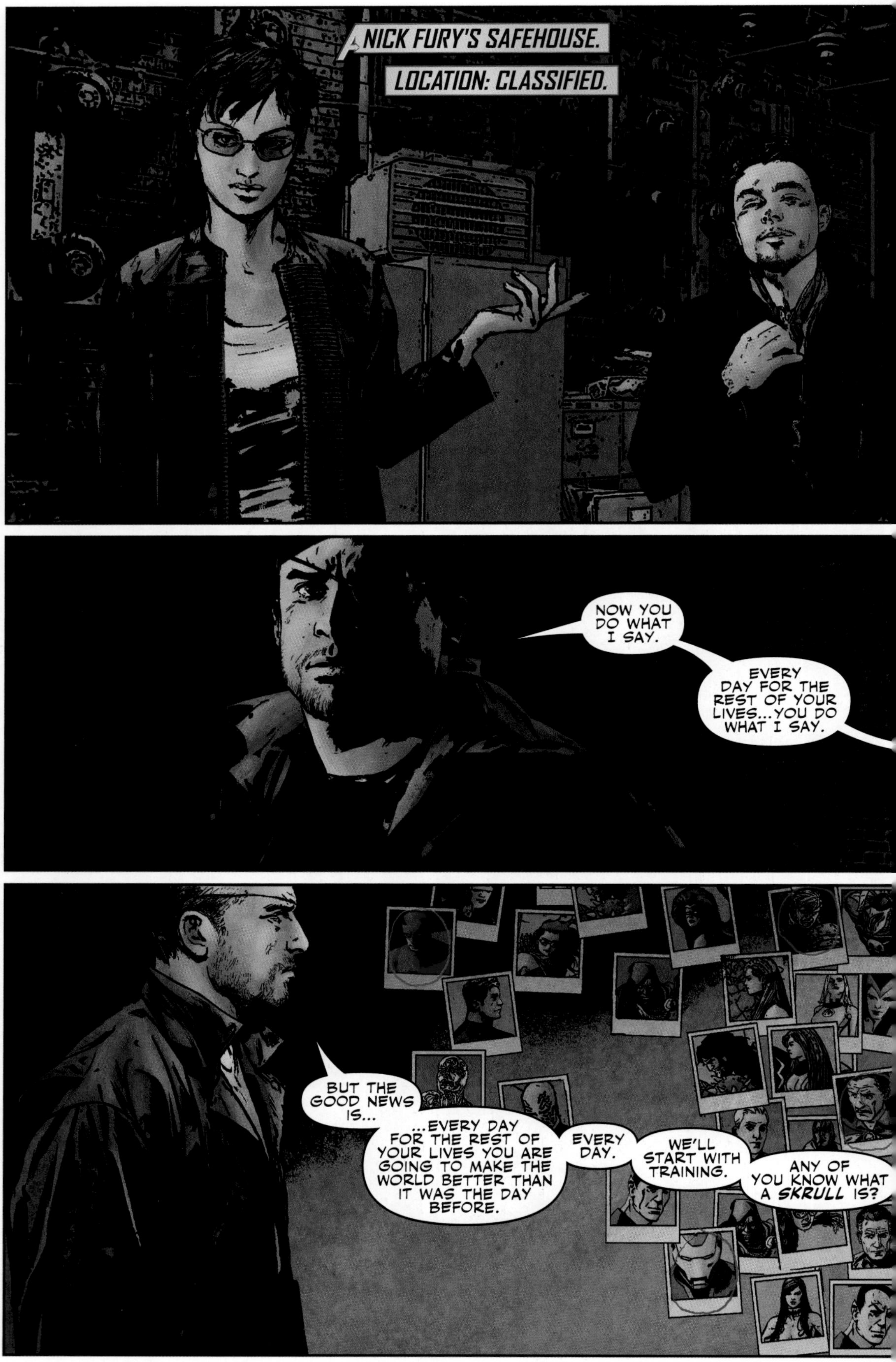
NICK FURY'S SAFEHOUSE.
LOCATION: CLASSIFIED.
NOW YOU DO WHAT I SAY.
EVERY DAY FOR THE REST OF YOUR LIVES...YOU DO WHAT I SAY.
BUT THE GOOD NEWS IS...
...EVERY DAY FOR THE REST OF YOUR LIVES YOU ARE GOING TO MAKE THE WORLD BETTER THAN IT WAS THE DAY BEFORE.
EVERY DAY.
WE'LL START WITH TRAINING.
ANY OF YOU KNOW WHAT A *SKRULL* IS?

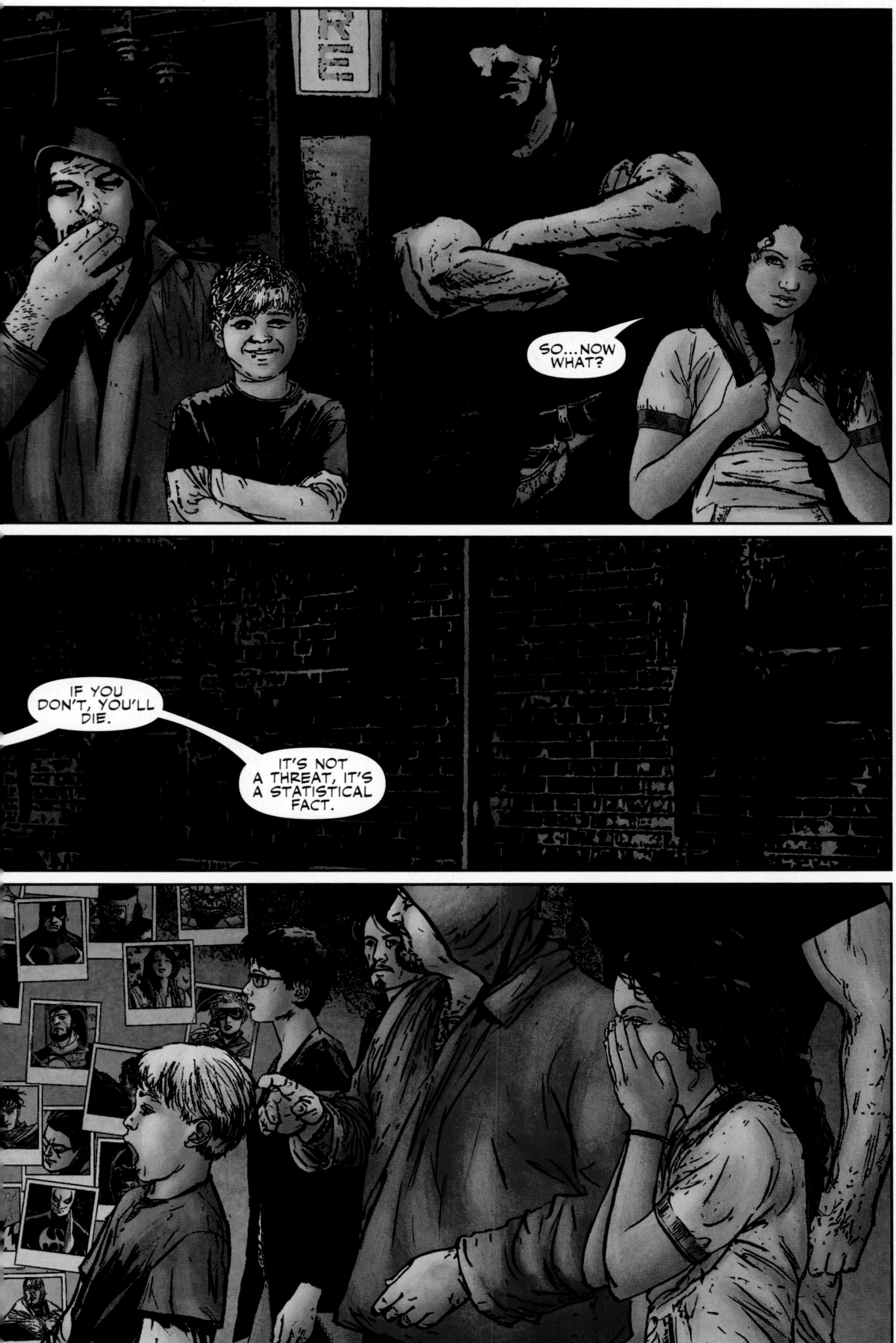
SO...NOW WHAT?
IF YOU DON'T, YOU'LL DIE.
IT'S NOT A THREAT, IT'S A STATISTICAL FACT.

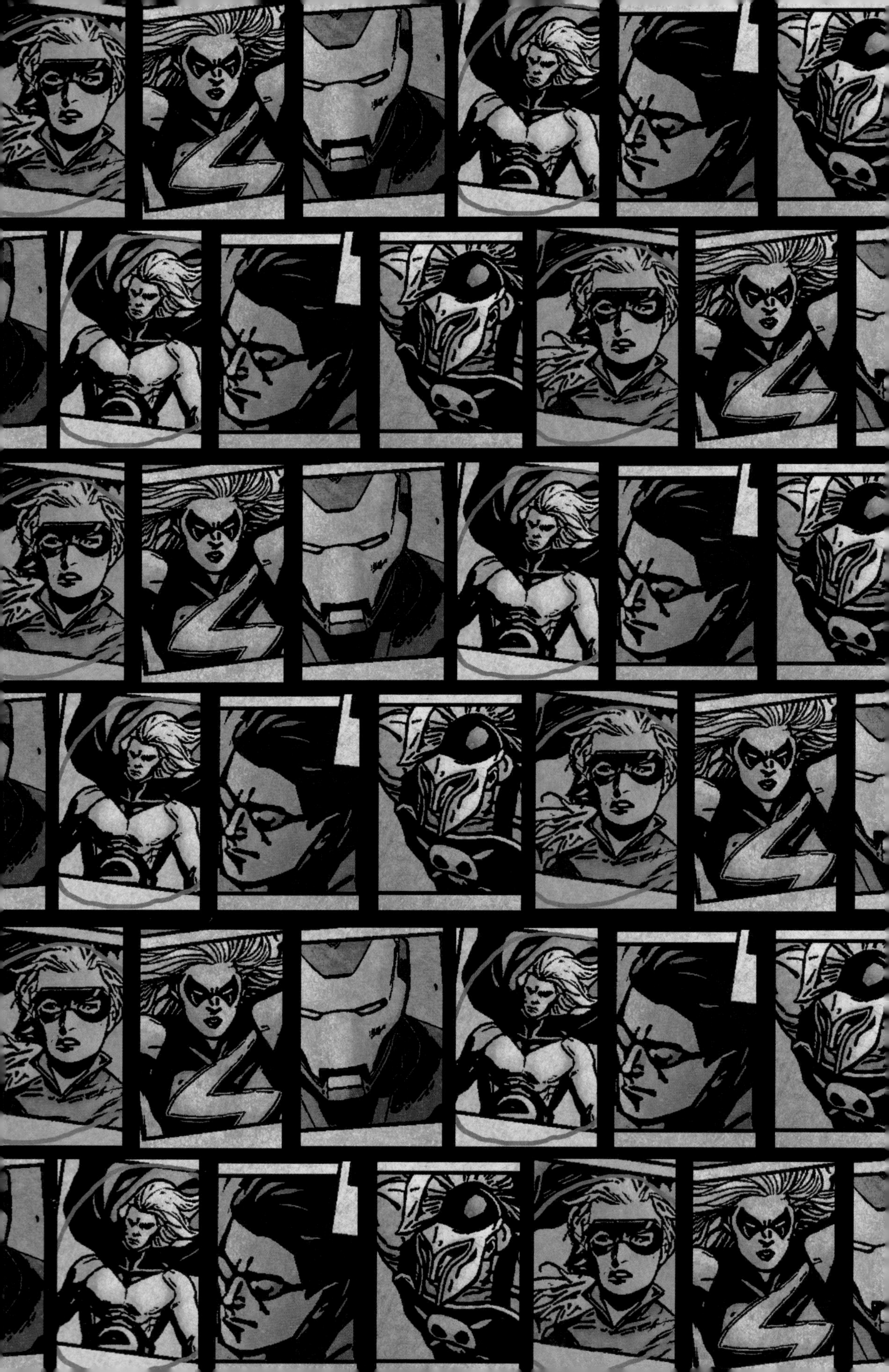

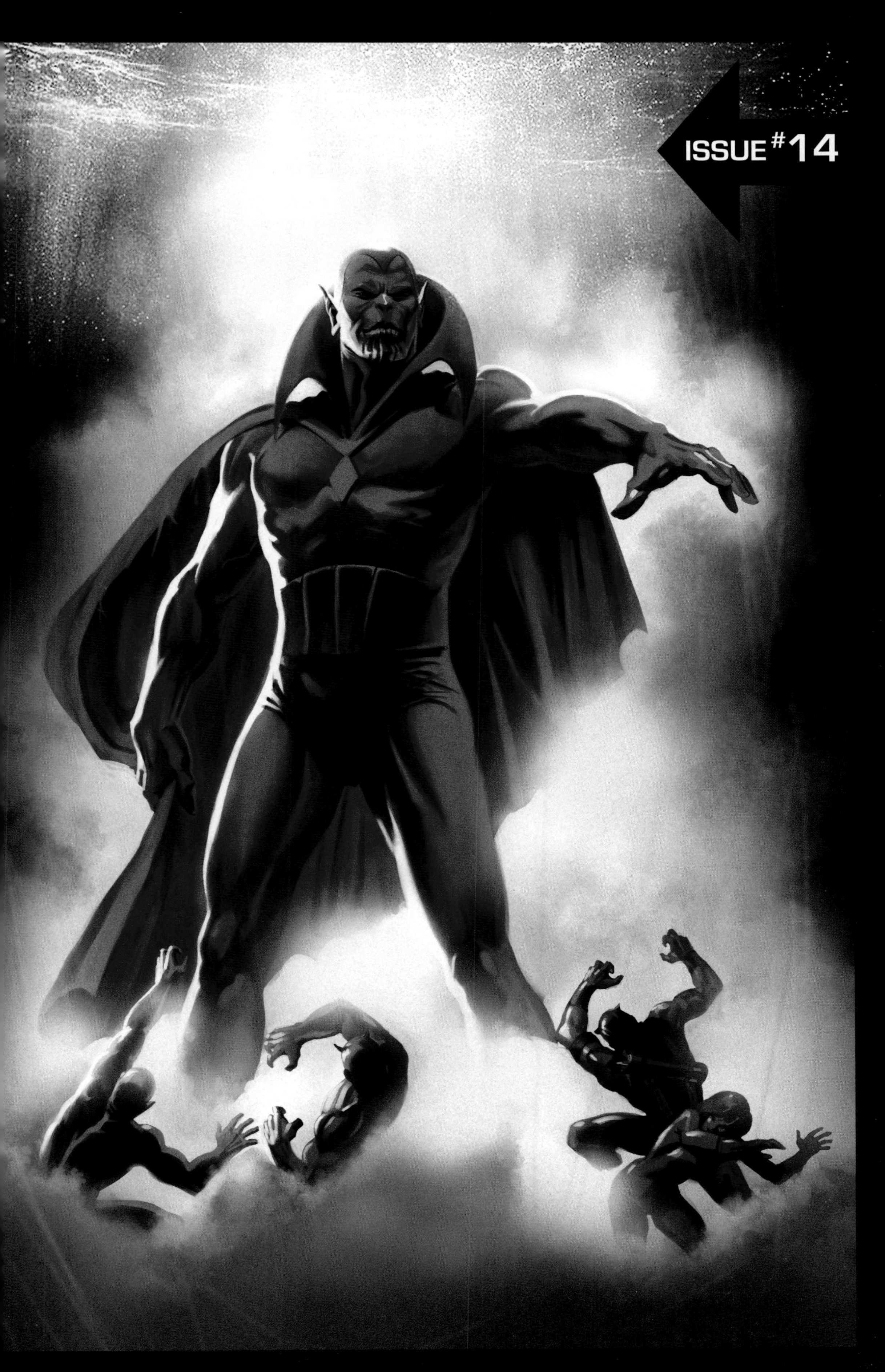
ISSUE #14

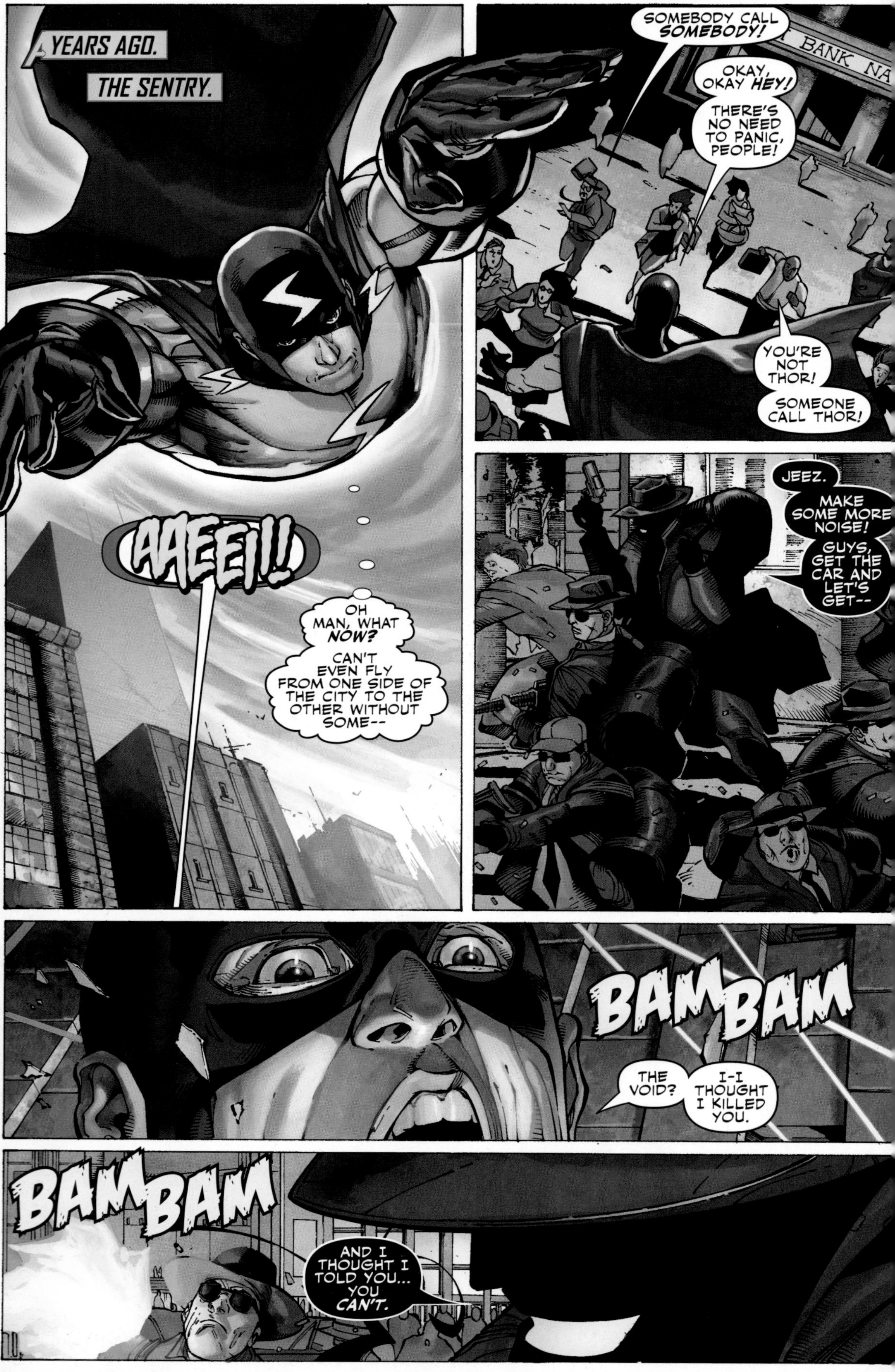
YEARS AGO.
THE SENTRY.
AAEEII!!
OH MAN, WHAT NOW? CAN'T EVEN FLY FROM ONE SIDE OF THE CITY TO THE OTHER WITHOUT SOME--
SOMEBODY CALL SOMEBODY!
OKAY, OKAY HEY!
THERE'S NO NEED TO PANIC, PEOPLE!
YOU'RE NOT THOR!
SOMEONE CALL THOR!
JEEZ.
MAKE SOME MORE NOISE!
GUYS, GET THE CAR AND LET'S GET--
BAM BAM
THE VOID?
I-I THOUGHT I KILLED YOU.
BAM BAM
AND I THOUGHT I TOLD YOU... YOU CAN'T.

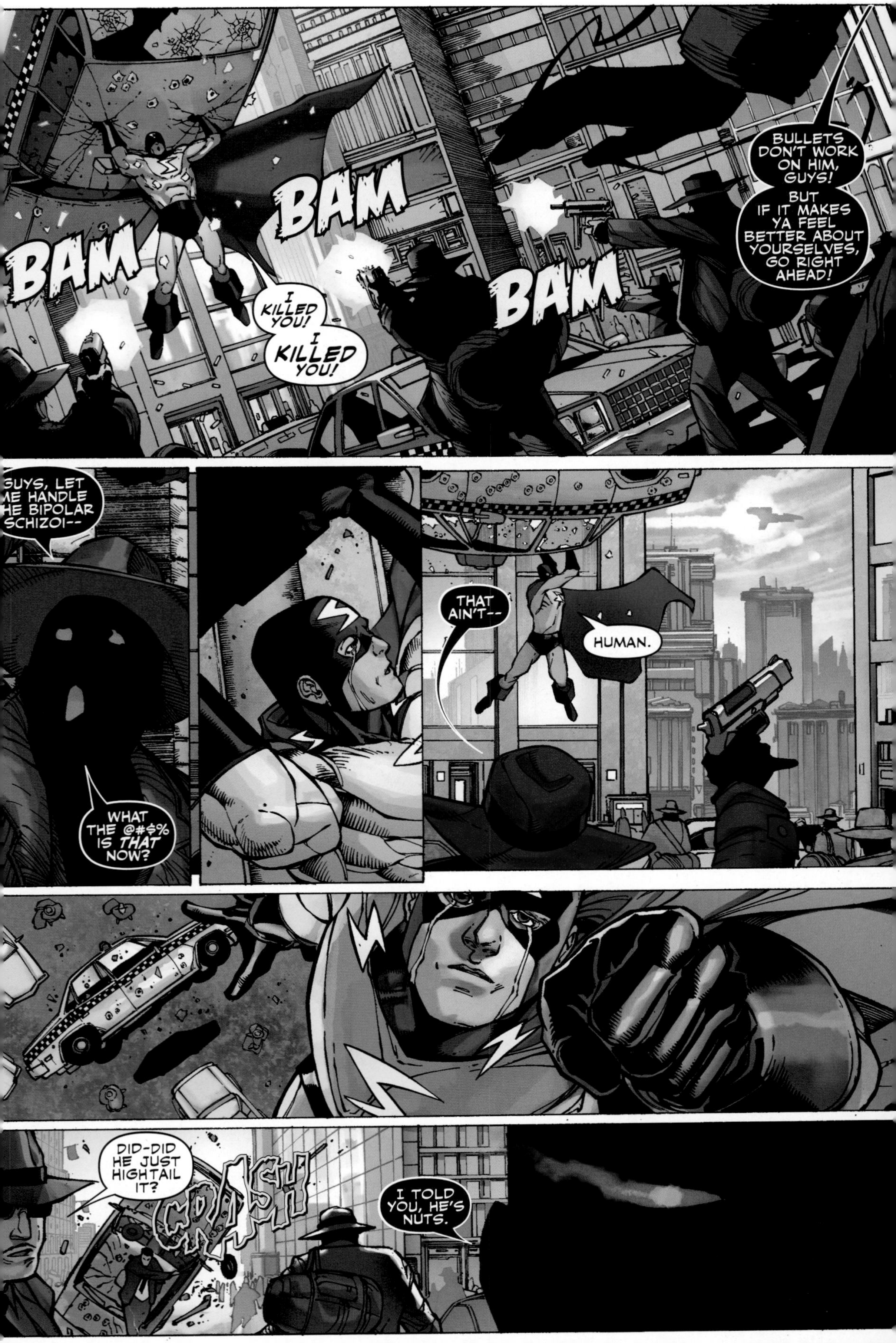

BAM
BAM
I KILLED YOU! I KILLED YOU!
BAM
BULLETS DON'T WORK ON HIM, GUYS!
BUT IF IT MAKES YA FEEL BETTER ABOUT YOURSELVES, GO RIGHT AHEAD!
GUYS, LET ME HANDLE HE BIPOLAR SCHIZOI--
WHAT THE @#$% IS THAT NOW?
THAT AIN'T--
HUMAN.
DID-DID HE JUST HIGHTAIL IT?
CRASH
I TOLD YOU, HE'S NUTS.

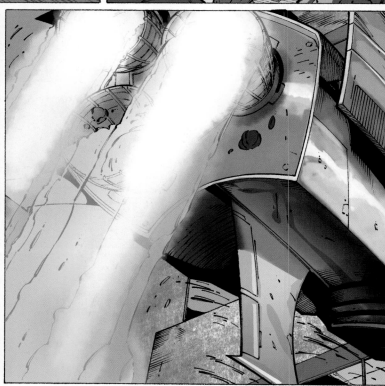

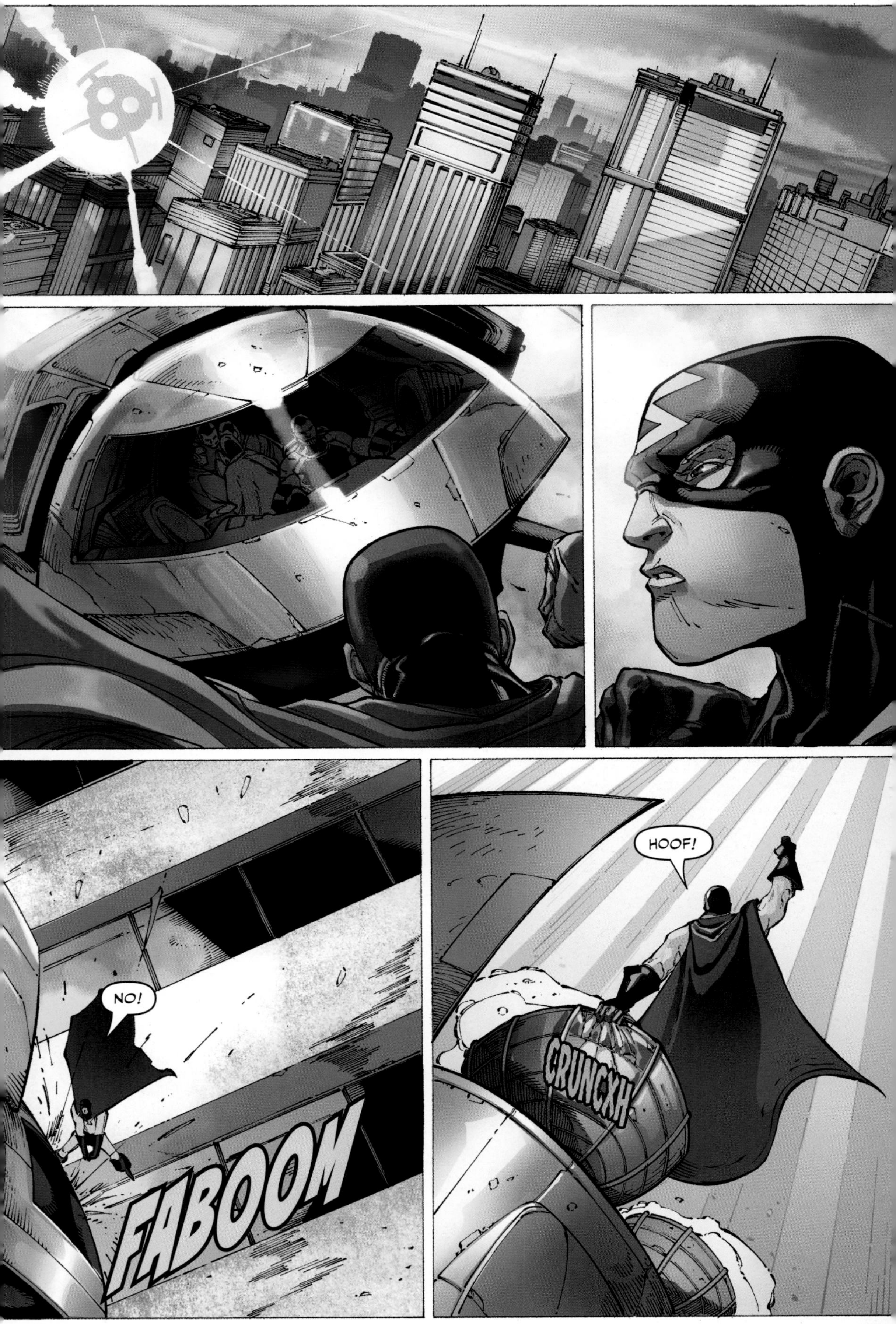
NO!
FABOOM
HOOF!
CRUNCXH

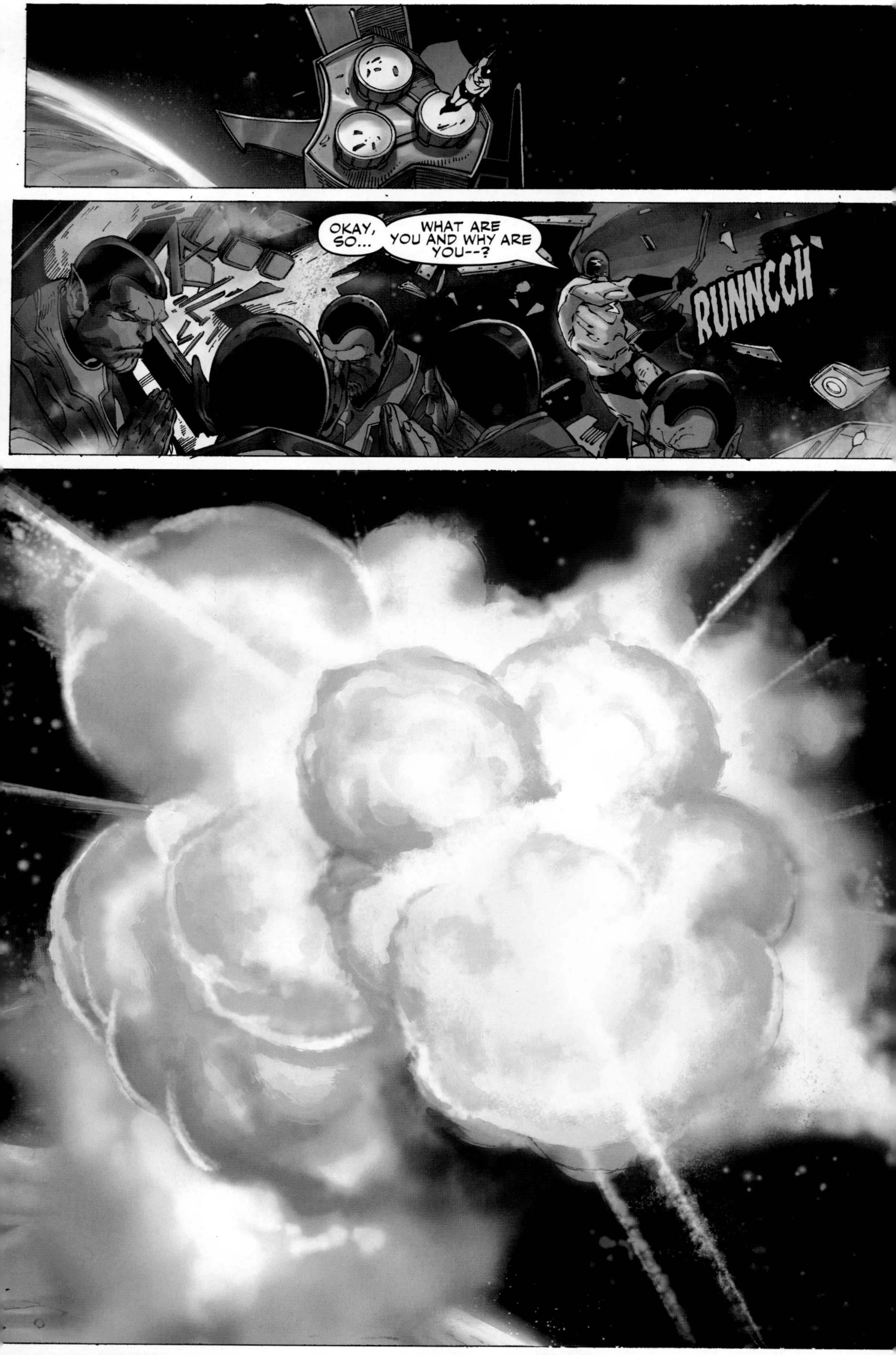
OKAY, SO...
WHAT ARE YOU AND WHY ARE YOU--?
RUNNCCH

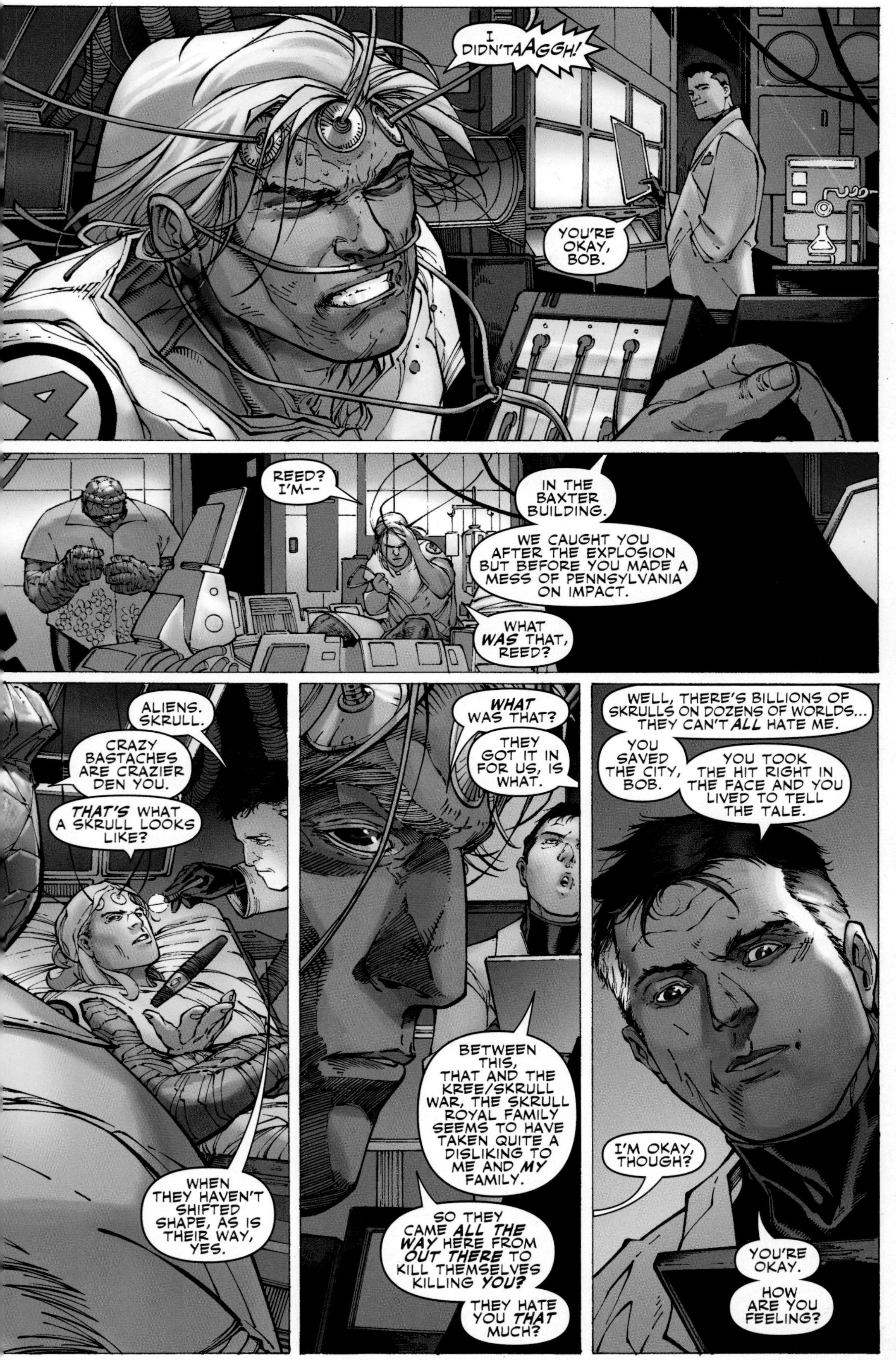
I DIDN'TAAGGH!
YOU'RE OKAY, BOB.
REED? I'M--
IN THE BAXTER BUILDING.
WE CAUGHT YOU AFTER THE EXPLOSION BUT BEFORE YOU MADE A MESS OF PENNSYLVANIA ON IMPACT.
WHAT WAS THAT, REED?
ALIENS. SKRULL.
CRAZY BASTACHES ARE CRAZIER DEN YOU.
THAT'S WHAT A SKRULL LOOKS LIKE?
WHEN THEY HAVEN'T SHIFTED SHAPE, AS IS THEIR WAY, YES.
WHAT WAS THAT?
THEY GOT IT IN FOR US, IS WHAT.
BETWEEN THIS, THAT AND THE KREE/SKRULL WAR, THE SKRULL ROYAL FAMILY SEEMS TO HAVE TAKEN QUITE A DISLIKING TO ME AND MY FAMILY.
SO THEY CAME ALL THE WAY HERE FROM OUT THERE TO KILL THEMSELVES KILLING YOU?
THEY HATE YOU THAT MUCH?
WELL, THERE'S BILLIONS OF SKRULLS ON DOZENS OF WORLDS... THEY CAN'T ALL HATE ME.
YOU SAVED THE CITY, BOB.
YOU TOOK THE HIT RIGHT IN THE FACE AND YOU LIVED TO TELL THE TALE.
I'M OKAY, THOUGH?
YOU'RE OKAY.
HOW ARE YOU FEELING?

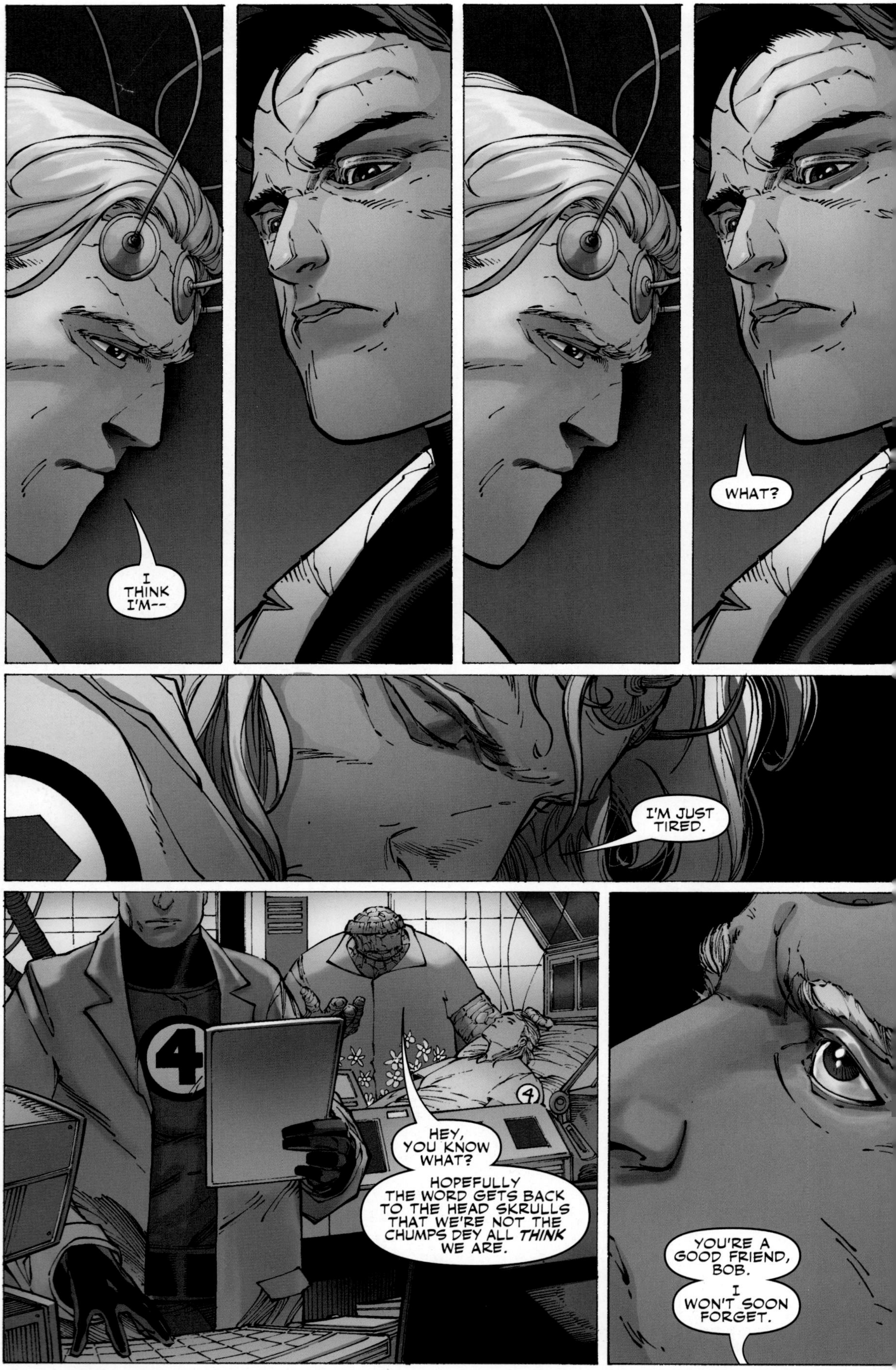
I THINK I'M--
WHAT?
I'M JUST TIRED.
HEY, YOU KNOW WHAT?
HOPEFULLY THE WORD GETS BACK TO THE HEAD SKRULLS THAT WE'RE NOT THE CHUMPS DEY ALL *THINK* WE ARE.
YOU'RE A GOOD FRIEND, BOB.
I WON'T SOON FORGET.

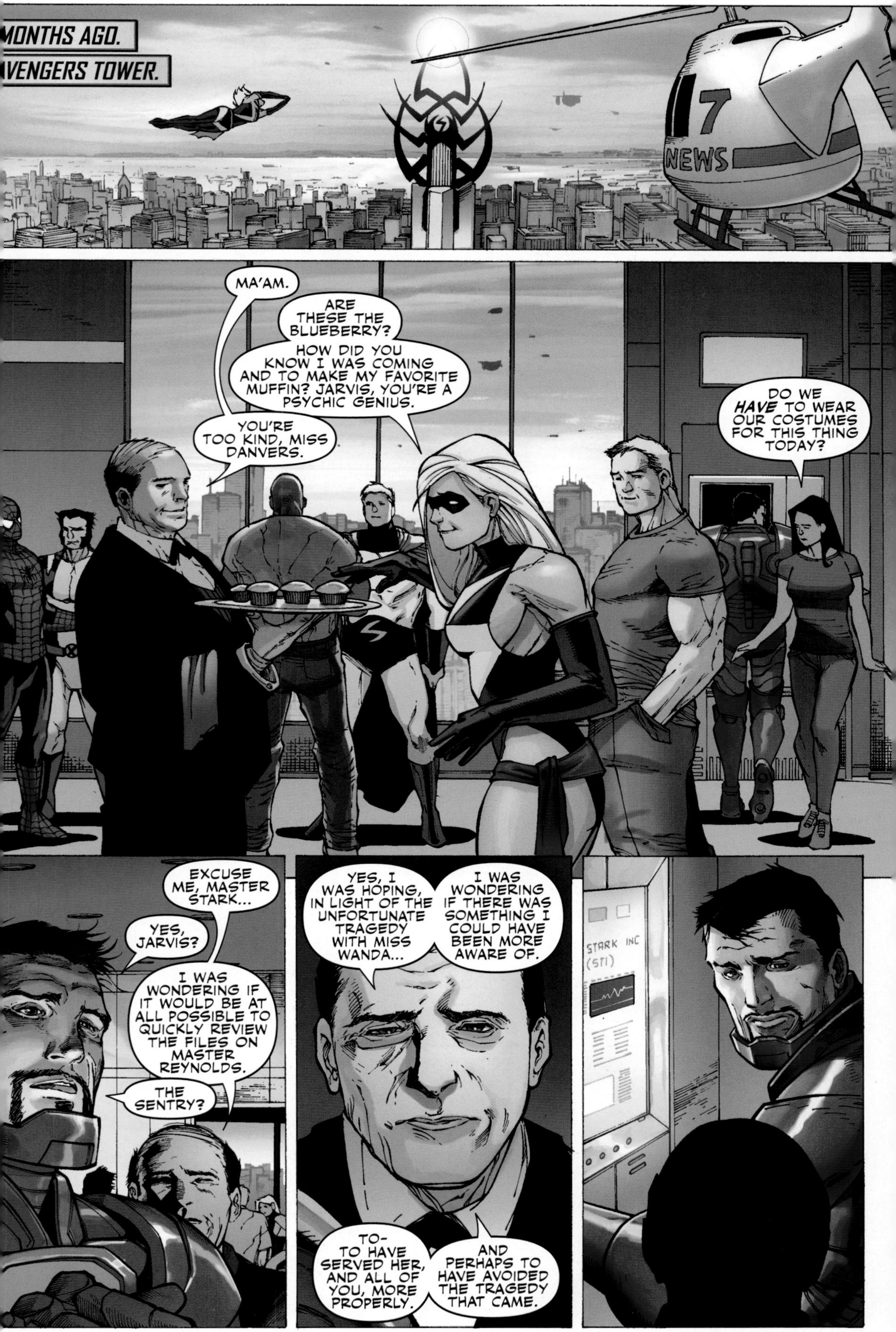

MONTHS AGO.
AVENGERS TOWER.
7 NEWS
MA'AM.
ARE THESE THE BLUEBERRY?
HOW DID YOU KNOW I WAS COMING AND TO MAKE MY FAVORITE MUFFIN? JARVIS, YOU'RE A PSYCHIC GENIUS.
YOU'RE TOO KIND, MISS DANVERS.
DO WE HAVE TO WEAR OUR COSTUMES FOR THIS THING TODAY?
EXCUSE ME, MASTER STARK...
YES, JARVIS?
I WAS WONDERING IF IT WOULD BE AT ALL POSSIBLE TO QUICKLY REVIEW THE FILES ON MASTER REYNOLDS.
THE SENTRY?
YES, I WAS HOPING, IN LIGHT OF THE UNFORTUNATE TRAGEDY WITH MISS WANDA...
I WAS WONDERING IF THERE WAS SOMETHING I COULD HAVE BEEN MORE AWARE OF.
TO- TO HAVE SERVED HER, AND ALL OF YOU, MORE PROPERLY.
AND PERHAPS TO HAVE AVOIDED THE TRAGEDY THAT CAME.
STARK INC
(STI)

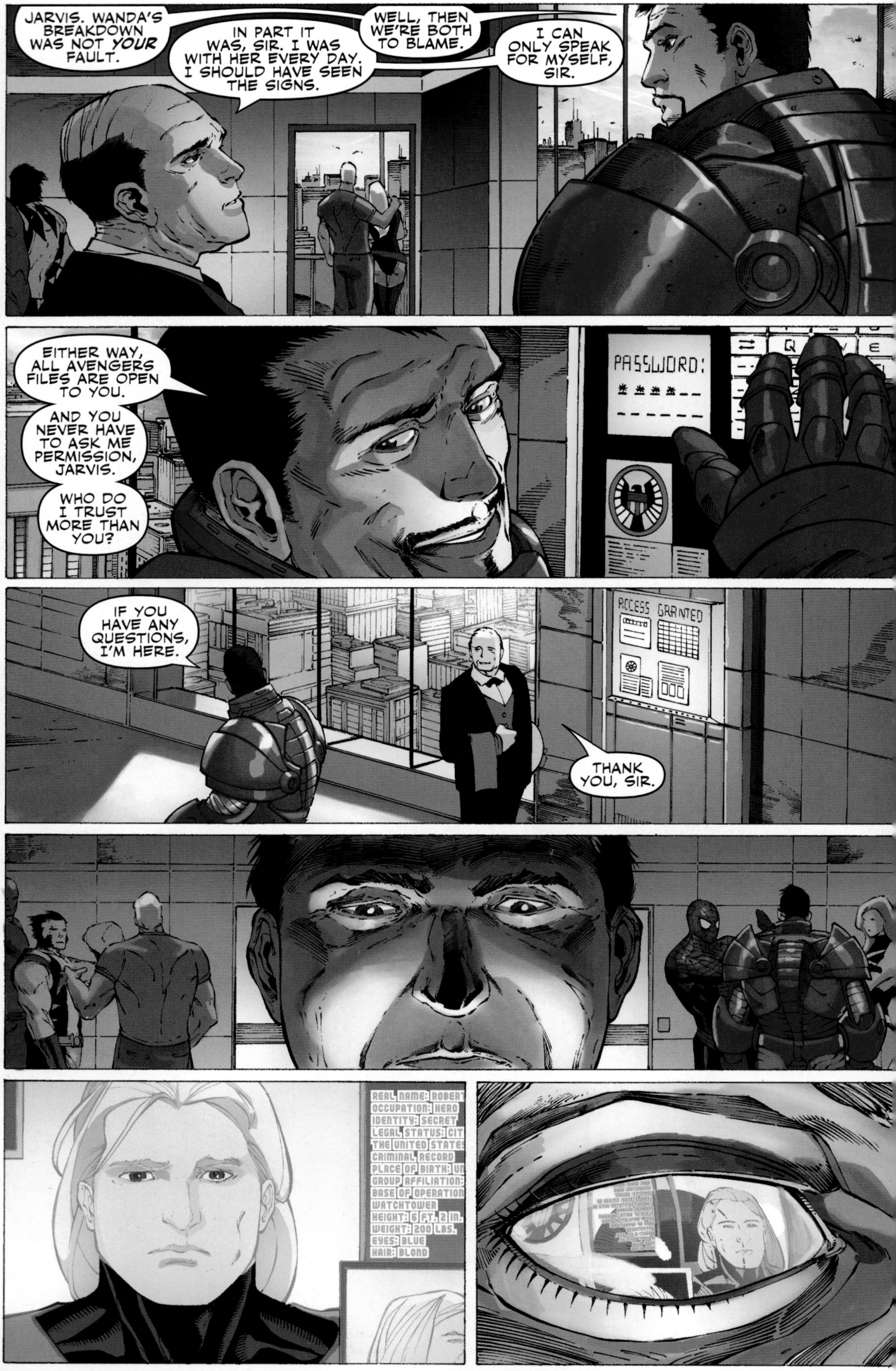
JARVIS. WANDA'S BREAKDOWN WAS NOT *YOUR* FAULT.
IN PART IT WAS, SIR. I WAS WITH HER EVERY DAY. I SHOULD HAVE SEEN THE SIGNS.
WELL, THEN WE'RE BOTH TO BLAME.
I CAN ONLY SPEAK FOR MYSELF, SIR.
EITHER WAY, ALL AVENGERS FILES ARE OPEN TO YOU.
AND YOU NEVER HAVE TO ASK ME PERMISSION, JARVIS.
WHO DO I TRUST MORE THAN YOU?
PASSWORD:
IF YOU HAVE ANY QUESTIONS, I'M HERE.
ACCESS GRANTED
THANK YOU, SIR.
REAL NAME: ROBERT
OCCUPATION: HERO
IDENTITY: SECRET
LEGAL STATUS: CIT
THE UNITED STATES
CRIMINAL RECORD
PLACE OF BIRTH: UN
GROUP AFFILIATION:
BASE OF OPERATION
WATCHTOWER
HEIGHT: 6 FT. 2 IN.
WEIGHT: 200 LBS.
EYES: BLUE
HAIR: BLOND

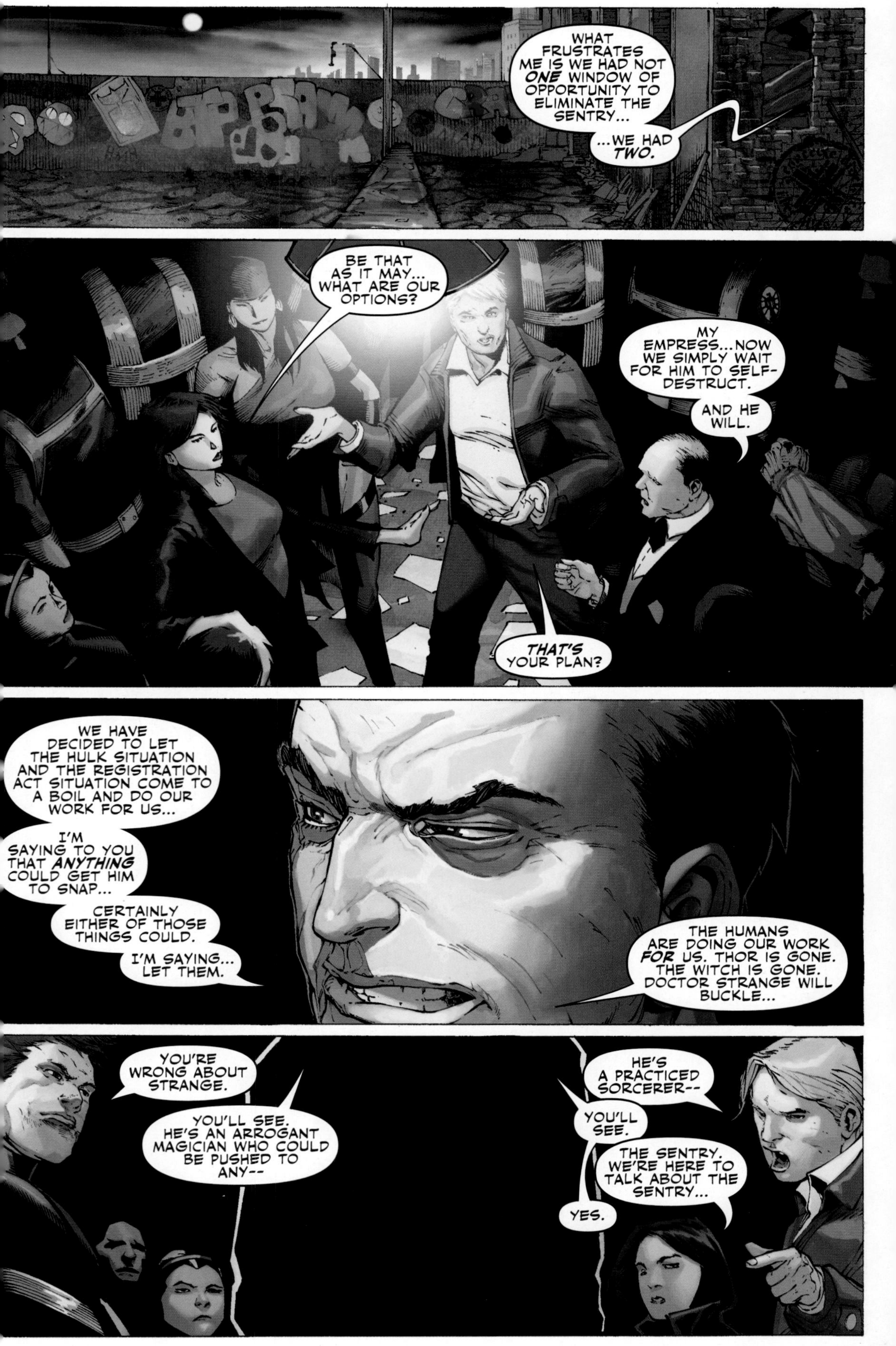
WHAT FRUSTRATES ME IS WE HAD NOT ONE WINDOW OF OPPORTUNITY TO ELIMINATE THE SENTRY...
...WE HAD TWO.
BE THAT AS IT MAY... WHAT ARE OUR OPTIONS?
MY EMPRESS...NOW WE SIMPLY WAIT FOR HIM TO SELF-DESTRUCT.
AND HE WILL.
THAT'S YOUR PLAN?
WE HAVE DECIDED TO LET THE HULK SITUATION AND THE REGISTRATION ACT SITUATION COME TO A BOIL AND DO OUR WORK FOR US...
I'M SAYING TO YOU THAT ANYTHING COULD GET HIM TO SNAP...
CERTAINLY EITHER OF THOSE THINGS COULD.
I'M SAYING... LET THEM.
THE HUMANS ARE DOING OUR WORK FOR US. THOR IS GONE. THE WITCH IS GONE. DOCTOR STRANGE WILL BUCKLE...
YOU'RE WRONG ABOUT STRANGE.
HE'S A PRACTICED SORCERER--
YOU'LL SEE.
YOU'LL SEE. HE'S AN ARROGANT MAGICIAN WHO COULD BE PUSHED TO ANY--
THE SENTRY. WE'RE HERE TO TALK ABOUT THE SENTRY...
YES.

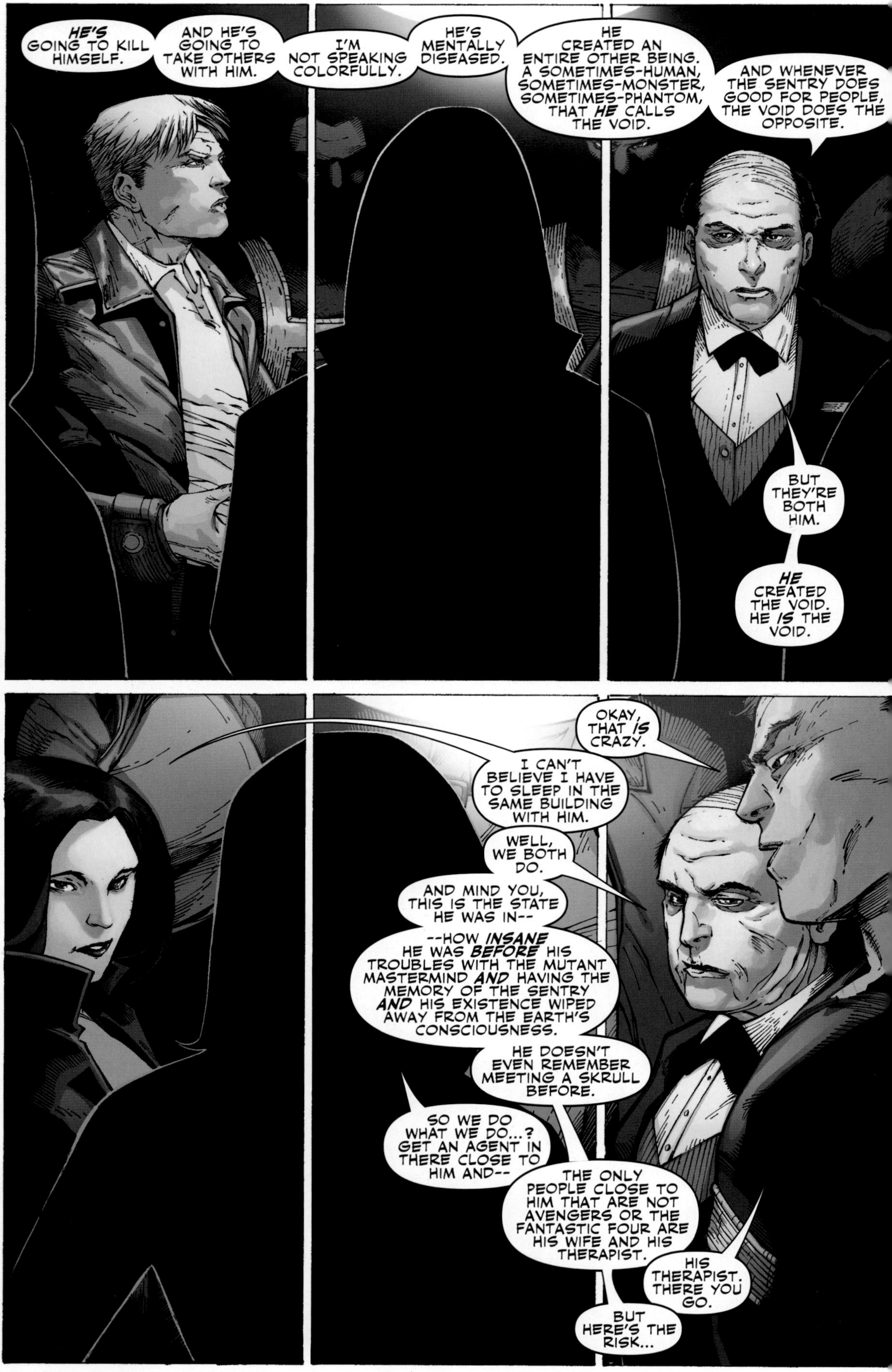
HE'S GOING TO KILL HIMSELF.
AND HE'S GOING TO TAKE OTHERS WITH HIM.
I'M NOT SPEAKING COLORFULLY.
HE'S MENTALLY DISEASED.
HE CREATED AN ENTIRE OTHER BEING. A SOMETIMES-HUMAN, SOMETIMES-MONSTER, SOMETIMES-PHANTOM, THAT HE CALLS THE VOID.
AND WHENEVER THE SENTRY DOES GOOD FOR PEOPLE, THE VOID DOES THE OPPOSITE.
BUT THEY'RE BOTH HIM.
HE CREATED THE VOID. HE IS THE VOID.
OKAY, THAT IS CRAZY.
I CAN'T BELIEVE I HAVE TO SLEEP IN THE SAME BUILDING WITH HIM.
WELL, WE BOTH DO.
AND MIND YOU, THIS IS THE STATE HE WAS IN--
--HOW INSANE HE WAS BEFORE HIS TROUBLES WITH THE MUTANT MASTERMIND AND HAVING THE MEMORY OF THE SENTRY AND HIS EXISTENCE WIPED AWAY FROM THE EARTH'S CONSCIOUSNESS.
HE DOESN'T EVEN REMEMBER MEETING A SKRULL BEFORE.
SO WE DO WHAT WE DO...? GET AN AGENT IN THERE CLOSE TO HIM AND--
THE ONLY PEOPLE CLOSE TO HIM THAT ARE NOT AVENGERS OR THE FANTASTIC FOUR ARE HIS WIFE AND HIS THERAPIST.
HIS THERAPIST. THERE YOU GO.
BUT HERE'S THE RISK...

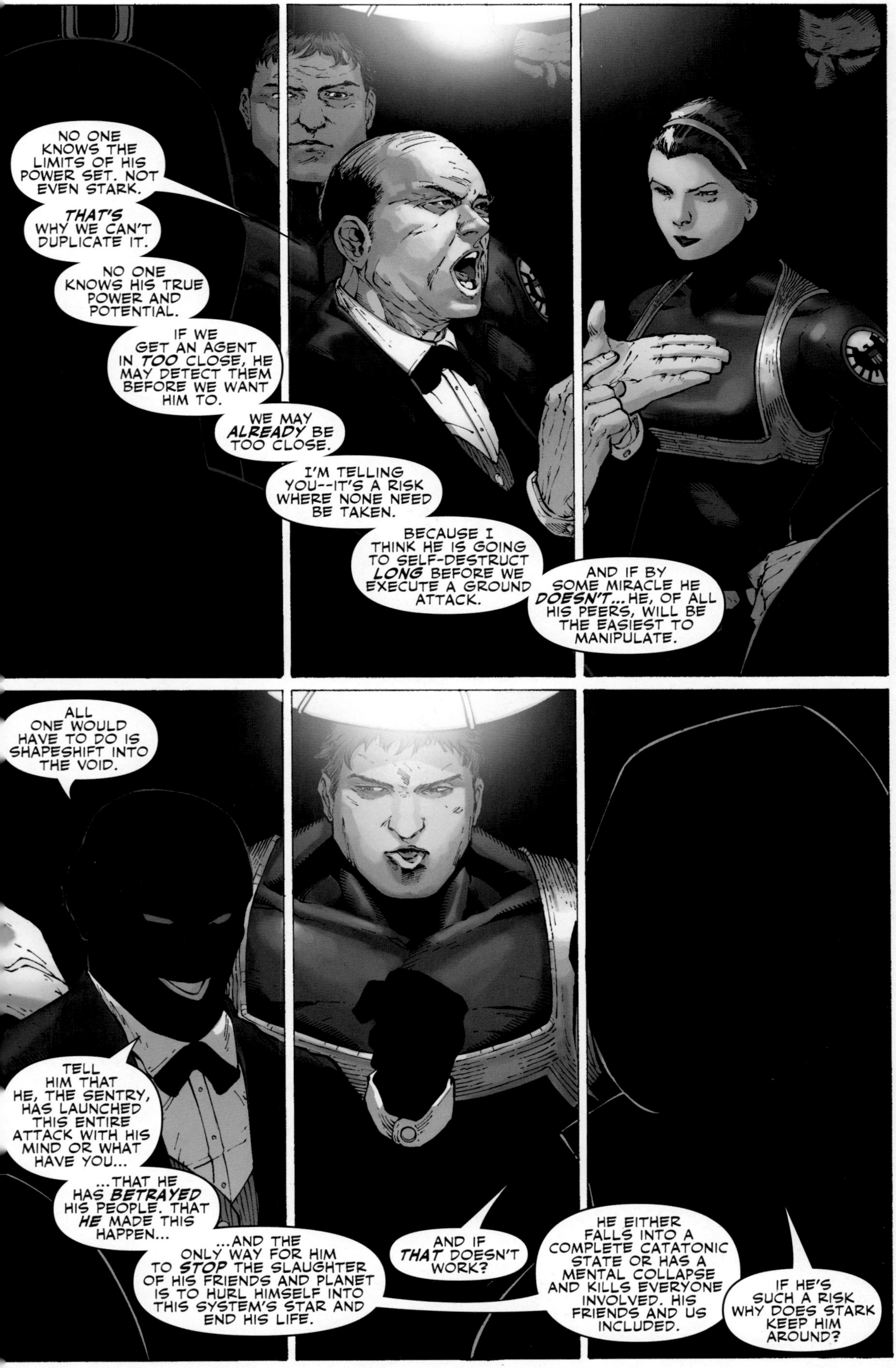
NO ONE KNOWS THE LIMITS OF HIS POWER SET. NOT EVEN STARK.
THAT'S WHY WE CAN'T DUPLICATE IT.
NO ONE KNOWS HIS TRUE POWER AND POTENTIAL.
IF WE GET AN AGENT IN TOO CLOSE, HE MAY DETECT THEM BEFORE WE WANT HIM TO.
WE MAY ALREADY BE TOO CLOSE.
I'M TELLING YOU--IT'S A RISK WHERE NONE NEED BE TAKEN.
BECAUSE I THINK HE IS GOING TO SELF-DESTRUCT LONG BEFORE WE EXECUTE A GROUND ATTACK.
AND IF BY SOME MIRACLE HE DOESN'T...HE, OF ALL HIS PEERS, WILL BE THE EASIEST TO MANIPULATE.
ALL ONE WOULD HAVE TO DO IS SHAPESHIFT INTO THE VOID.
TELL HIM THAT HE, THE SENTRY, HAS LAUNCHED THIS ENTIRE ATTACK WITH HIS MIND OR WHAT HAVE YOU...
...THAT HE HAS BETRAYED HIS PEOPLE. THAT HE MADE THIS HAPPEN...
...AND THE ONLY WAY FOR HIM TO STOP THE SLAUGHTER OF HIS FRIENDS AND PLANET IS TO HURL HIMSELF INTO THIS SYSTEM'S STAR AND END HIS LIFE.
AND IF THAT DOESN'T WORK?
HE EITHER FALLS INTO A COMPLETE CATATONIC STATE OR HAS A MENTAL COLLAPSE AND KILLS EVERYONE INVOLVED. HIS FRIENDS AND US INCLUDED.
IF HE'S SUCH A RISK WHY DOES STARK KEEP HIM AROUND?

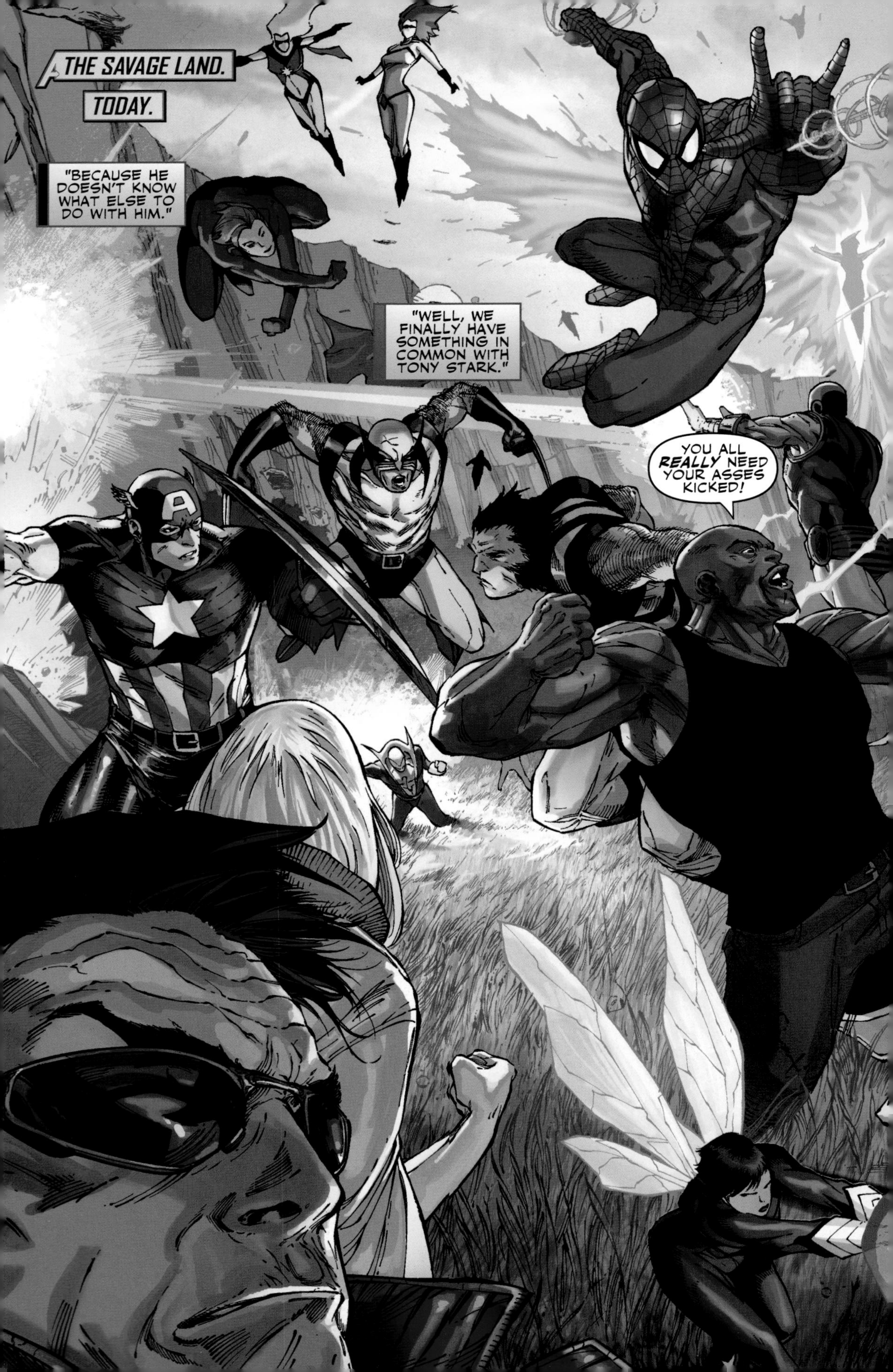
THE SAVAGE LAND.
TODAY.
"BECAUSE HE DOESN'T KNOW WHAT ELSE TO DO WITH HIM."
"WELL, WE FINALLY HAVE SOMETHING IN COMMON WITH TONY STARK."
YOU ALL REALLY NEED YOUR ASSES KICKED!

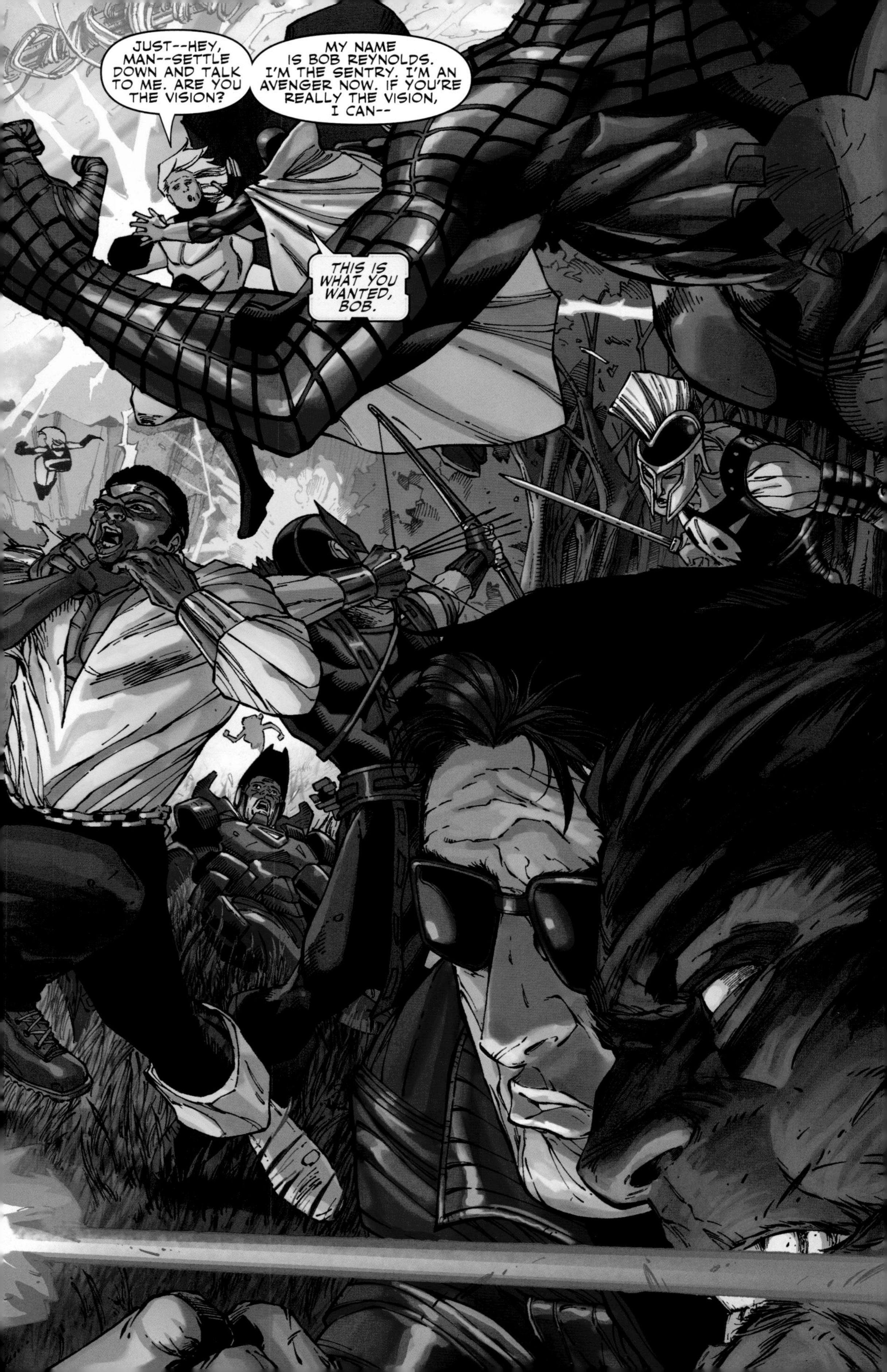
JUST--HEY, MAN--SETTLE DOWN AND TALK TO ME. ARE YOU THE VISION?
MY NAME IS BOB REYNOLDS. I'M THE SENTRY. I'M AN AVENGER NOW. IF YOU'RE REALLY THE VISION, I CAN--
THIS IS WHAT YOU WANTED, BOB.

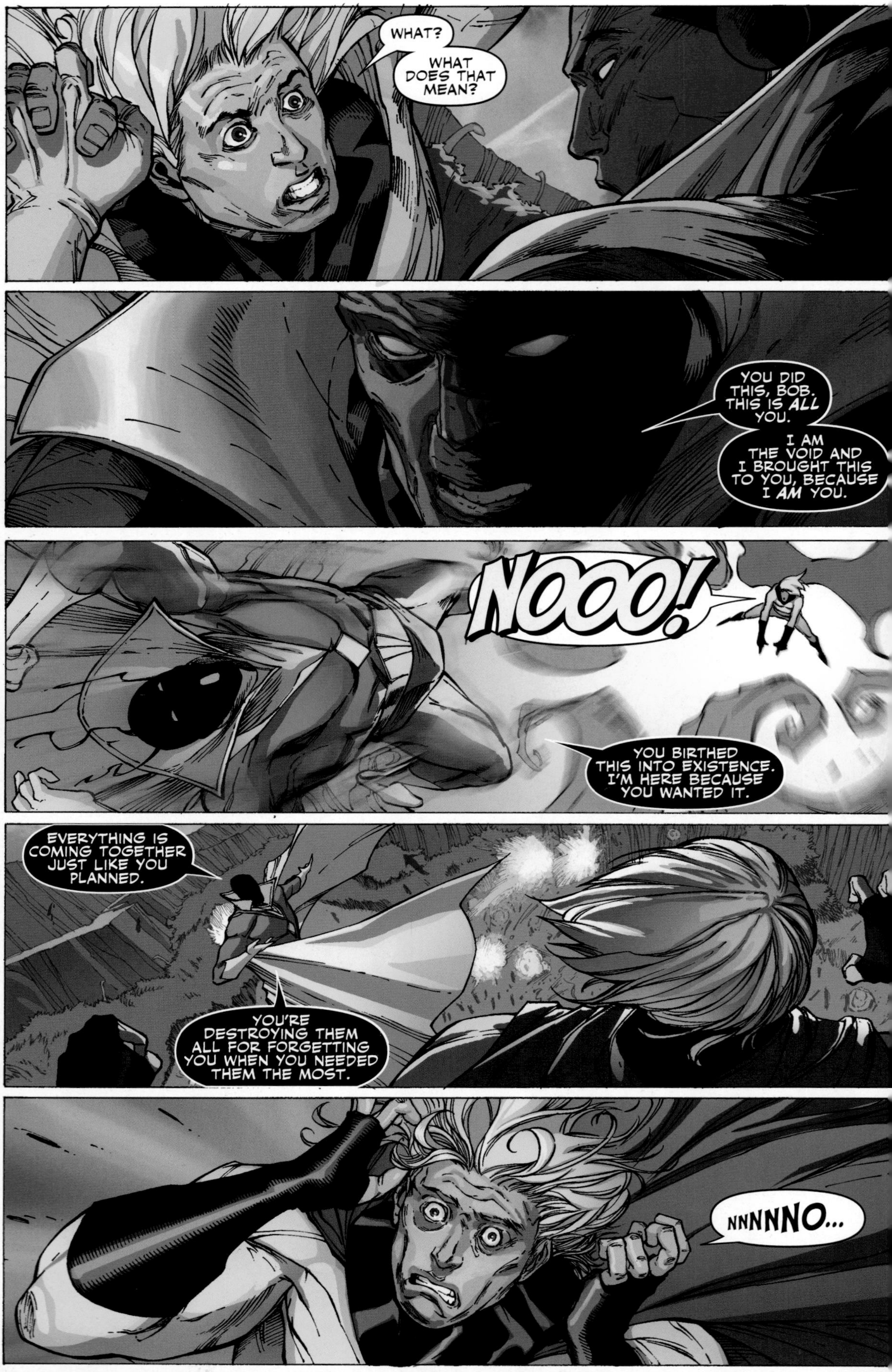

WHAT?
WHAT DOES THAT MEAN?
YOU DID THIS, BOB. THIS IS *ALL* YOU.
I AM THE VOID AND I BROUGHT THIS TO YOU, BECAUSE I *AM* YOU.
NOOO!
YOU BIRTHED THIS INTO EXISTENCE. I'M HERE BECAUSE YOU WANTED IT.
EVERYTHING IS COMING TOGETHER JUST LIKE YOU PLANNED.
YOU'RE DESTROYING THEM ALL FOR FORGETTING YOU WHEN YOU NEEDED THEM THE MOST.
NNNNNO...

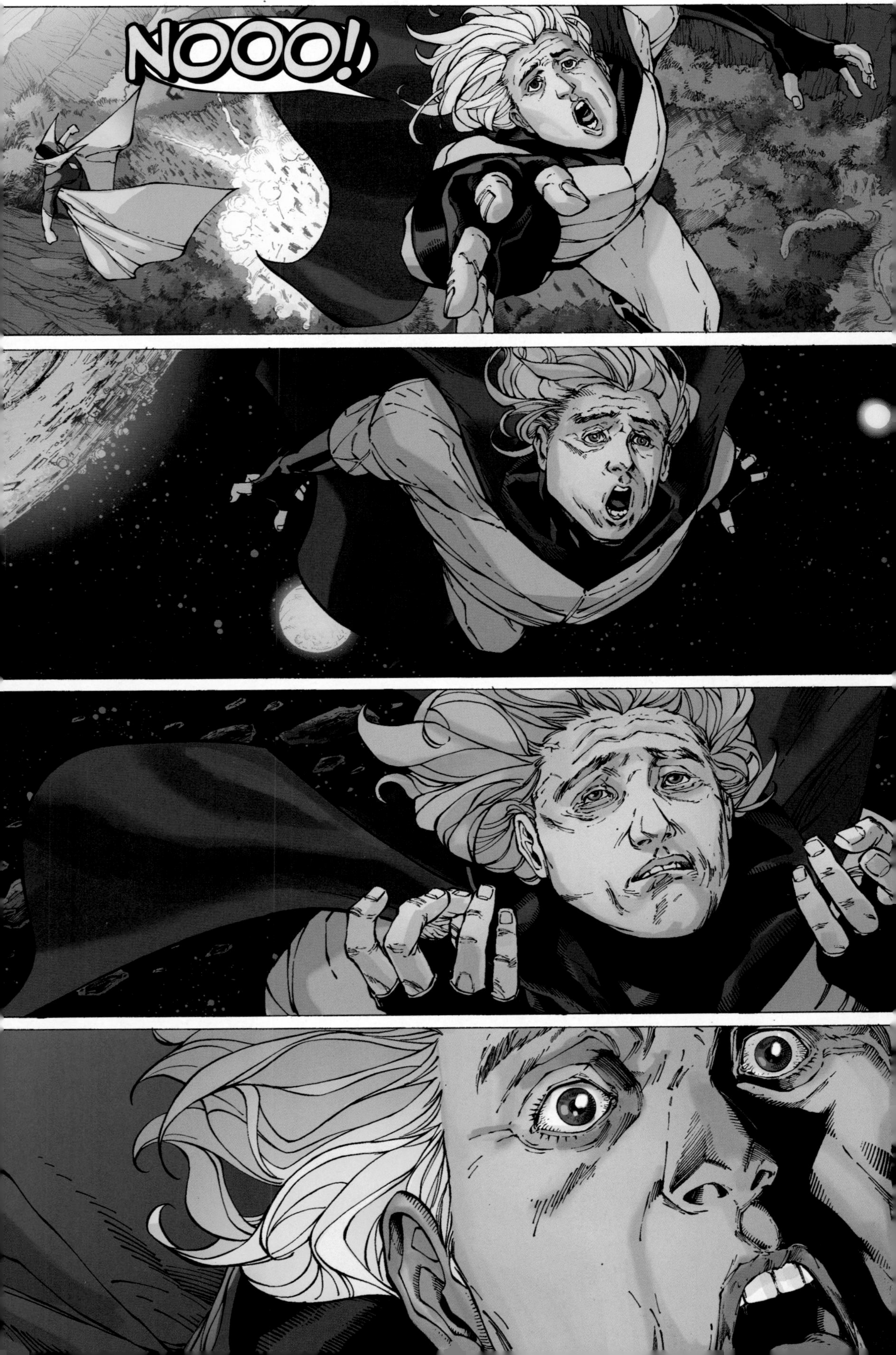
NOOO!

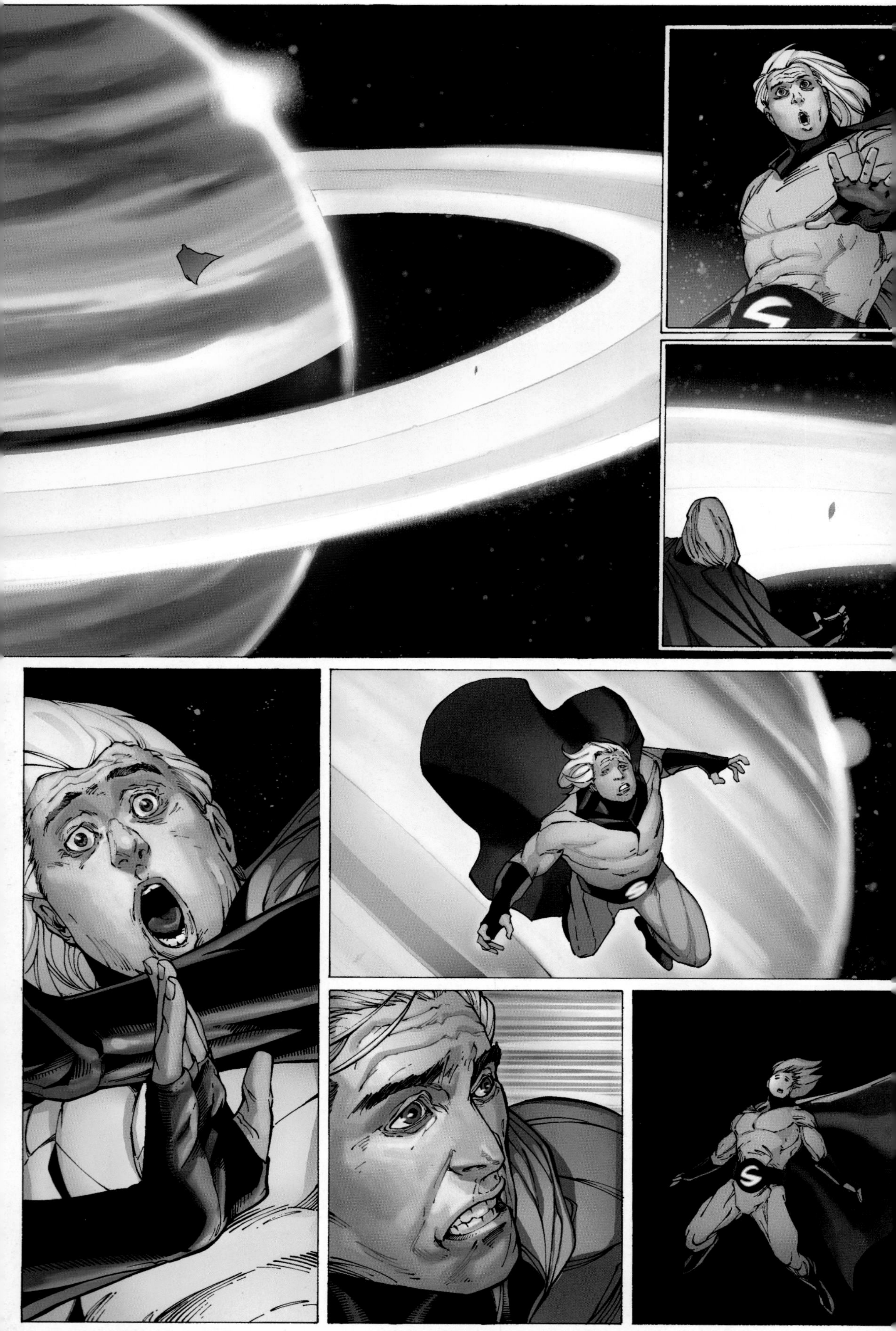

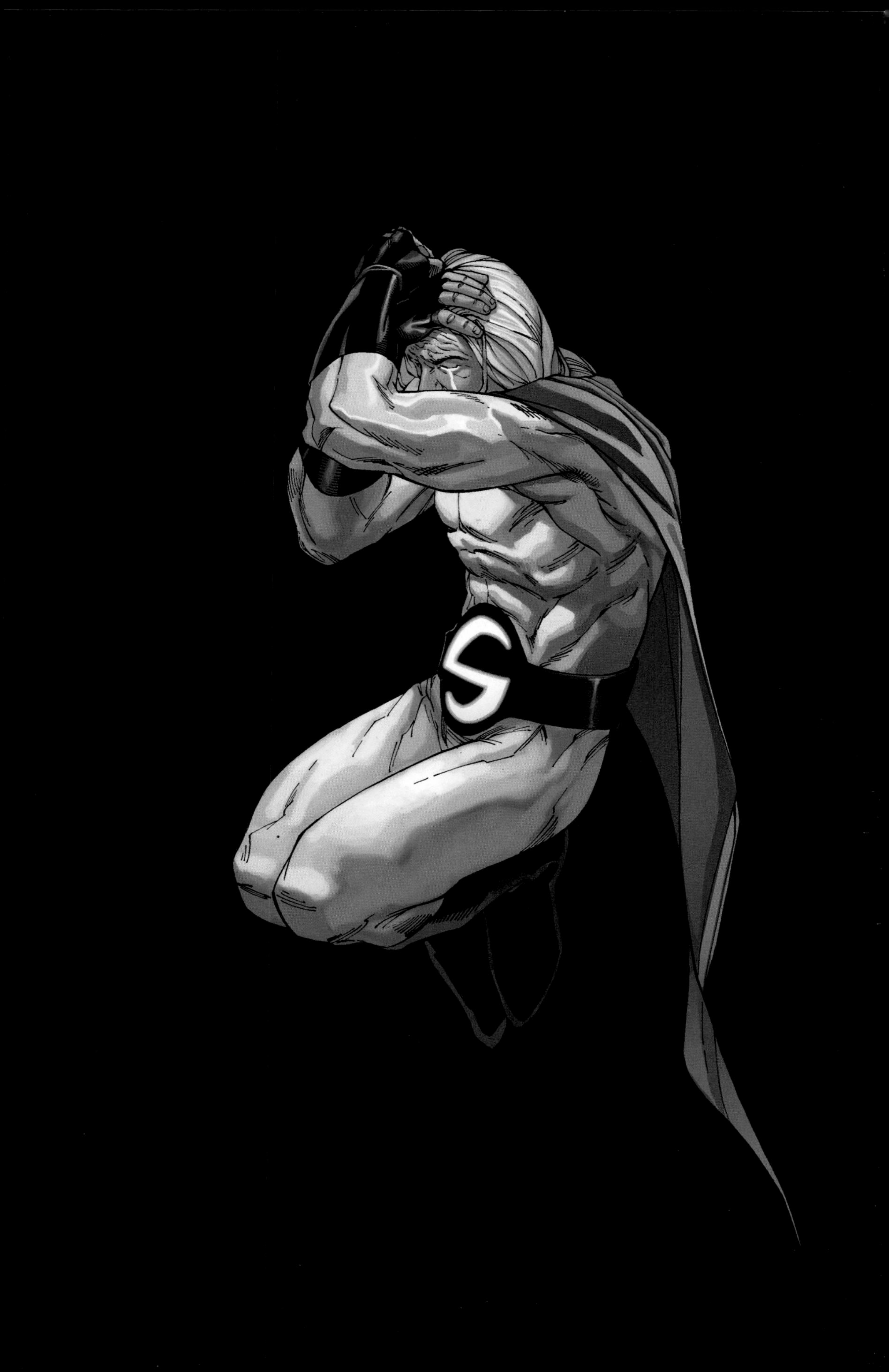

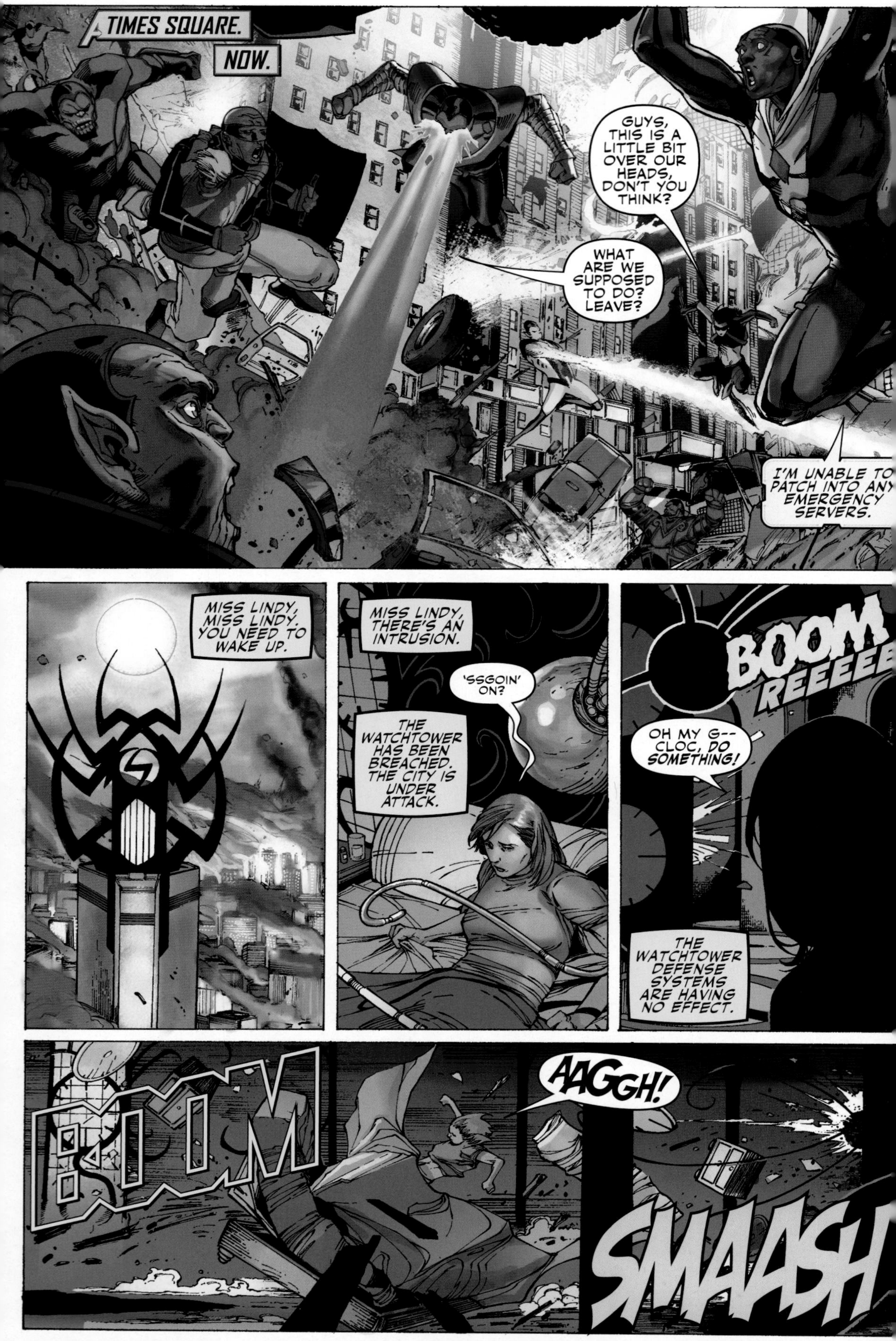
TIMES SQUARE.
NOW.
GUYS, THIS IS A LITTLE BIT OVER OUR HEADS, DON'T YOU THINK?
WHAT ARE WE SUPPOSED TO DO? LEAVE?
I'M UNABLE TO PATCH INTO ANY EMERGENCY SERVERS.
MISS LINDY, MISS LINDY. YOU NEED TO WAKE UP.
MISS LINDY, THERE'S AN INTRUSION.
'SSGOIN' ON?
THE WATCHTOWER HAS BEEN BREACHED. THE CITY IS UNDER ATTACK.
BOOM
REEEEE
OH MY G-- CLOC, DO SOMETHING!
THE WATCHTOWER DEFENSE SYSTEMS ARE HAVING NO EFFECT.
AAGGH!
SMAASH

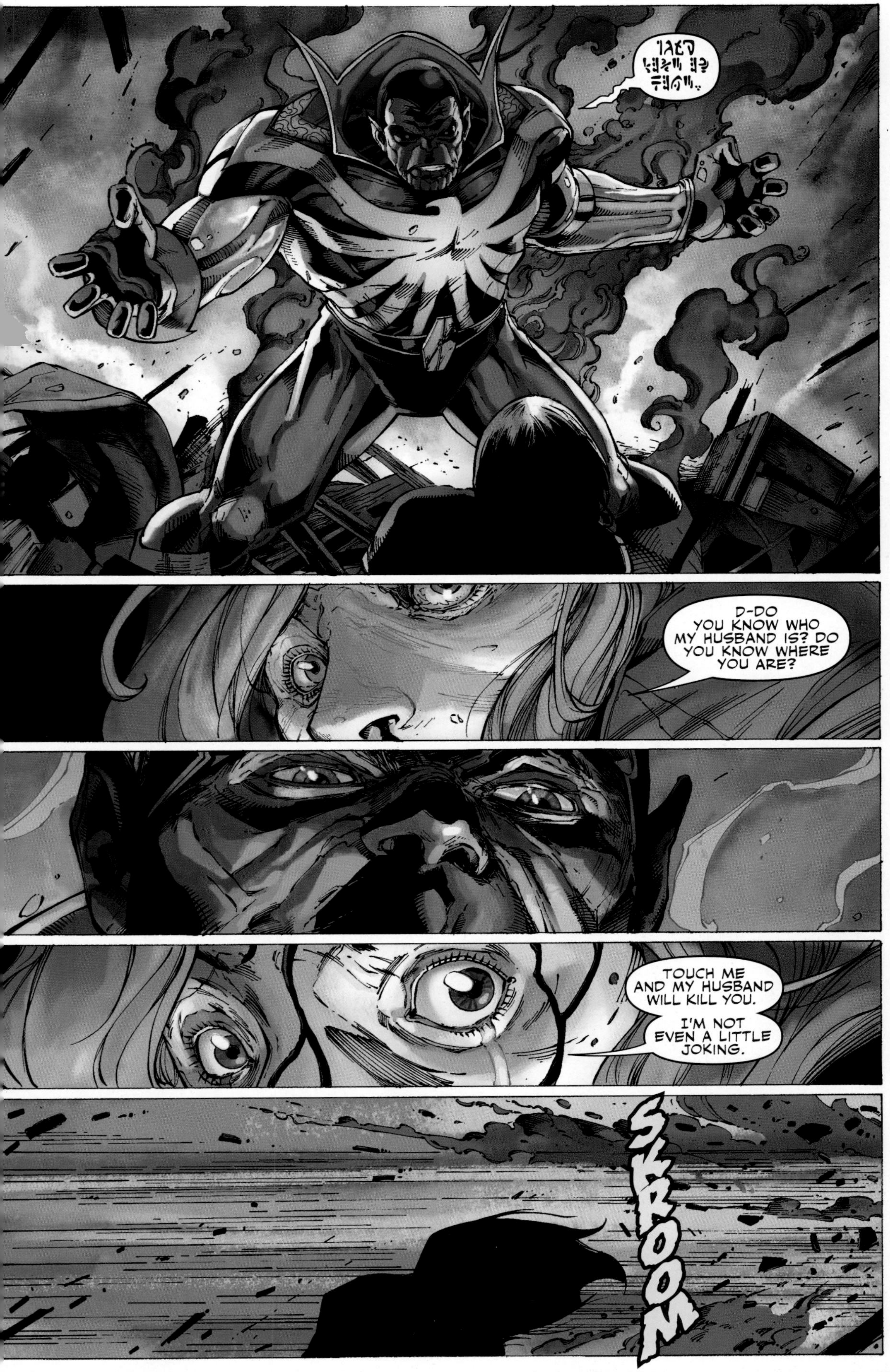
D-DO YOU KNOW WHO MY HUSBAND IS? DO YOU KNOW WHERE YOU ARE?
TOUCH ME AND MY HUSBAND WILL KILL YOU.
I'M NOT EVEN A LITTLE JOKING.
SKROOM

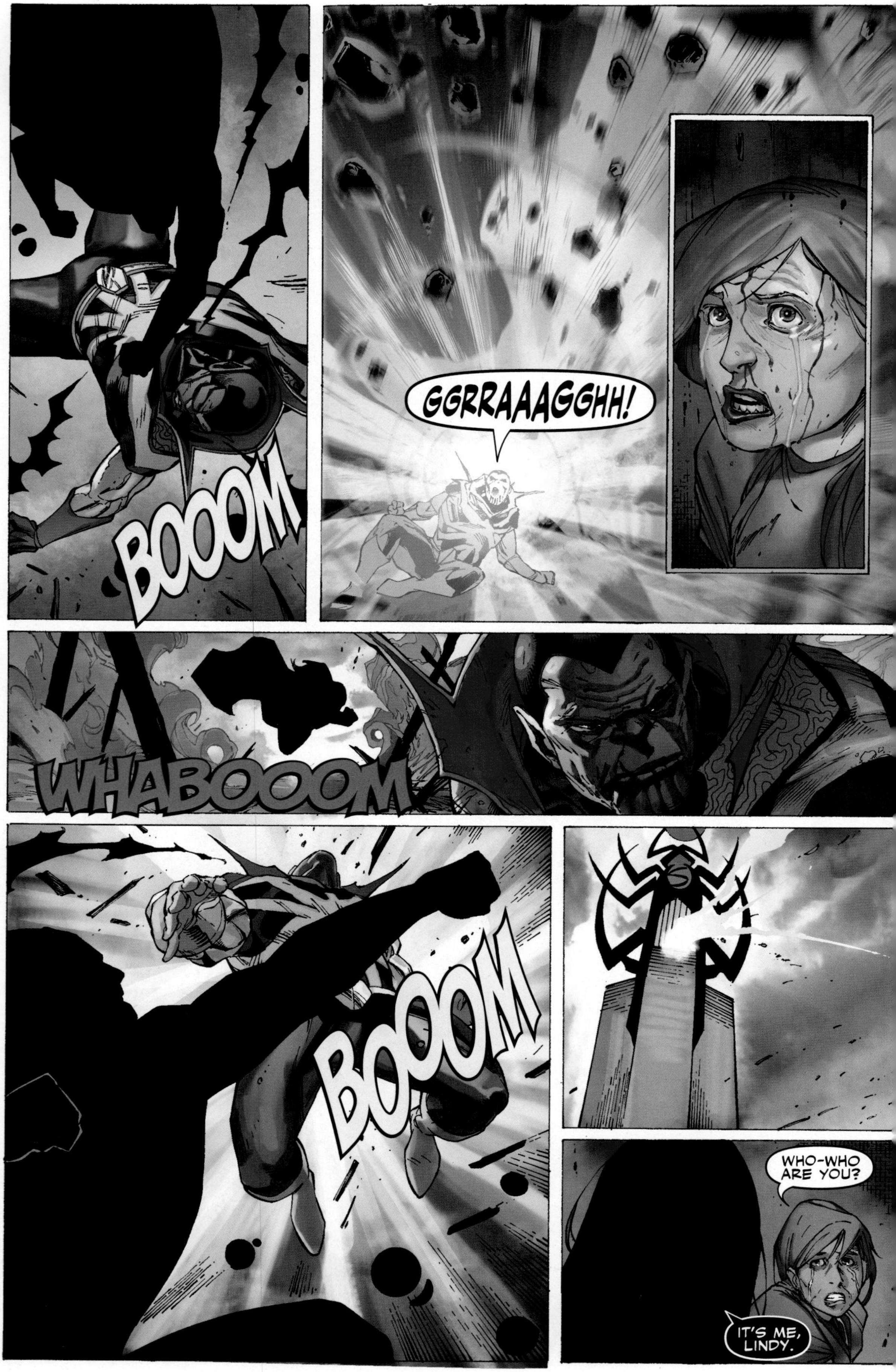
BOOOM
GGRRAAAGGHH!
WHABOOOM
BOOOM
WHO-WHO ARE YOU?
IT'S ME, LINDY.

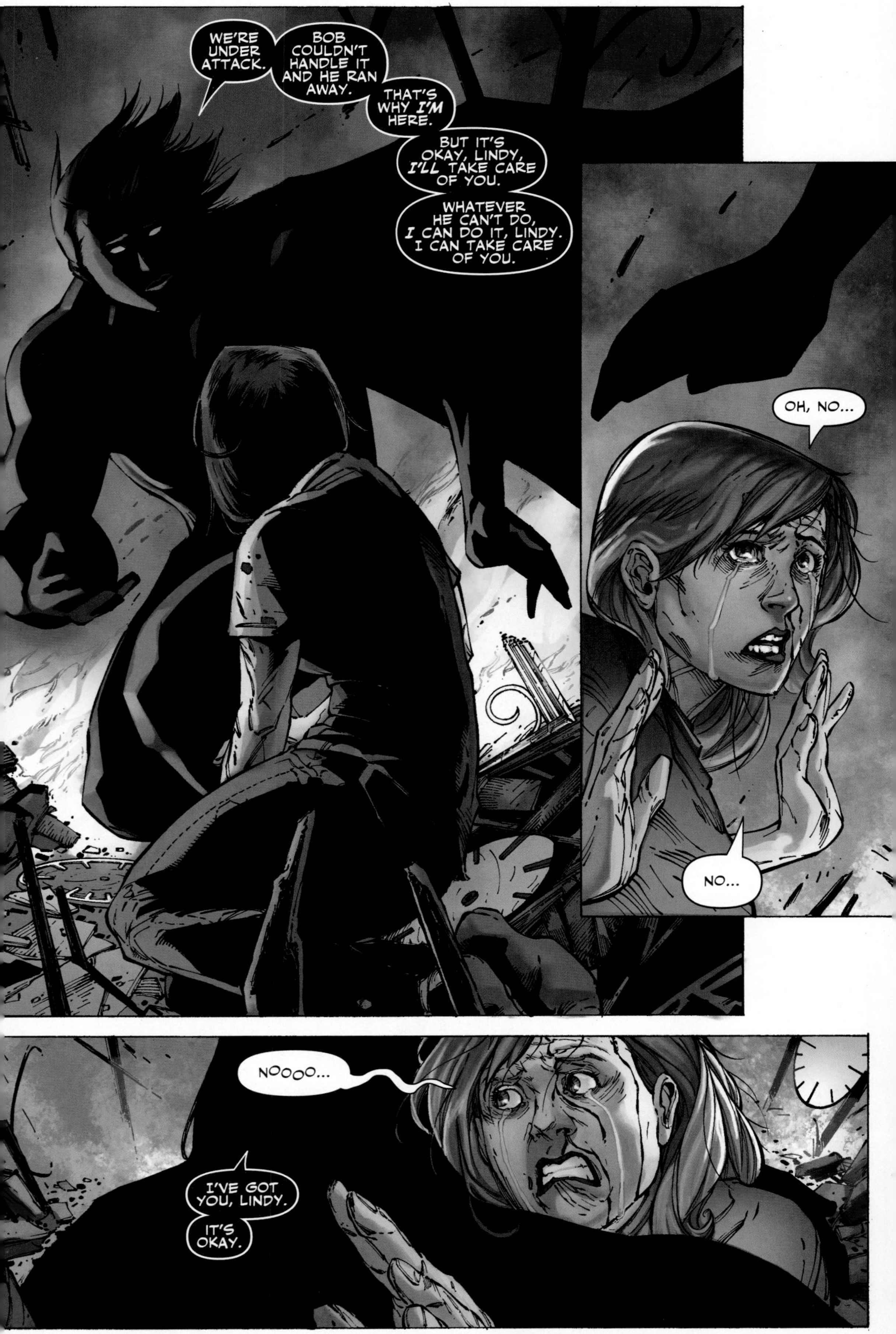
WE'RE UNDER ATTACK.
BOB COULDN'T HANDLE IT AND HE RAN AWAY.
THAT'S WHY *I'M* HERE.
BUT IT'S OKAY, LINDY, *I'LL* TAKE CARE OF YOU.
WHATEVER HE CAN'T DO, *I* CAN DO IT, LINDY. I CAN TAKE CARE OF YOU.
OH, NO...
NO...
NOOOO...
I'VE GOT YOU, LINDY.
IT'S OKAY.

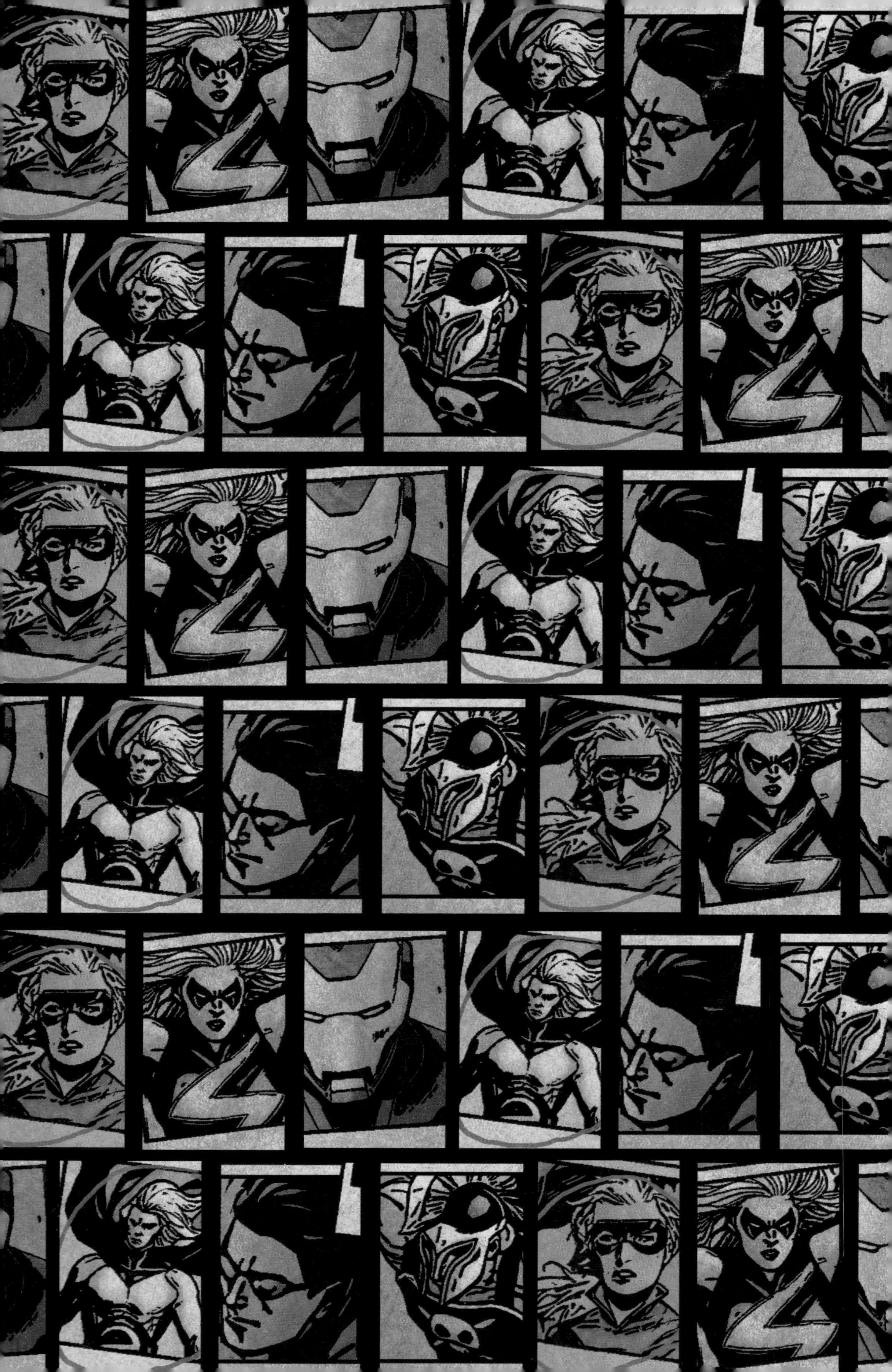

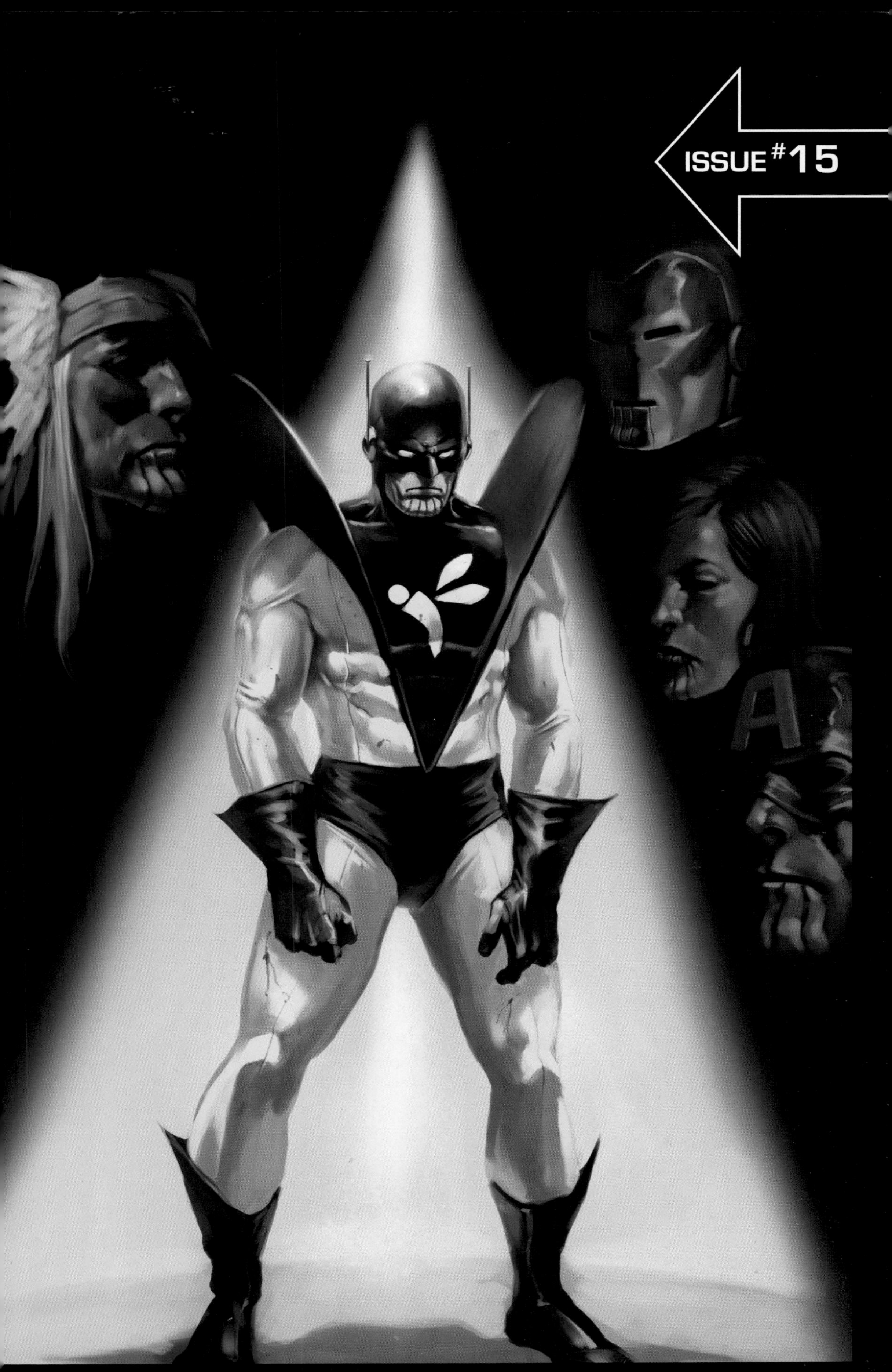
ISSUE #15

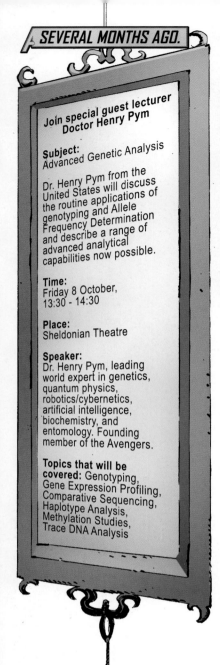

Join special guest lecturer
Doctor Henry Pym

Subject:
Advanced Genetic Analysis

Dr. Henry Pym from the
United States will discuss
the routine applications of
genotyping and Allele
Frequency Determination
and describe a range of
advanced analytical
capabilities now possible.

Time:
Friday 8 October,
13:30 - 14:30

Place:
Sheldonian Theatre

Speaker:
Dr. Henry Pym, leading
world expert in genetics,
quantum physics,
robotics/cybernetics,
artificial intelligence,
biochemistry, and
entomology. Founding
member of the Avengers.

**Topics that will be
covered:** Genotyping,
Gene Expression Profiling,
Comparative Sequencing,
Haplotype Analysis,
Methylation Studies,
Trace DNA Analysis

YES. OF
COURSE.

BUT
EVERYTHING
AND ANYTHING
CAN CHANGE
ONE'S WORLD
VIEW.

A, UH,
AN ASSOCIATE
OF MINE
TOLD ME HE
HAD HIS BIGGEST
RESEARCH
BREAKTHROUGH
AFTER WATCHING
HIS SON
PLAY WITH
BLOCKS.

JUST SOMETHING
ABOUT WATCHING THA
THE SIMPLEST OF CHIL
ACTIVITIES, INSPIRED
IDEA THAT CHANGED HI
ENTIRE LIFE.

AND *THIS* IS
A MAJOR PLAYER
IN THE--OKAY, IT WAS
REED RICHARDS.

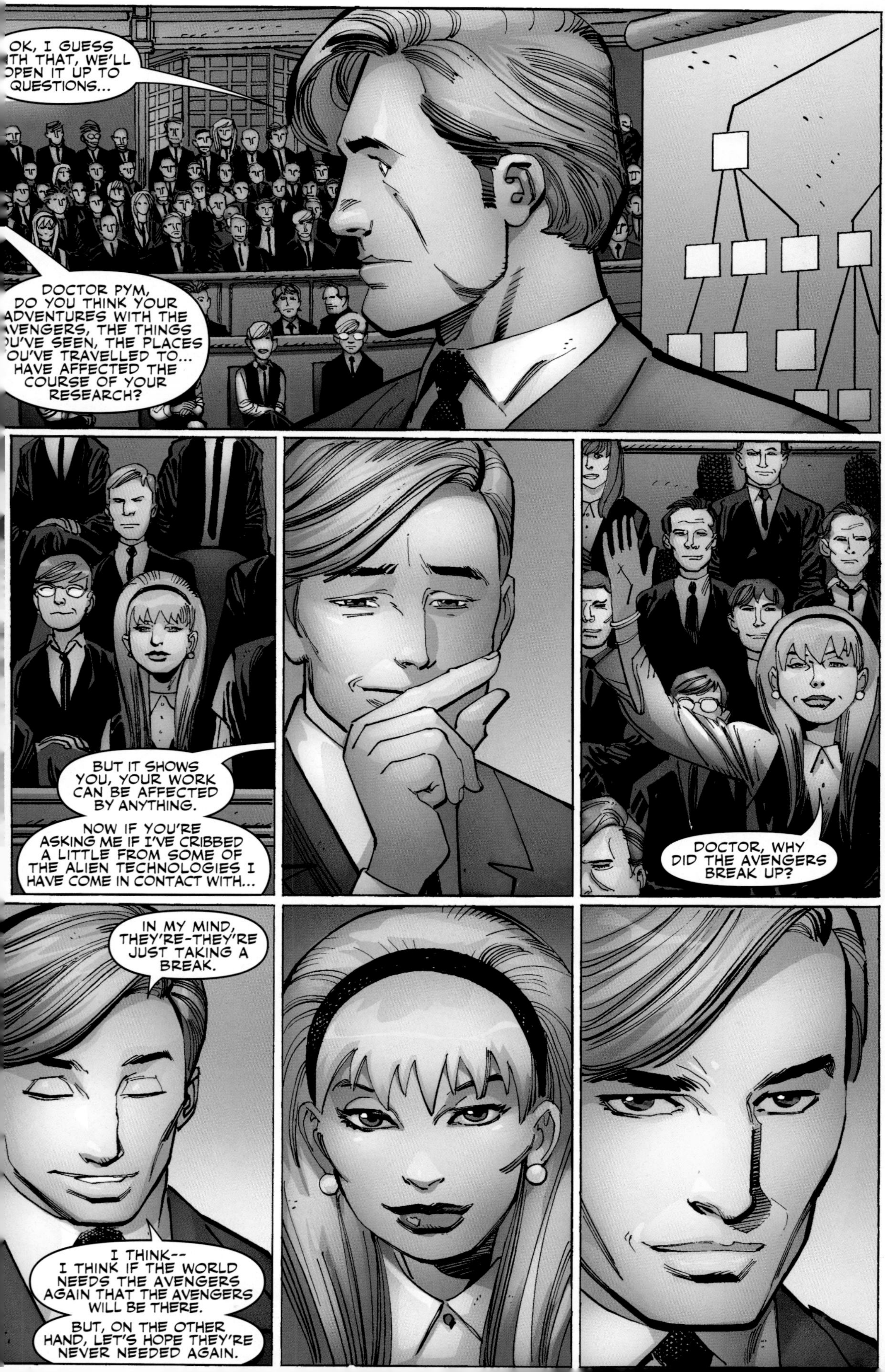
OK, I GUESS ITH THAT, WE'LL OPEN IT UP TO QUESTIONS...
DOCTOR PYM, DO YOU THINK YOUR ADVENTURES WITH THE AVENGERS, THE THINGS OU'VE SEEN, THE PLACES OU'VE TRAVELLED TO... HAVE AFFECTED THE COURSE OF YOUR RESEARCH?
BUT IT SHOWS YOU, YOUR WORK CAN BE AFFECTED BY ANYTHING.
NOW IF YOU'RE ASKING ME IF I'VE CRIBBED A LITTLE FROM SOME OF THE ALIEN TECHNOLOGIES I HAVE COME IN CONTACT WITH...
DOCTOR, WHY DID THE AVENGERS BREAK UP?
IN MY MIND, THEY'RE-THEY'RE JUST TAKING A BREAK.
I THINK-- I THINK IF THE WORLD NEEDS THE AVENGERS AGAIN THAT THE AVENGERS WILL BE THERE.
BUT, ON THE OTHER HAND, LET'S HOPE THEY'RE NEVER NEEDED AGAIN.

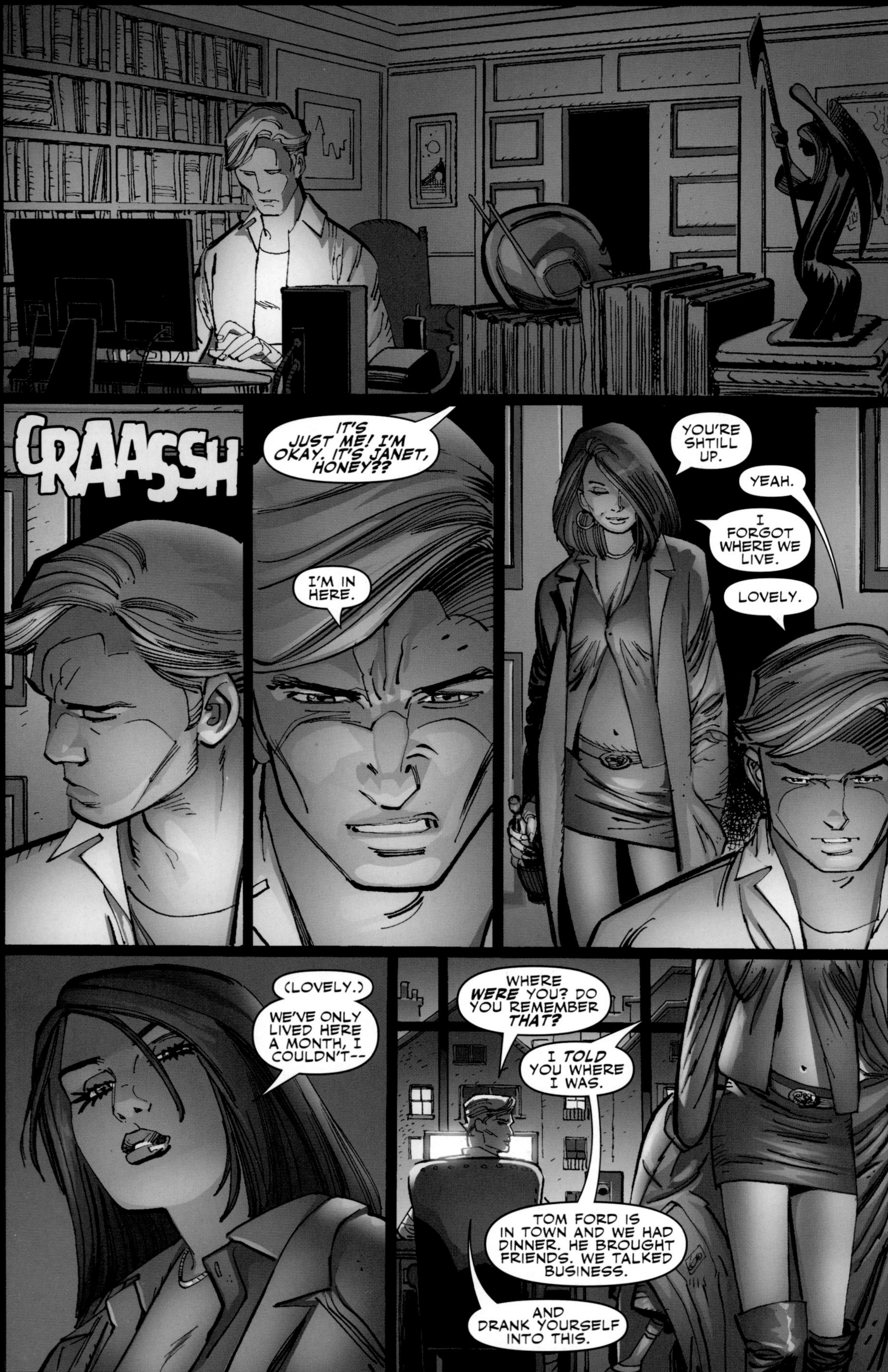
CRAASSH
IT'S JUST ME! I'M OKAY. IT'S JANET, HONEY??
I'M IN HERE.
YOU'RE SHTILL UP.
YEAH.
I FORGOT WHERE WE LIVE.
LOVELY.
(LOVELY.)
WE'VE ONLY LIVED HERE A MONTH, I COULDN'T--
WHERE *WERE* YOU? DO YOU REMEMBER *THAT?*
I *TOLD* YOU WHERE I WAS.
TOM FORD IS IN TOWN AND WE HAD DINNER. HE BROUGHT FRIENDS. WE TALKED BUSINESS.
AND DRANK YOURSELF INTO THIS.

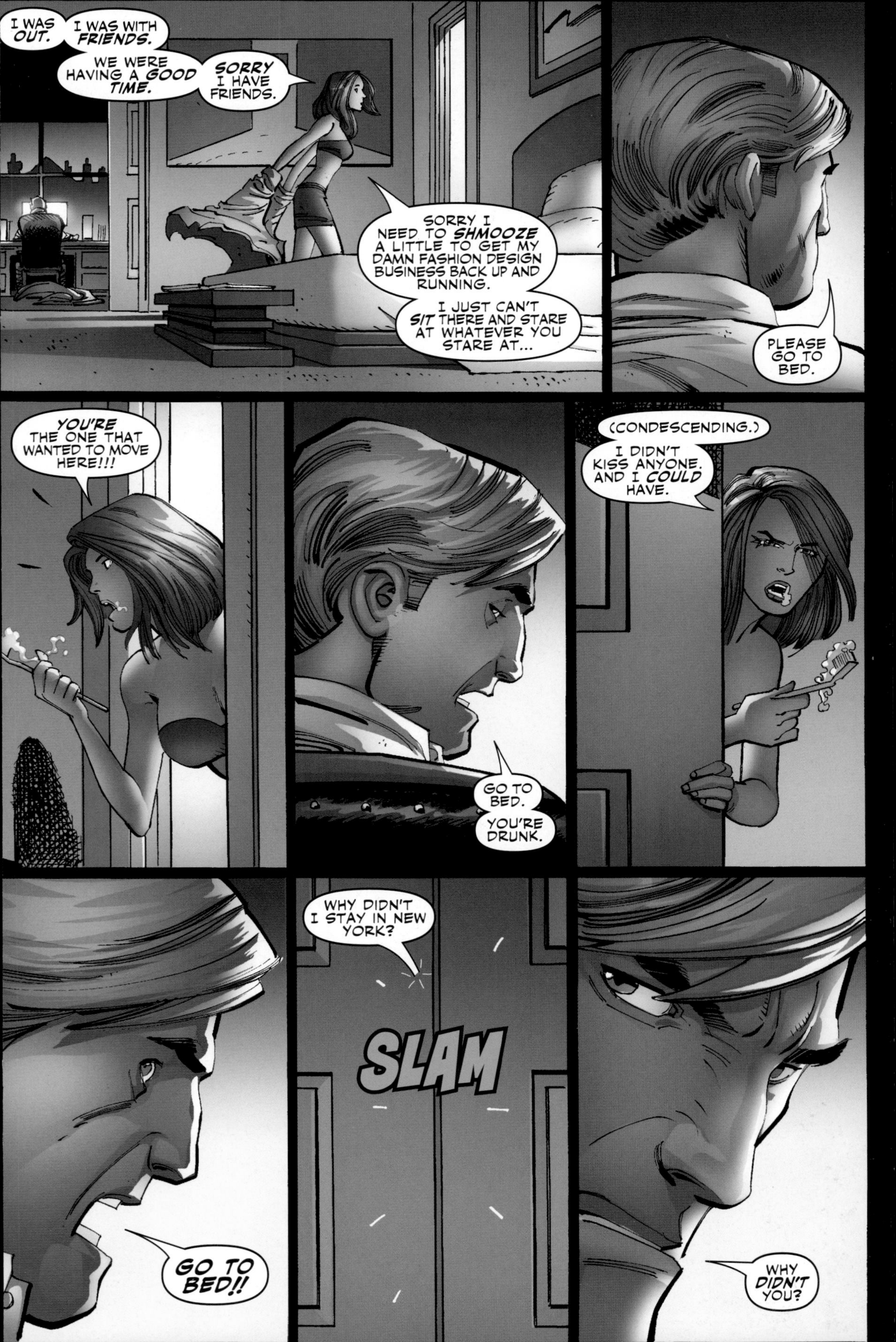
I WAS OUT.
I WAS WITH FRIENDS.
WE WERE HAVING A GOOD TIME.
SORRY I HAVE FRIENDS.
SORRY I NEED TO SHMOOZE A LITTLE TO GET MY DAMN FASHION DESIGN BUSINESS BACK UP AND RUNNING.
I JUST CAN'T SIT THERE AND STARE AT WHATEVER YOU STARE AT...
PLEASE GO TO BED.
YOU'RE THE ONE THAT WANTED TO MOVE HERE!!!
GO TO BED.
YOU'RE DRUNK.
(CONDESCENDING.)
I DIDN'T KISS ANYONE. AND I COULD HAVE.
GO TO BED!!
WHY DIDN'T I STAY IN NEW YORK?
SLAM
WHY DIDN'T YOU?

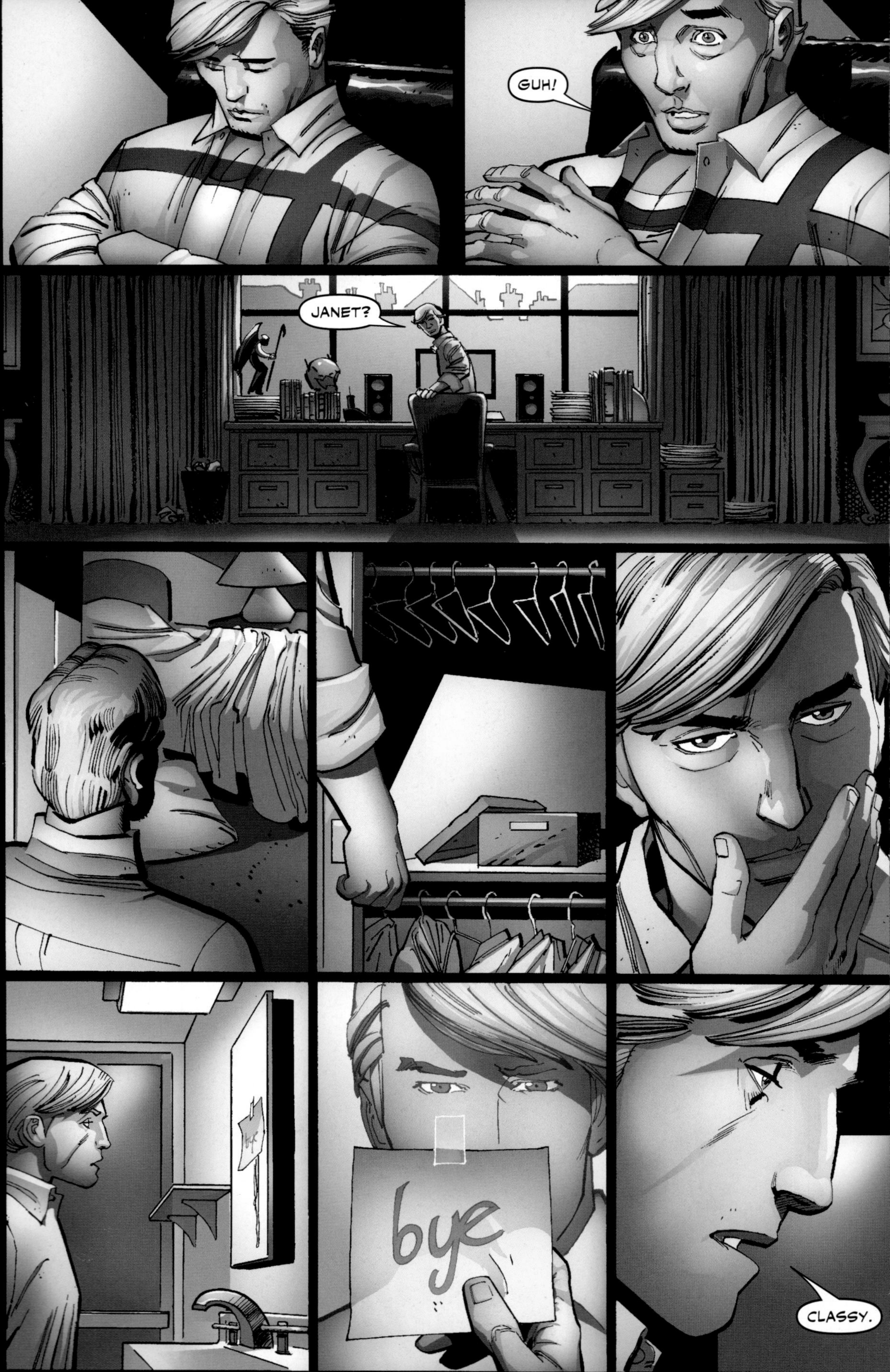
GUH!
JANET?
bye
CLASSY.

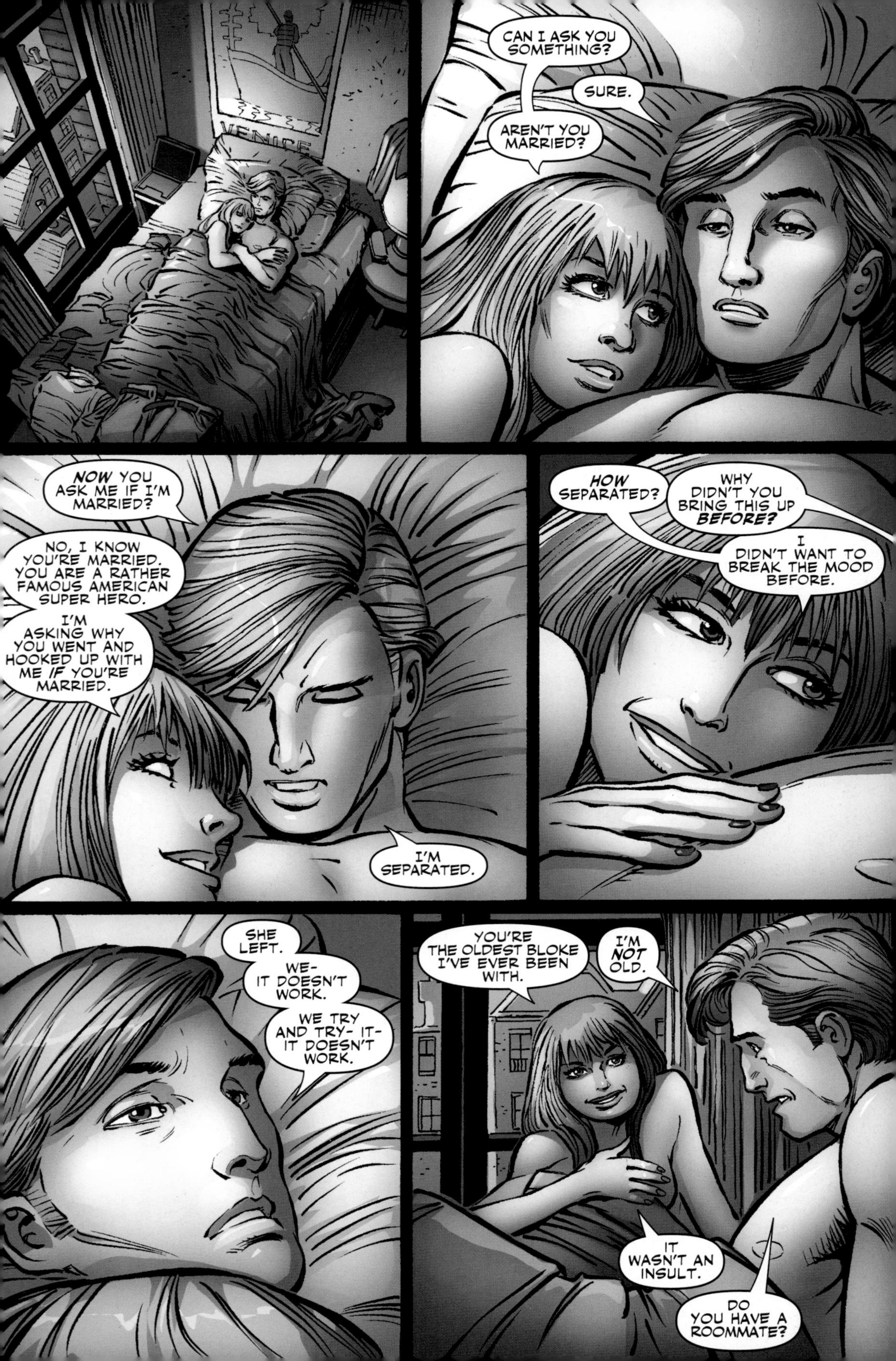
VENICE
CAN I ASK YOU SOMETHING?
SURE.
AREN'T YOU MARRIED?
NOW YOU ASK ME IF I'M MARRIED?
NO, I KNOW YOU'RE MARRIED. YOU ARE A RATHER FAMOUS AMERICAN SUPER HERO.
I'M ASKING WHY YOU WENT AND HOOKED UP WITH ME IF YOU'RE MARRIED.
I'M SEPARATED.
HOW SEPARATED?
WHY DIDN'T YOU BRING THIS UP BEFORE?
I DIDN'T WANT TO BREAK THE MOOD BEFORE.
SHE LEFT.
WE- IT DOESN'T WORK.
WE TRY AND TRY- IT- IT DOESN'T WORK.
YOU'RE THE OLDEST BLOKE I'VE EVER BEEN WITH.
I'M NOT OLD.
IT WASN'T AN INSULT.
DO YOU HAVE A ROOMMATE?

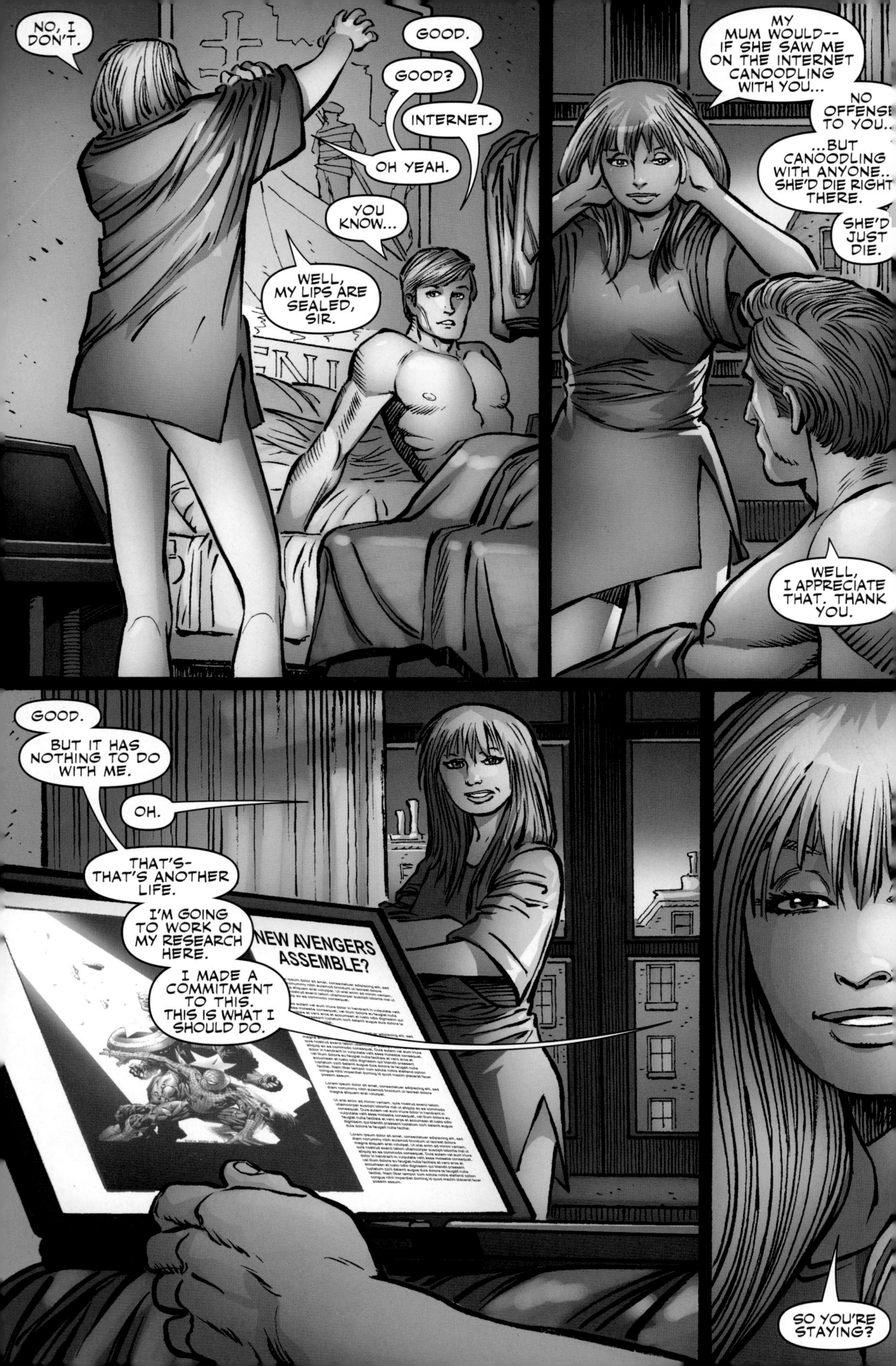
NO, I DON'T.
GOOD.
GOOD?
INTERNET.
OH YEAH.
YOU KNOW...
WELL, MY LIPS ARE SEALED, SIR.
MY MUM WOULD-- IF SHE SAW ME ON THE INTERNET CANOODLING WITH YOU...
NO OFFENSE TO YOU..
...BUT CANOODLING WITH ANYONE.. SHE'D DIE RIGHT THERE.
SHE'D JUST DIE.
WELL, I APPRECIATE THAT. THANK YOU.
GOOD.
BUT IT HAS NOTHING TO DO WITH ME.
OH.
THAT'S- THAT'S ANOTHER LIFE.
I'M GOING TO WORK ON MY RESEARCH HERE.
I MADE A COMMITMENT TO THIS. THIS IS WHAT I SHOULD DO.
NEW AVENGERS ASSEMBLE?
SO YOU'RE STAYING?

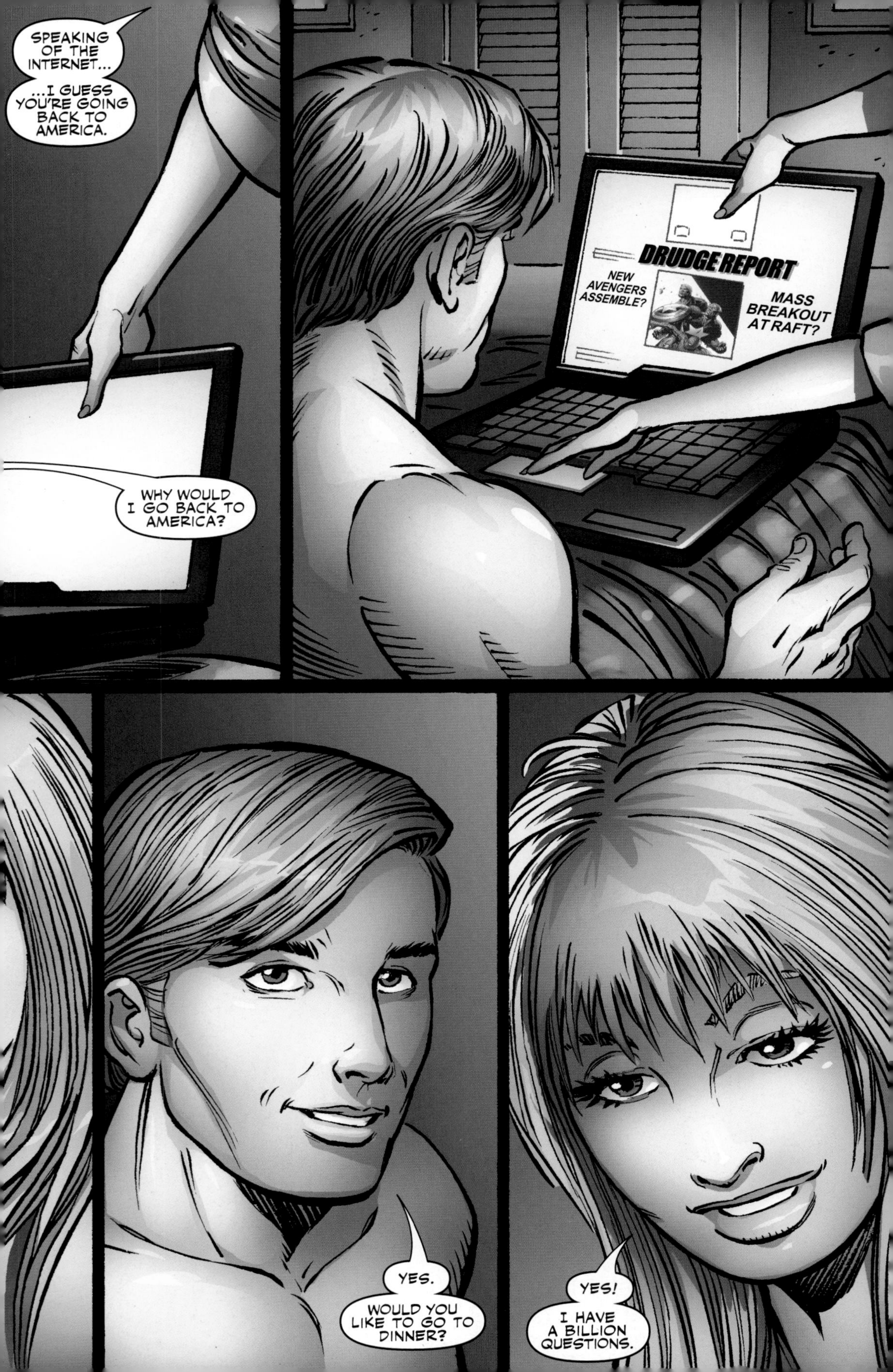
SPEAKING OF THE INTERNET...
...I GUESS YOU'RE GOING BACK TO AMERICA.
WHY WOULD I GO BACK TO AMERICA?
DRUDGE REPORT
NEW AVENGERS ASSEMBLE?
MASS BREAKOUT AT RAFT?
YES.
WOULD YOU LIKE TO GO TO DINNER?
YES!
I HAVE A BILLION QUESTIONS.

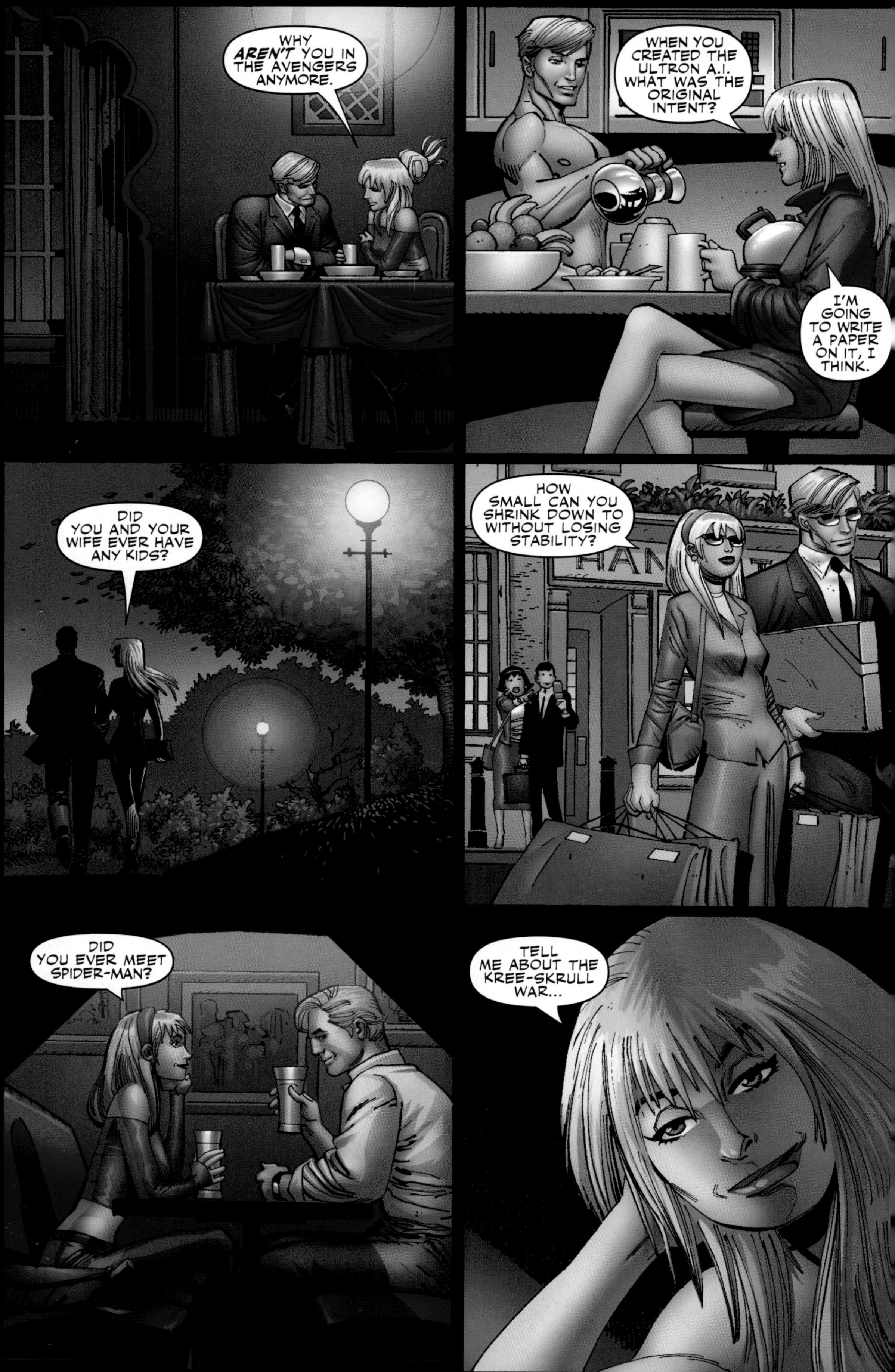
WHY *AREN'T* YOU IN THE AVENGERS ANYMORE.
WHEN YOU CREATED THE ULTRON A.I. WHAT WAS THE ORIGINAL INTENT?
I'M GOING TO WRITE A PAPER ON IT, I THINK.
DID YOU AND YOUR WIFE EVER HAVE ANY KIDS?
HOW SMALL CAN YOU SHRINK DOWN TO WITHOUT LOSING STABILITY?
DID YOU EVER MEET SPIDER-MAN?
TELL ME ABOUT THE KREE-SKRULL WAR...

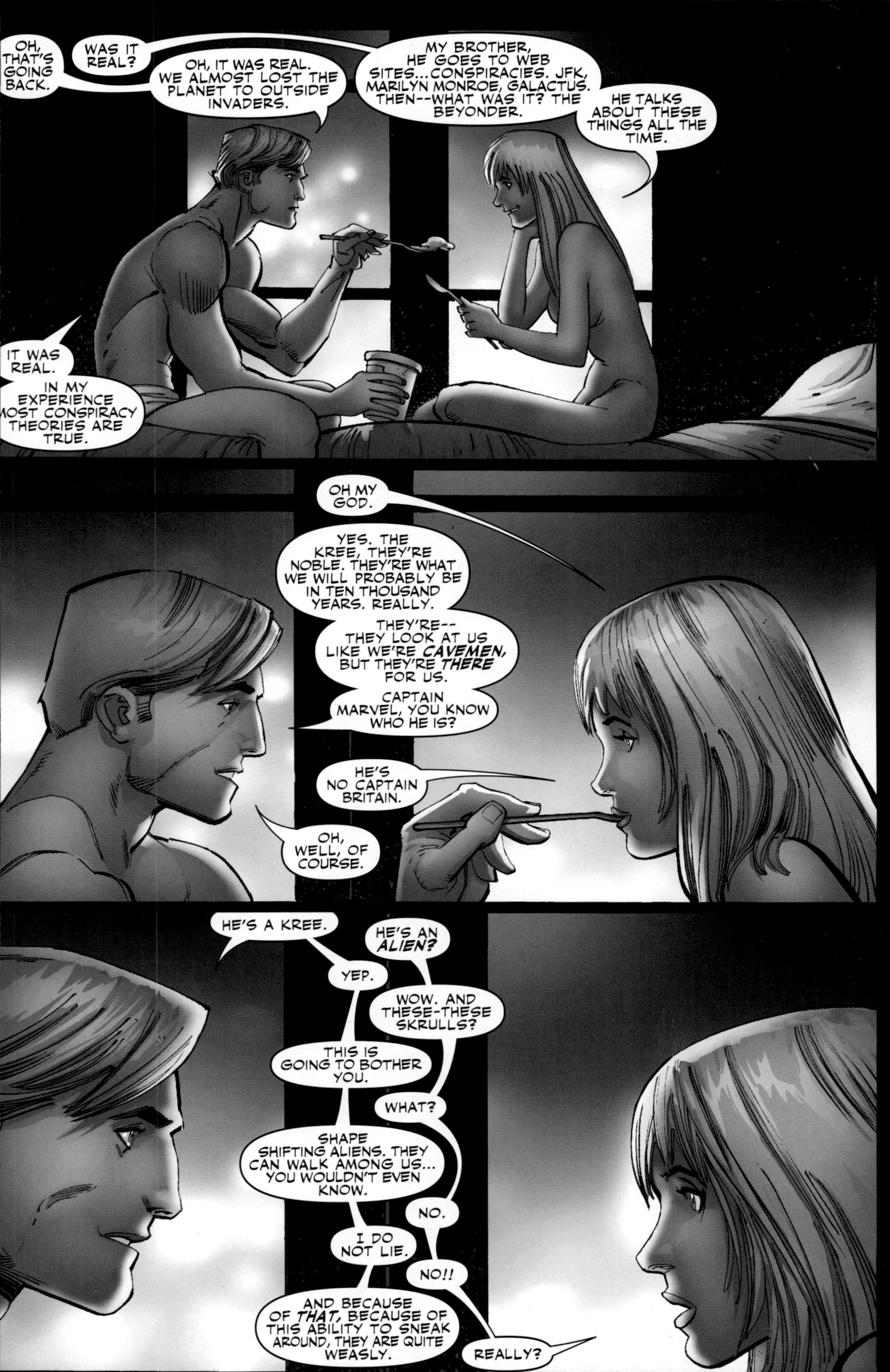
WAS IT REAL?
OH, THAT'S GOING BACK.
OH, IT WAS REAL. WE ALMOST LOST THE PLANET TO OUTSIDE INVADERS.
MY BROTHER, HE GOES TO WEB SITES...CONSPIRACIES. JFK, MARILYN MONROE, GALACTUS. THEN--WHAT WAS IT? THE BEYONDER.
HE TALKS ABOUT THESE THINGS ALL THE TIME.
IT WAS REAL.
IN MY EXPERIENCE MOST CONSPIRACY THEORIES ARE TRUE.
OH MY GOD.
YES. THE KREE, THEY'RE NOBLE. THEY'RE WHAT WE WILL PROBABLY BE IN TEN THOUSAND YEARS. REALLY.
THEY'RE-- THEY LOOK AT US LIKE WE'RE *CAVEMEN,* BUT THEY'RE *THERE* FOR US.
CAPTAIN MARVEL, YOU KNOW WHO HE IS?
HE'S NO CAPTAIN BRITAIN.
OH, WELL, OF COURSE.
HE'S A KREE.
HE'S AN *ALIEN?*
YEP.
WOW. AND THESE-THESE SKRULLS?
THIS IS GOING TO BOTHER YOU.
WHAT?
SHAPE SHIFTING ALIENS. THEY CAN WALK AMONG US... YOU WOULDN'T EVEN KNOW.
NO.
I DO NOT LIE.
NO!!
AND BECAUSE OF *THAT,* BECAUSE OF THIS ABILITY TO SNEAK AROUND, THEY ARE QUITE WEASLY.
REALLY?

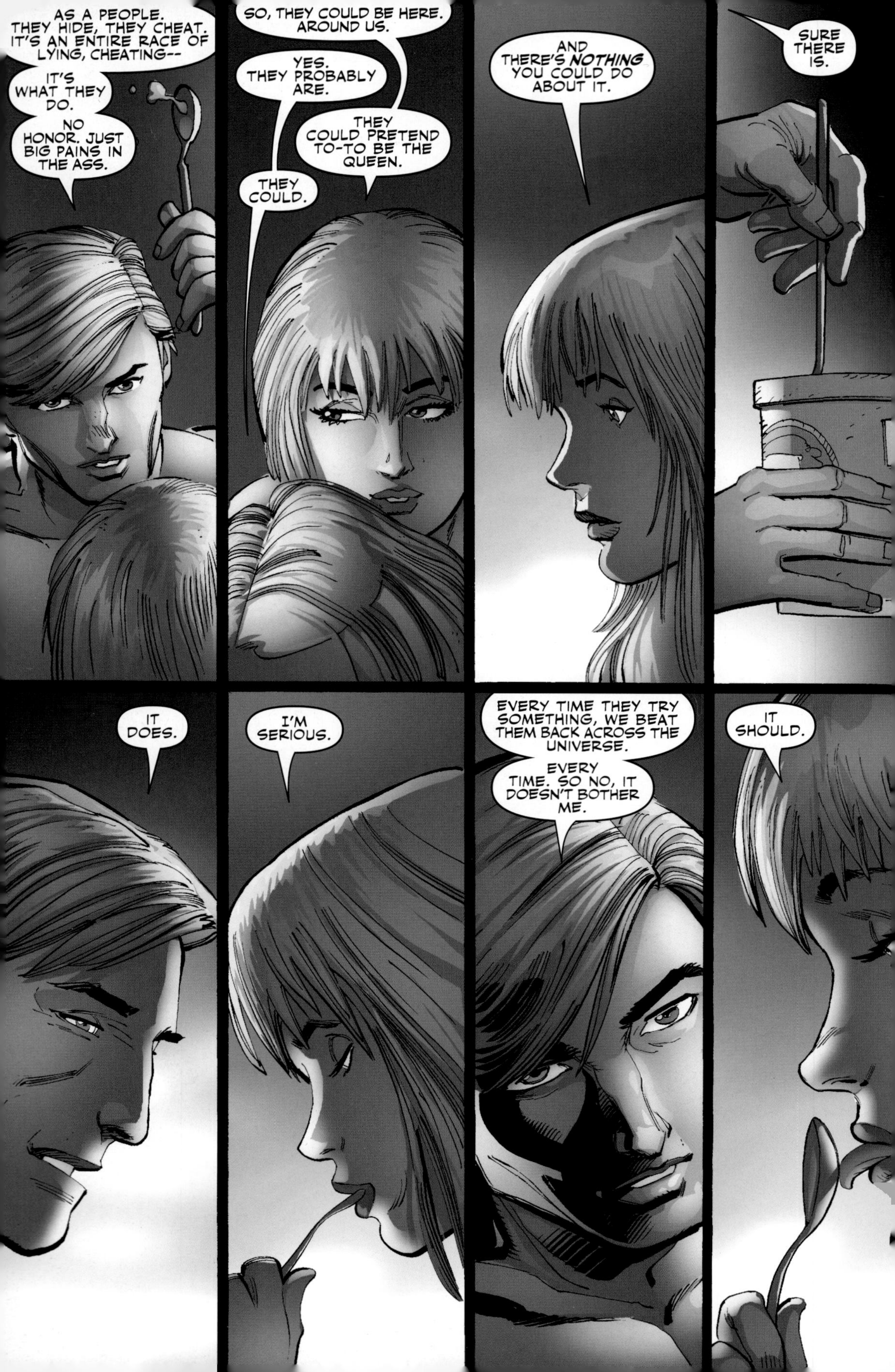
AS A PEOPLE. THEY HIDE, THEY CHEAT. IT'S AN ENTIRE RACE OF LYING, CHEATING--
IT'S WHAT THEY DO.
NO HONOR. JUST BIG PAINS IN THE ASS.
SO, THEY COULD BE HERE. AROUND US.
YES. THEY PROBABLY ARE.
THEY COULD PRETEND TO-TO BE THE QUEEN.
THEY COULD.
AND THERE'S NOTHING YOU COULD DO ABOUT IT.
SURE THERE IS.
IT DOES.
I'M SERIOUS.
EVERY TIME THEY TRY SOMETHING, WE BEAT THEM BACK ACROSS THE UNIVERSE.
EVERY TIME. SO NO, IT DOESN'T BOTHER ME.
IT SHOULD.

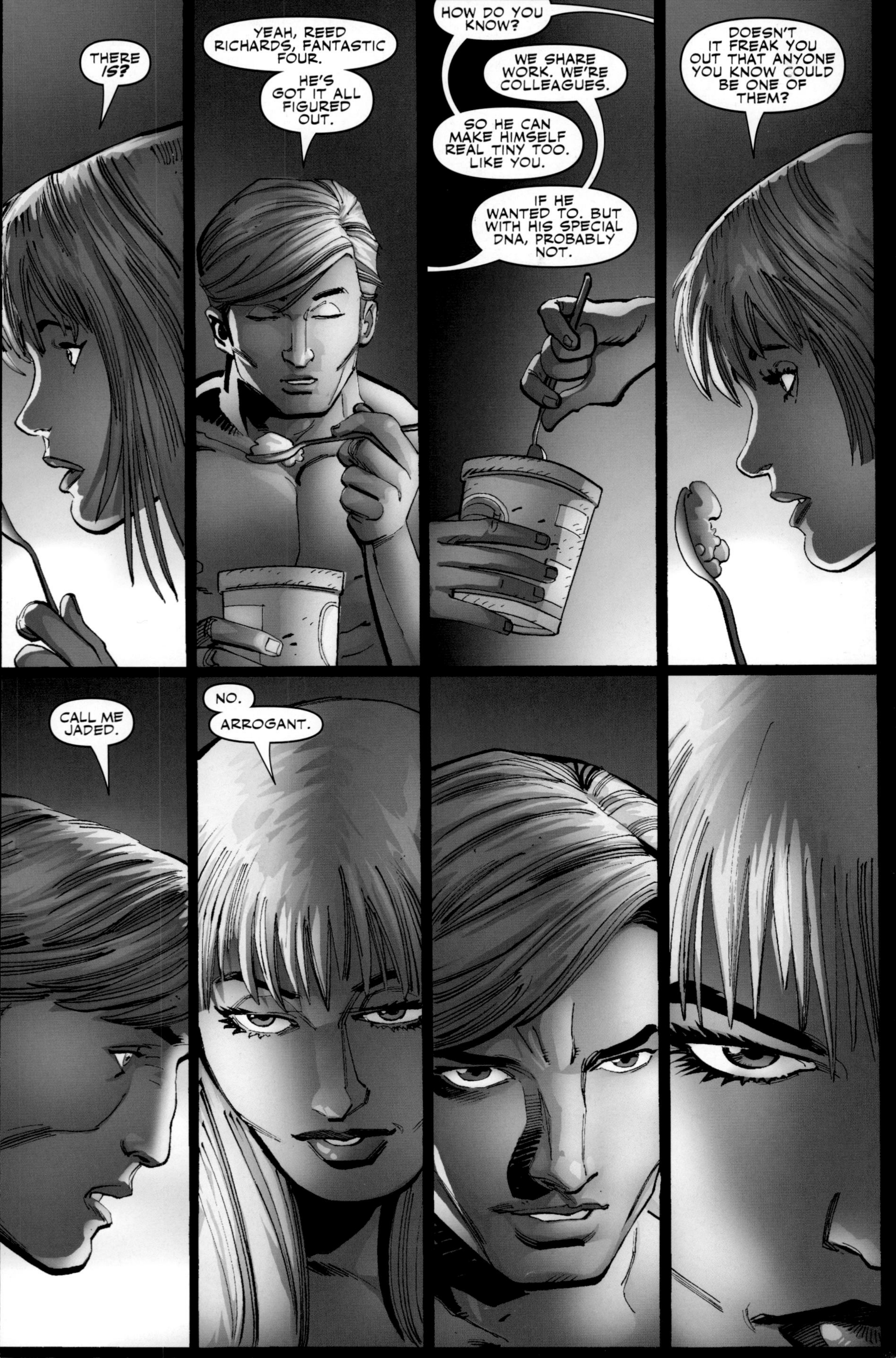
THERE IS?
YEAH, REED RICHARDS, FANTASTIC FOUR.
HE'S GOT IT ALL FIGURED OUT.
HOW DO YOU KNOW?
WE SHARE WORK. WE'RE COLLEAGUES.
SO HE CAN MAKE HIMSELF REAL TINY TOO. LIKE YOU.
IF HE WANTED TO. BUT WITH HIS SPECIAL DNA, PROBABLY NOT.
DOESN'T IT FREAK YOU OUT THAT ANYONE YOU KNOW COULD BE ONE OF THEM?
CALL ME JADED.
NO.
ARROGANT.

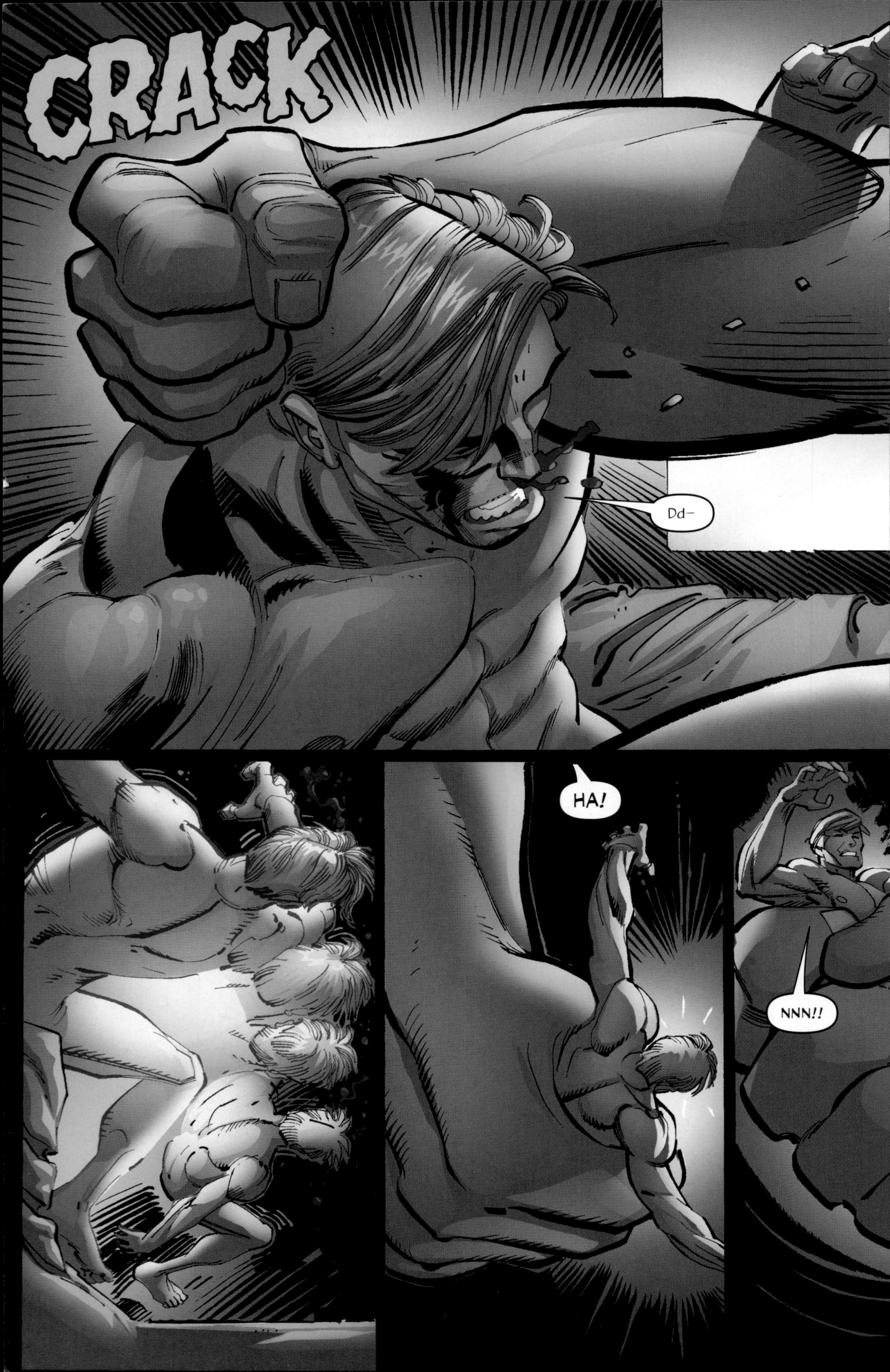
CRACK
Dd—
HA!
NNN!!

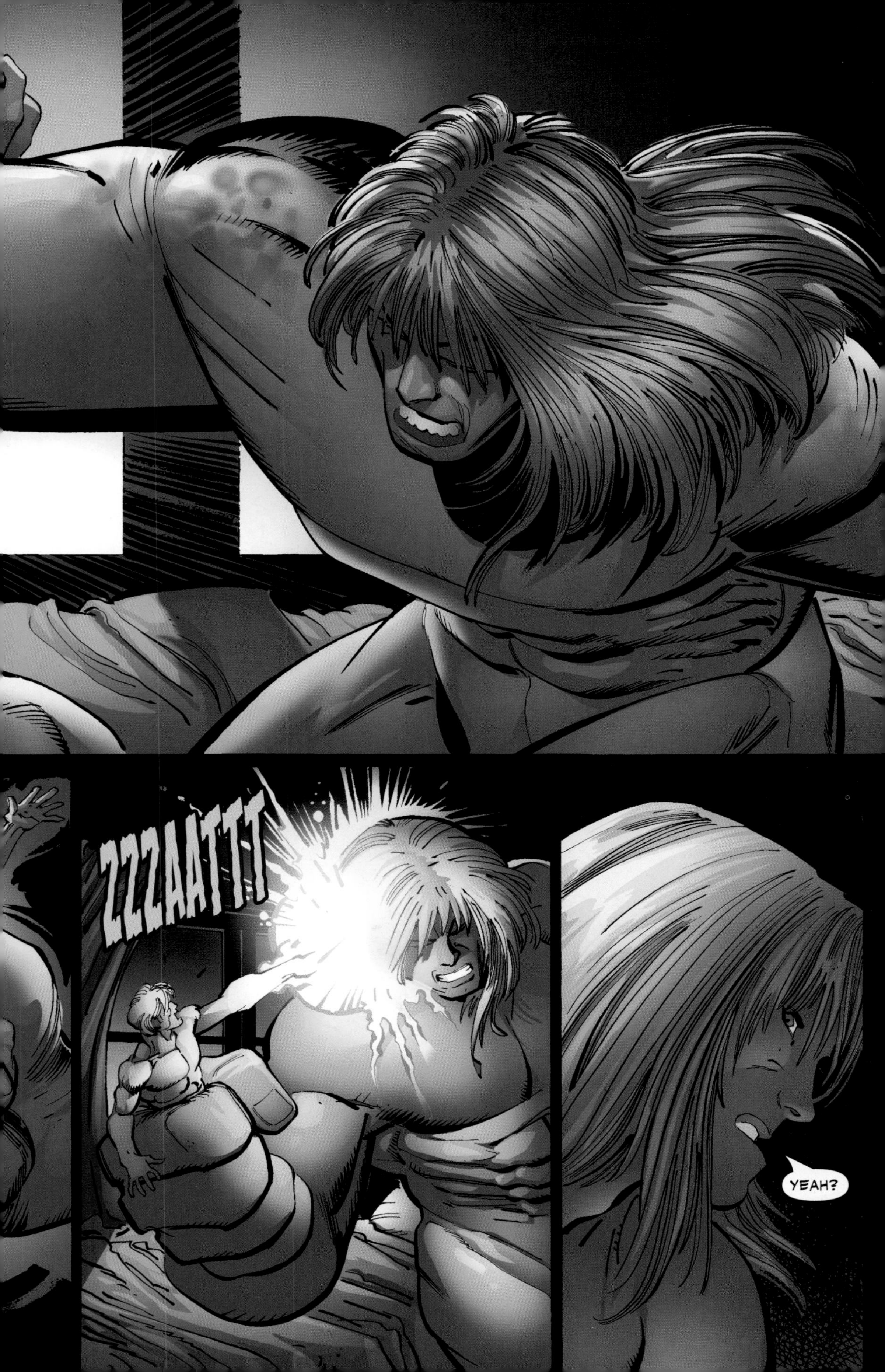
ZZZAATTT
YEAH?

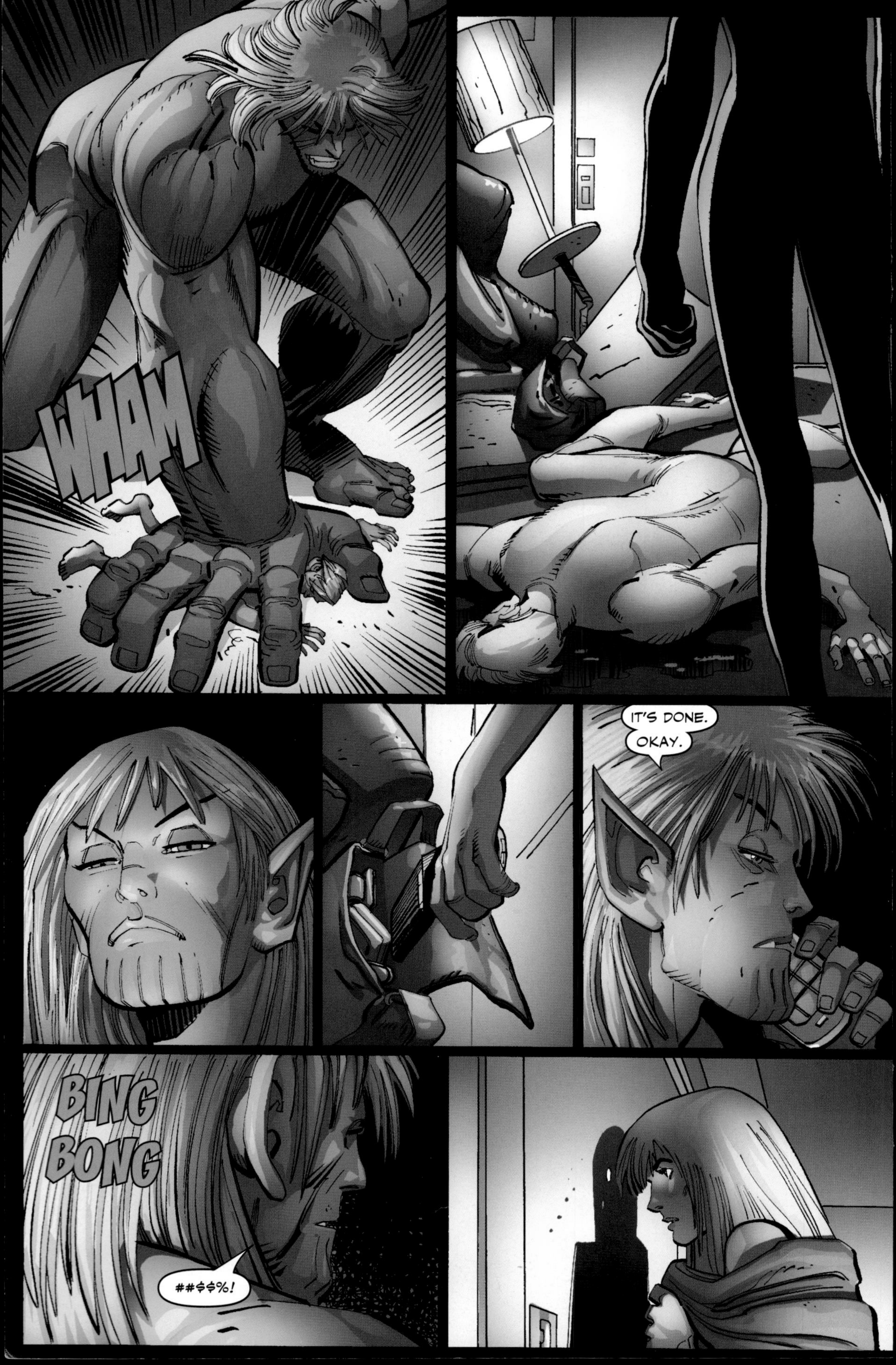
WHAM
IT'S DONE.
OKAY.
BING
BONG
##$$%!

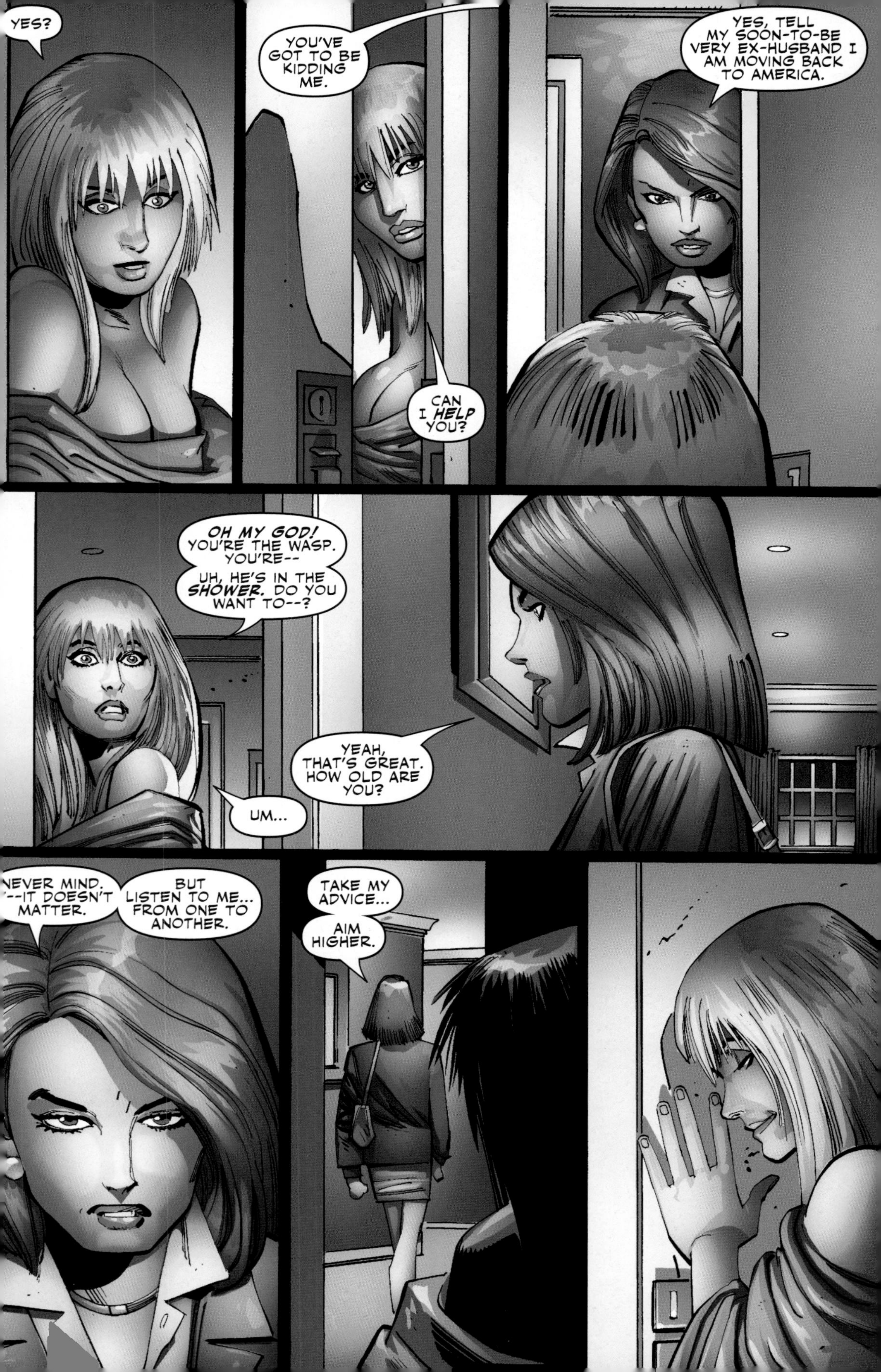
YES?
YOU'VE GOT TO BE KIDDING ME.
CAN I HELP YOU?
YES, TELL MY SOON-TO-BE VERY EX-HUSBAND I AM MOVING BACK TO AMERICA.
OH MY GOD! YOU'RE THE WASP. YOU'RE--
UH, HE'S IN THE SHOWER. DO YOU WANT TO--?
YEAH, THAT'S GREAT. HOW OLD ARE YOU?
UM...
NEVER MIND. --IT DOESN'T MATTER.
BUT LISTEN TO ME... FROM ONE TO ANOTHER.
TAKE MY ADVICE...
AIM HIGHER.

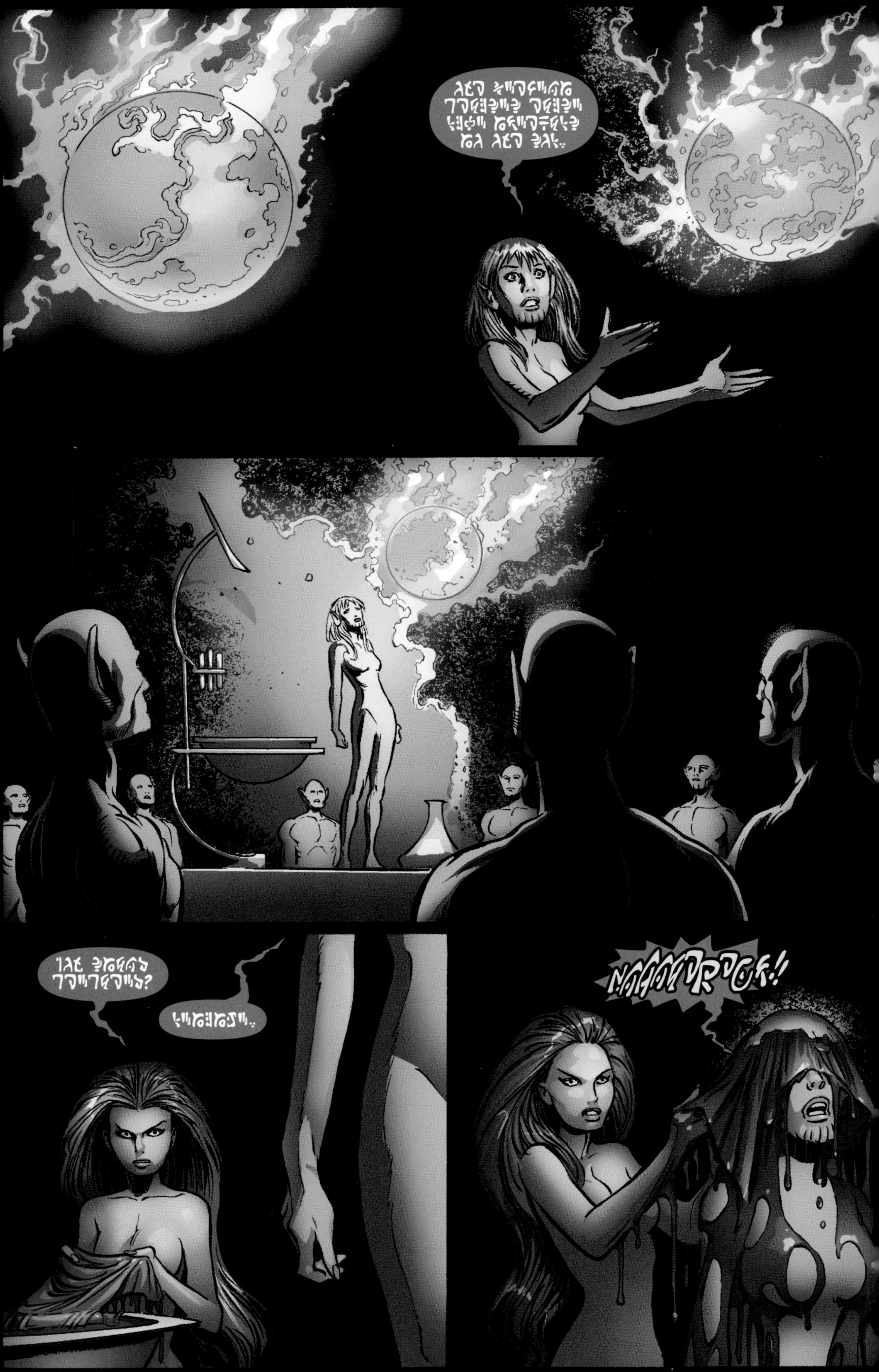

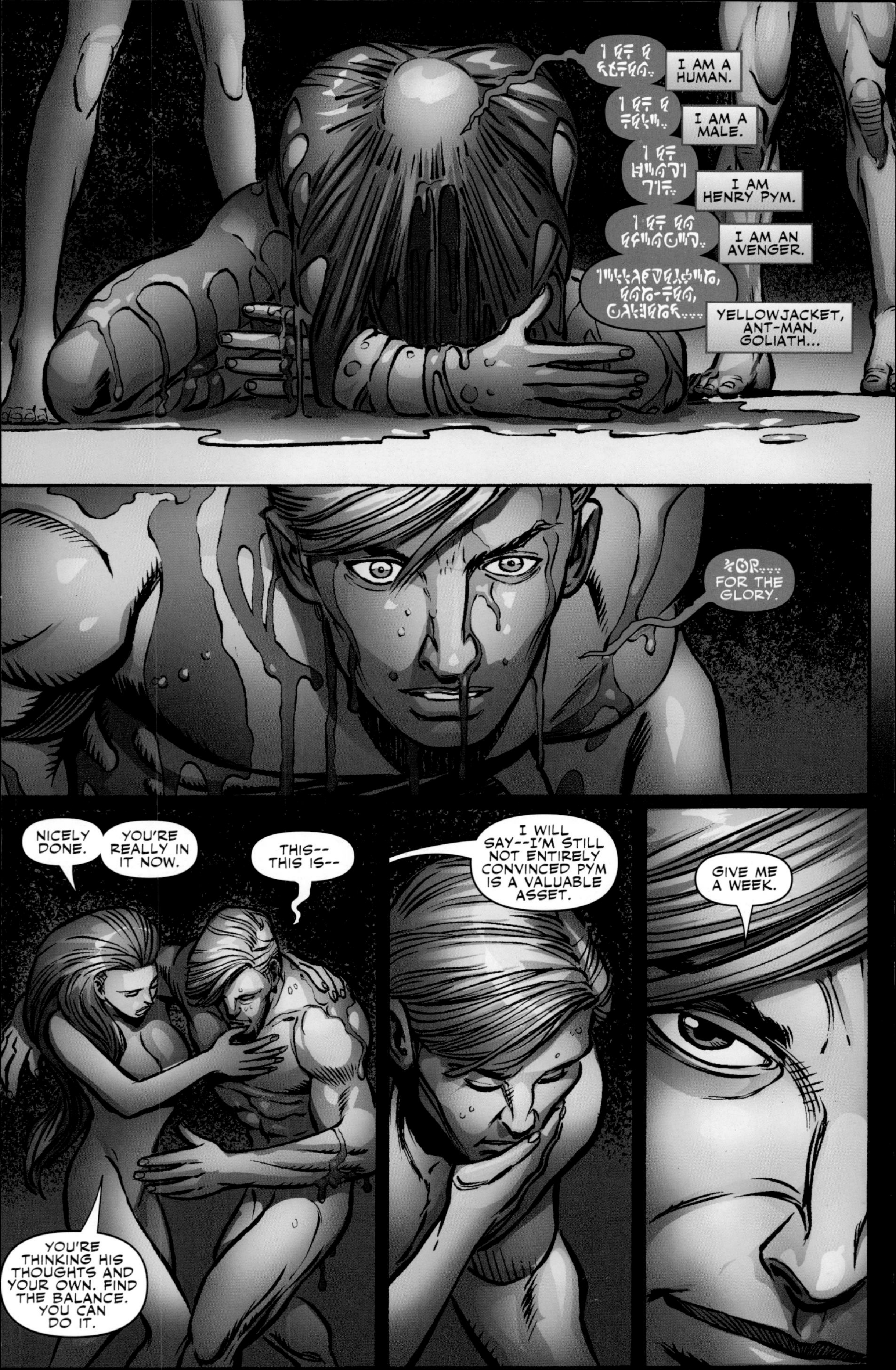
I AM A HUMAN.
I AM A MALE.
I AM HENRY PYM.
I AM AN AVENGER.
YELLOWJACKET, ANT-MAN, GOLIATH...
FOR THE GLORY.
NICELY DONE.
YOU'RE REALLY IN IT NOW.
THIS-- THIS IS--
YOU'RE THINKING HIS THOUGHTS AND YOUR OWN. FIND THE BALANCE. YOU CAN DO IT.
I WILL SAY--I'M STILL NOT ENTIRELY CONVINCED PYM IS A VALUABLE ASSET.
GIVE ME A WEEK.

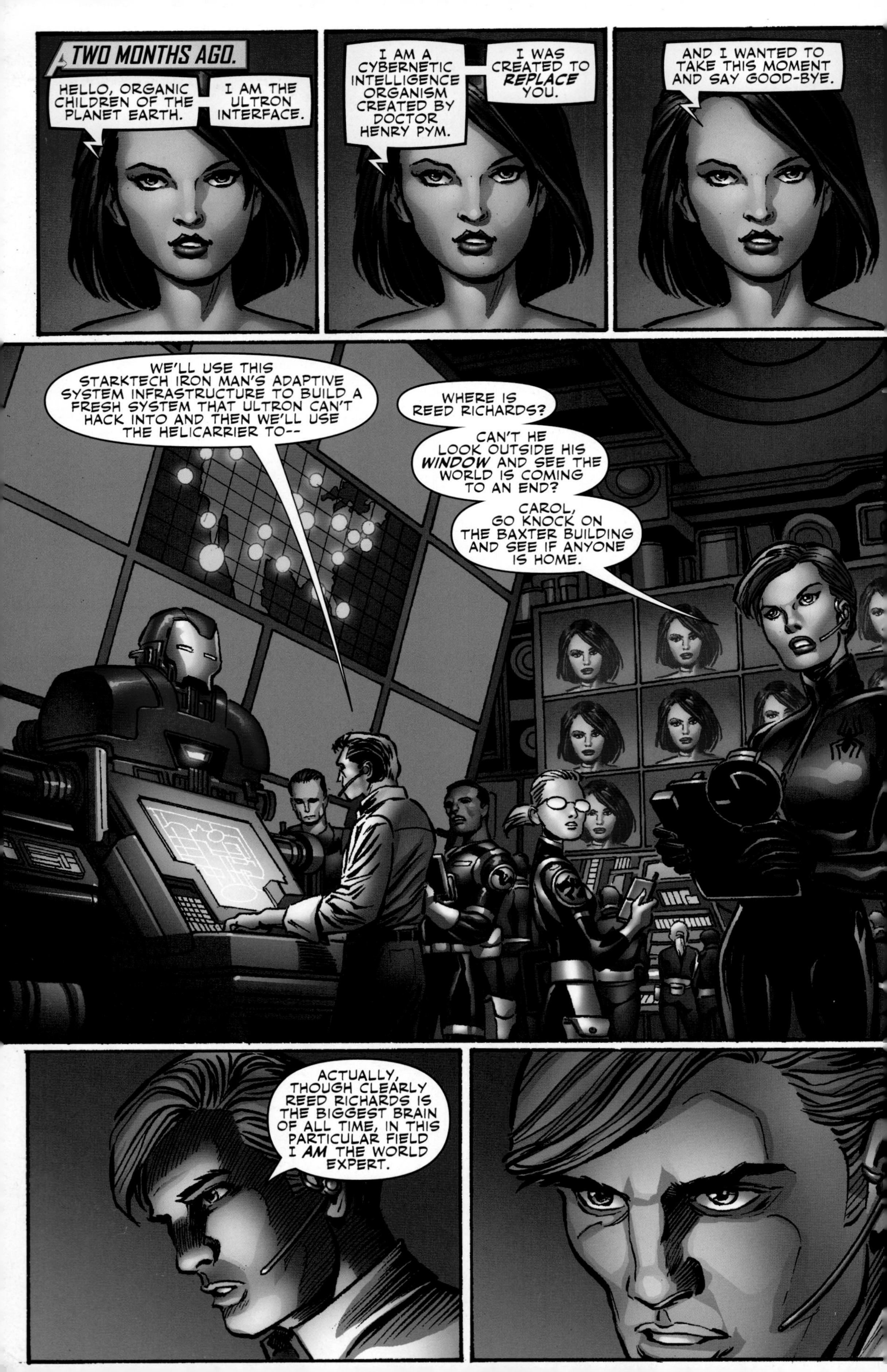

TWO MONTHS AGO.
HELLO, ORGANIC CHILDREN OF THE PLANET EARTH.
I AM THE ULTRON INTERFACE.
I AM A CYBERNETIC INTELLIGENCE ORGANISM CREATED BY DOCTOR HENRY PYM.
I WAS CREATED TO REPLACE YOU.
AND I WANTED TO TAKE THIS MOMENT AND SAY GOOD-BYE.
WE'LL USE THIS STARKTECH IRON MAN'S ADAPTIVE SYSTEM INFRASTRUCTURE TO BUILD A FRESH SYSTEM THAT ULTRON CAN'T HACK INTO AND THEN WE'LL USE THE HELICARRIER TO--
WHERE IS REED RICHARDS?
CAN'T HE LOOK OUTSIDE HIS WINDOW AND SEE THE WORLD IS COMING TO AN END?
CAROL, GO KNOCK ON THE BAXTER BUILDING AND SEE IF ANYONE IS HOME.
ACTUALLY, THOUGH CLEARLY REED RICHARDS IS THE BIGGEST BRAIN OF ALL TIME, IN THIS PARTICULAR FIELD I AM THE WORLD EXPERT.

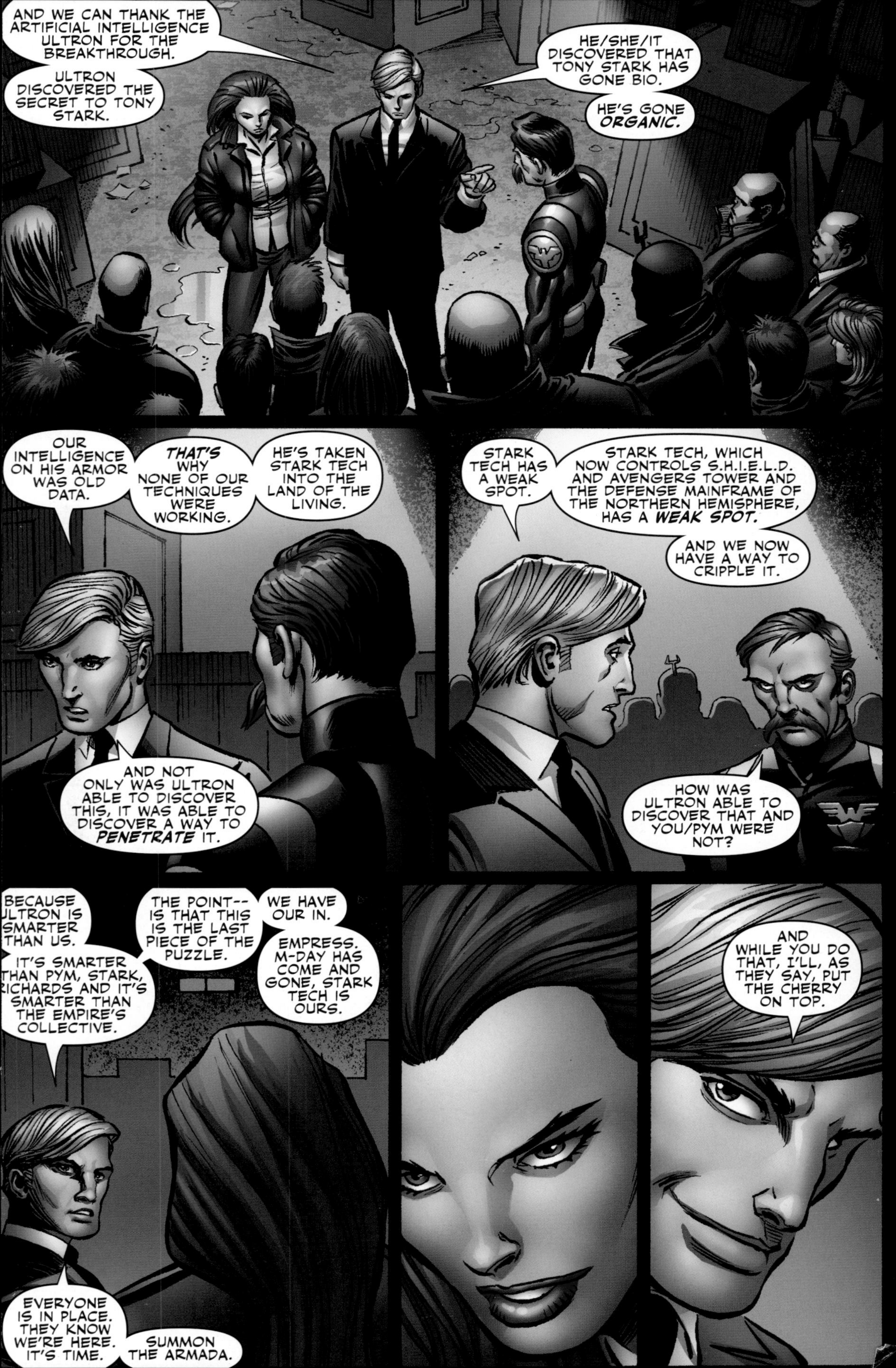
AND WE CAN THANK THE ARTIFICIAL INTELLIGENCE ULTRON FOR THE BREAKTHROUGH.
ULTRON DISCOVERED THE SECRET TO TONY STARK.
HE/SHE/IT DISCOVERED THAT TONY STARK HAS GONE BIO.
HE'S GONE ORGANIC.
OUR INTELLIGENCE ON HIS ARMOR WAS OLD DATA.
THAT'S WHY NONE OF OUR TECHNIQUES WERE WORKING.
HE'S TAKEN STARK TECH INTO THE LAND OF THE LIVING.
AND NOT ONLY WAS ULTRON ABLE TO DISCOVER THIS, IT WAS ABLE TO DISCOVER A WAY TO PENETRATE IT.
STARK TECH HAS A WEAK SPOT.
STARK TECH, WHICH NOW CONTROLS S.H.I.E.L.D. AND AVENGERS TOWER AND THE DEFENSE MAINFRAME OF THE NORTHERN HEMISPHERE, HAS A WEAK SPOT.
AND WE NOW HAVE A WAY TO CRIPPLE IT.
HOW WAS ULTRON ABLE TO DISCOVER THAT AND YOU/PYM WERE NOT?
BECAUSE ULTRON IS SMARTER THAN US.
IT'S SMARTER THAN PYM, STARK, RICHARDS AND IT'S SMARTER THAN THE EMPIRE'S COLLECTIVE.
THE POINT-- IS THAT THIS IS THE LAST PIECE OF THE PUZZLE.
WE HAVE OUR IN.
EMPRESS. M-DAY HAS COME AND GONE, STARK TECH IS OURS.
EVERYONE IS IN PLACE. THEY KNOW WE'RE HERE. IT'S TIME.
SUMMON THE ARMADA.
AND WHILE YOU DO THAT, I'LL, AS THEY SAY, PUT THE CHERRY ON TOP.

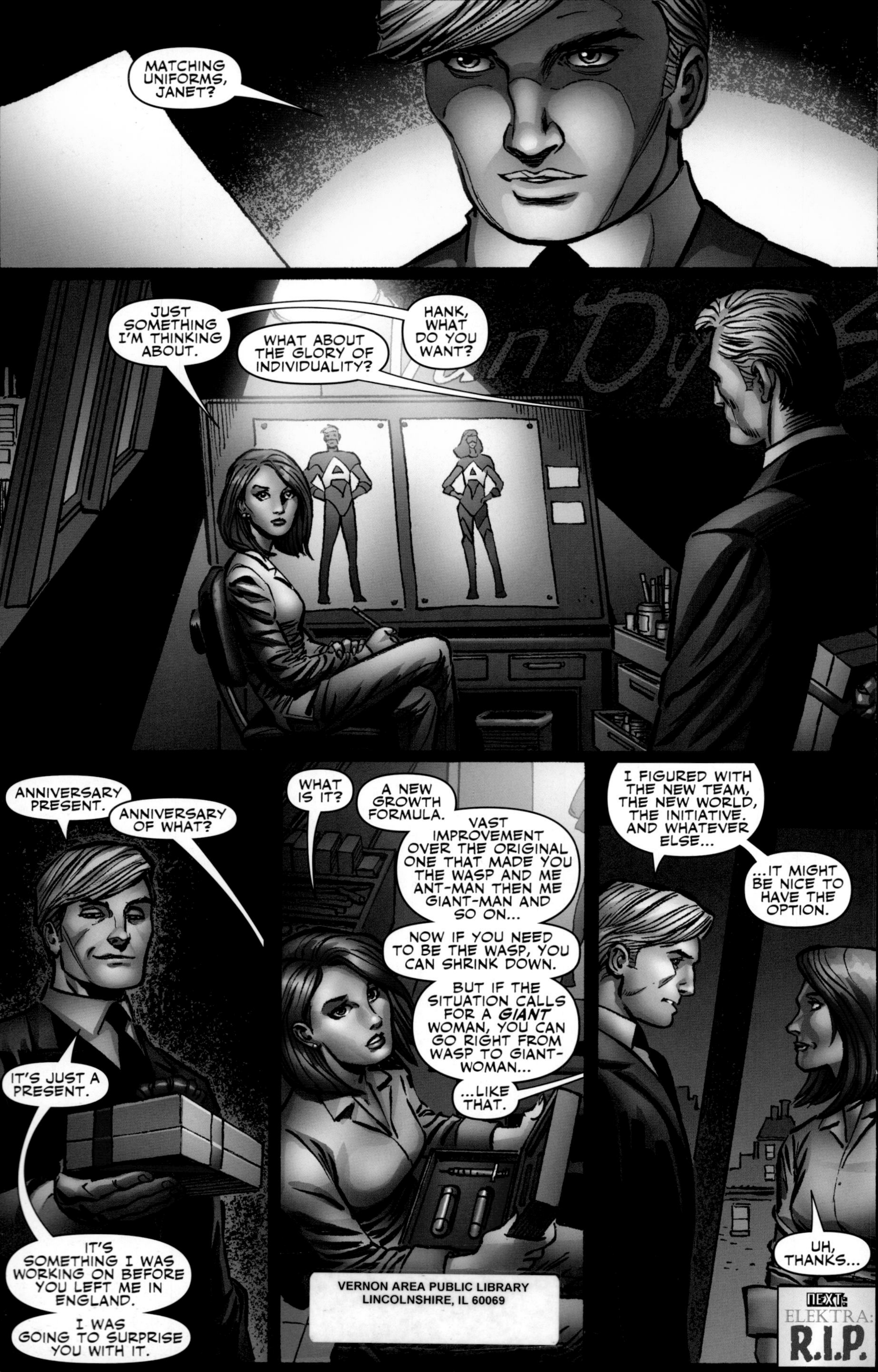
MATCHING UNIFORMS, JANET?
JUST SOMETHING I'M THINKING ABOUT.
WHAT ABOUT THE GLORY OF INDIVIDUALITY?
HANK, WHAT DO YOU WANT?
ANNIVERSARY PRESENT.
ANNIVERSARY OF WHAT?
IT'S JUST A PRESENT.
IT'S SOMETHING I WAS WORKING ON BEFORE YOU LEFT ME IN ENGLAND.
I WAS GOING TO SURPRISE YOU WITH IT.
WHAT IS IT?
A NEW GROWTH FORMULA.
VAST IMPROVEMENT OVER THE ORIGINAL ONE THAT MADE YOU THE WASP AND ME ANT-MAN THEN ME GIANT-MAN AND SO ON...
NOW IF YOU NEED TO BE THE WASP, YOU CAN SHRINK DOWN.
BUT IF THE SITUATION CALLS FOR A *GIANT* WOMAN, YOU CAN GO RIGHT FROM WASP TO GIANT-WOMAN...
...LIKE THAT.
I FIGURED WITH THE NEW TEAM, THE NEW WORLD, THE INITIATIVE. AND WHATEVER ELSE...
...IT MIGHT BE NICE TO HAVE THE OPTION.
UH, THANKS...
NEXT: ELEKTRA: R.I.P.

MIGHTY AVENGERS

By Brian Michael Bendis
Issue 12

Alex- the spy that came in from the cold, Munich, the parallax view, three days of the condor.

Break out your art style we're planning for the Spider-Woman series. This issue represents a tone very close to what the series will be. This is a good place to work towards it.

Page 1-
RECAP AND CREDIT PAGE.
Earth's Mightiest Heroes united against a common threat! On that day The Avengers were born - to fight foes that no single hero could withstand!

Previously in the Mighty Avengers...

One year ago! Nick Fury, director of S.H.I.E.L.D., the world peacekeeping task force and international espionage coalition, discovers the alarming fact that dozens of low-rent technology-based super-criminals are being secretly funded by what America thinks is a new ally. The new prime minister of Latveria.

When Fury tells the president his alarming news, that these criminals are now technically terrorists, he is blown off and dismissed.

Fury, in a panic, knowing that something big is brewing, something nightmarish, vows to do something to stop this even if his government won't.

Fury gathered some of the world's most colorful and, misunderstood heroes Wolverine, Daredevil, Spider-Man, Captain America, Black Widow, and Luke Cage for a covert trip to Latveria.

What the heroes did not know is that Fury brought them there to violently overthrow the terrorist Latverian government. After the violence had occurred and the day was won, Fury erased the horrible memory from the heroes' minds.

It was only later, when Latervia launched a revenge attack that they discovered the nature of Fury's betrayal.

Page 2-
Same as Page 28, of issue 5 of Secret War number 5. The last appearance of Nick fury. Ask tom for reference.
1- Ext. Manhattan/ piers- night

From behind Fury, Fury turns around just in time for Logan to lunge up and swing his claws wide and slice Nick Fury hard in the stomach. Berserker rage takes hold of him.

In the background, everyone is horrified!! the X-men, The Fantastic Four, Spider-man, Luke cage, Daredevil... all battle worn and tired. They were all listening to fury's confession. No one expected this.

Logan slices him wide. Its horrible. Everyone is diving to stop it.

Reads: ONE YEAR AGO

2- Low, looking up. Nick falls backwards to the messy pier, Logan on top of him. Another slash is coming. Beserker rage overpowers his intellect. One mind-wipe too many.

We don't get a good look at Fury yet.

LOGAN
You don't touch my head!!!!!

3- From over Daisy Johnson's (think young Angelina Jolie in a S.H.I.E.L.D. uniform) head and shoulder, Reed Richards stretches and grabs Logan's arms and Spidey webs him back to try and help stop this.

And the X-Men are already there holding him back. Logan lunges for Daisy next. Totally out of control.

Sue Storm was going to block it with a force field but wasn't given the chance.

SPIDER-MAN
Whoah!!

CYCLOPS
Logan!!

LOGAN
You don't touch my head!!!!

4- Daisy stands her ground and points her finger. She has earthquake powers and will use them. And yells right at us.

S.H.I.E.L.D. AGENT DAISY JOHNSON
Stop.

Page 3-
Images from page 30 of Secret War 5 mixed in with new images.

1- From over Daredevil, The Thing and Reed Richards' heads looking down at the ground- at what they thought would be the bleeding body of Nick Fury.

But there's no blood, just blobs of orange. It's not Fury. Its a life model decoy.

Richards stretches in to examine it. Daisy stands over the odd sight lying on the wet pier.

S.H.I.E.L.D. AGENT DAISY JOHNSON
Yeah, um...

The colonel excused himself from the scene once the threat was done.

2- Low, looking up, the gathered heroes are shocked. Logan is in an insane amount of pain but already healing. The X-Men tend to him.

REED RICHARDS
That's a... life model decoy?

THE THING
Wow, they're making them good now.

3- The shocked group of heroes p.o.v. Nick's fake body lies there and gurgles orange.

NICK FURY
New design.
I know you're sssssteamin' but don't worry.
This was my biiiiig finish.
I'm done.

I ddddodged the politics of this once- I ccccan't do it again.

4- Int. Nick Fury's hideaway bunker- Same
Tight profile, on Nick Fury's scruffy lips speaking into a thin microphone. Silhouette.

NICK FURY
You'll never see or hear from me again.

There's nothing more I can do here.

5- Ext. Manhattan/piers- night
The shocked group of heroes. Spider-Woman isn't satisfied. Neither is Daredevil. Reed is looking up and around.

NICK FURY
That's why I came ccccclean with ya here.

Let you hhhhhear it straight from me.

CAPTAIN AMERICA
Where is he?

REED RICHARDS
He's broadcasting from somewhere.
6- Int. Nick Fury's hideaway bunker- Same
Same as 4, but wider. Nick talks into his microphone. Silhouette. Behind him, a hint of the hidden, covert bunker he is hiding away in.

NICK FURY
You are heroes. More than me.

Maybe one day you'll look around and you'll see the world like I have to and you'll know I did the right thing.

Or at least you'll understand why I did it.
7- Ext. Manhattan/piers- night

Fury's LMD doesn't move. He's not there anymore. The life model decoy is non-operational.

NICK FURY
Signin' offfffffffffff.

Page 4-
1- Int. Sewer safehouse- Same
Behind Nick Fury, backlit, he sits back and looks at the stacked monitors in front of him.

Nick Fury's underground safehouse.

Backlit to a dim industrial yellow light. One of those lights like they use in tunnels that runs on its own generator and is always on.

The room itself is shown in Civil War two and NA 21. a dark, dank, underground safehouse built and tucked away by Nick Fury.

A handful of stacked monitors and computer terminals. It's all pieced together. Not high tech. The opposite. But effective, none the less.

A few trunks and crates and boxes unboxed. A couple of chairs. A cot. Really, a place to go at the end of the world.

This room is very shadow-laden. Shadows and cobwebs. Except for the screens that show five different angles of the scene on the docks. The agitated heroes.

We imagine the life model decoy is still broadcasting a low, looking up view. Daisy has a view from her belt buckle.

And Nick has an eye in the sky somewhere looking wide of the scene.

2- Tight on Nick Fury, looking in pain at the life he now has to leave behind.

This is not an easy choice. This hurts. Those are his friends, comrades and soldiers. He betrayed them and now he is abandoning them.

3- Nick is leaving the room and walking away from us and the monitors in the foreground, profile, right. He has turned everything off. Closed the crates. Taken what he has needed.

He has a bag over his shoulder and is walking into the shadows of the hidden sewers.

He is leaving his life behind. Head hung low.

Page 5-
1- Ext. Mexico City- day
Wide of a cobblestone street off the main street of Mexico City. Small, run down, yet ornate buildings all around. An orange sun rises. a blanket dries on a laundry line.

In the background, a man, a couple of stories up, a bald man with a handlebar mustache, a paunch and an eyepatch is drinking a bottled water and looking out at the world. Lost in thought.

He stands on the smallish balcony of his not entirely horrible, but not great, hotel.
Reads: ONE MONTH LATER

2- Tighter on the balcony. Mid shot of the man, a bald man with a handlebar mustache, a paunch and an eyepatch is drinking a bottled water and looking out at the world. Lost in thought.

This is Nick Fury in disguise.

3- Int. Hotel room- Same
Nick turns and looks into his room when he hears a noise at the door.

We see the room is barely lived in. There's one suitcase of clothes and nothing that says he is the superspy of superspies.

4- Nick's p.o.v. of the door to the room. Someone is jiggling the lock.
Spx: rattle

5- Tight on Nick, he approaches the side of the door next to the small closet. Ready to take all comers. He has pulled a small but clearly high tech revolver. The sun hits it.

6- Over Nick's shoulder, a handsome middle-aged Italian woman with a throw of blonde hair and a handsome, but rugged outfit, stumbles into the room with wide eyes and a big smile. This is Countess Valentina Allegro DeFontaine in disguise, a big bag over her shoulder. An expensive one.

S.H.I.E.L.D. AGENT VALENTINA
Oh I'm sorry, I must have the wrong room.

7- In the foreground, her silhouetted hand closes the door, with her on the inside. Nick squints at her.

S.H.I.E.L.D. AGENT VALENTINA
So...
Do you like?

NICK FURY
Were you followed?

Page 6-
1- Over Nick's shoulder, Countess Valentina Allegro DeFontaine pulls off her wig to reveal her trademark skunk hair and beauty.

S.H.I.E.L.D. AGENT VALENTINA
Would I come here if I was?

2- Nick puts the gun away as Valentina takes her hug. A hug she knows she has to take because he doesn't give them out freely. Nick is surprised to hear what she is saying.

NICK FURY
How's the real world doing without me?

S.H.I.E.L.D. AGENT VALENTINA
They cleaned house.

NICK FURY
You're out.

S.H.I.E.L.D. AGENT VALENTINA
S.H.I.E.L.D. Agent Countess Valentina Allegro DeFontaine has been decommissioned.

Anyone who knew you is out. Sam, Jenny, Quartermain, everyone except Dugan.

3- Same but tighter. She really relaxes into him. He doesn't relax.

NICK FURY
What are ya gonna do now?

S.H.I.E.L.D. AGENT VALENTINA
What are you going to do now?

NICK FURY
I guess we're supposed to live happily ever after.

4- Over Nick's shoulder, she breaks the hug and smiles at him knowingly. She knows he is incapable.

S.H.I.E.L.D. AGENT VALENTINA
That would be nice.

You certainly earned it. We both earned it.

5- He looks at her. Lost and lonely and she is the face of everything he should have ever needed.

NICK FURY
Feels odd though, don't it?

6- Same as 4,

S.H.I.E.L.D. AGENT VALENTINA
You did what you had to do.

History will be kind.

7- Nick's not so sure. He did it, but what now?

8- Same as 6, she touches his face.

S.H.I.E.L.D. AGENT VALENTINA
Hey...

Page 7-
1- They are about to kiss. She tiptoes up. Lips close. She smiles. Teasing. Seducing.

S.H.I.E.L.D. AGENT VALENTINA
I went out of my way to make my disguise something you'd like.

NICK FURY
Didn't say I didn't.

S.H.I.E.L.D. AGENT VALENTINA
And what are you supposed to be?

NICK FURY
Disguised.

S.H.I.E.L.D. AGENT VALENTINA
Would it have killed you to try something a little less... bald?

2- They kiss. Hard. Passionate. Lovers in a dangerous world. For a long long time.

They are both mostly silhouettes in the sunlight outside the window.

3- Countess Valentina Allegro DeFontaine almost attacks him with the second kiss. The passion is so intense. She doesn't even realize she is doing it. Her hand on the back of his head.

4- Pulling past them out to the patio and the sun outside.

5- Tighter on the hot orange Mexican sun.

6- Int. Hotel bedroom- dusk

The sun has dissolved to a tight shot of Nick Fury's good eye. Staring at nothing. At us. The sun's glow bounces off of it.

Page 8-
1- Int. Hotel bedroom- dusk

High looking down, Nick Fury, not in disguise, lies in bed, covered in a sheet. The late day sun sliding over their roughed-up bedroom. They have made love.

He was lost in thought but just notices that Valentina is getting dressed and getting ready to go.

NICK FURY
Where ya going?

S.H.I.E.L.D. AGENT VALENTINA
I'm going to go get whatever that amazing smell outside is.

NICK FURY
Want me to come?

2- Valentina puts on her wig and smiles as she adjusts it.

S.H.I.E.L.D. AGENT VALENTINA
No, I'll bring you breakfast... or dinner... in bed.

3- She leans in and kisses him on the temple. He doesn't budge. Just a slight smirk.

4- Nick, in profile, doesn't seem to look her way as she leaves the way she came in.
Spx: clump

5- He sits up. As if he was waiting for her to leave to do so.

6- Over Nick's shoulder. He hides behind the curtain and looks down to the street. He watches her leave in a certain direction.

7- Ext. Mexican street/ alley- Same
Valentina is walking away from the restaurant that is cooking a pig on its patio. She is walking by a broken old column and looking around to see if she is being followed.

Page 9-
1- Same, but Valentina is off panel and Nick, in his disguise, is peeking around the same column she just passed Serious. Focussed.

2- Tighter on Nick. He touches a button on his watch and looks to see that no one is watching.
Spx: gleek

3- Same, Nick disappears. He turns invisible. It's a cloak. We can still see a light Photoshop outline. Like Sue Storm in the Fantastic Four movies.

4- Nick's p.o.v. Valentina is a block away, walking through a crowd. Her blonde hair sticks out among the Mexicans. She is turning a male head or two.

5- Nick, invisible, walks towards us and though the same crowd unseen. Everyone goes about their life.

6- Nick's p.o.v. Valentina is turning a corner. Almost out of sight.

7- Nick, stops at the entrance of a alley way/ walk through street. Voices off-panel to the right.

MAN
Did you get them?

S.H.I.E.L.D. AGENT VALENTINA
I got his confidence. It will take a week at least.

MAN
A week?

Page 10-

1- Over Nick's invisible shoulder. Valentina is talking to a thin, agitated black man. They are not friendly. All business.

S.H.I.E.L.D. AGENT VALENTINA
He's not a stupid man.

MAN
Get his passcodes to his private S.H.I.E.L.D. files and eliminate him.

S.H.I.E.L.D. AGENT VALENTINA
Calm down.

MAN
You-

S.H.I.E.L.D. AGENT VALENTINA
Calm down!

Tell the queen I'm in place.

2- Nick's p.o.v. Valentina is really annoyed to be talked to like this. He is very nervous and itchy. Like an addict.

MAN
You should get the-

S.H.I.E.L.D. AGENT VALENTINA
Tell the queen. You do your task. OK?

MAN
The more time you spend with him the riskier the-

S.H.I.E.L.D. AGENT VALENTINA
Stop talking.

Go.

I'll find you.

3- Over Nick's invisible shoulder. Valentina walks right past invisible Nick. She doesn't notice Fury. Leaving the agitated man in the alley.

4- Nick's p.o.v. The man is very nervous and itchy. Like an addict. He is walking away but turns back. Like he feels he is being watched.

5- Tight on the invisible Nick Fury. Blank-faced in the face of betrayal.

6- Int. Hotel bedroom- late dusk
Valentina comes back into the room with yummy ethnic dinner and drinks. A box of food and paper plates with a smile.

VALENTINA
OK, so it smells better than it looks, but that's the-

7- Same but tighter, Valentina's face drops. As she looks down to the bed.

Page 11-

1- Int. Hotel bedroom- dusk
Nick is sitting there. With a very shiny, high tech, silencer gun pointed right at her.

NICK FURY
Who are you... really?

2- Valentina calmly puts the food down and approaches. Cautiously.

S.H.I.E.L.D. AGENT VALENTINA
Come on, Nicholas...

Really?

3- Same as 1, he doesn't budge.

4- Valentina puts her back against the doorway. Respecting his position. But not giving in to it.

VALENTINA
Are you cracking?

Put it down, or I'm leaving.

5- Same as 3.

NICK FURY
One more time.

Who are you really?

6- Same as 4, Valentina sighs. She doesn't know what's wrong with him.

S.H.I.E.L.D. AGENT VALENTINA
This is very dissa-

7- Same. Nick shoots her in the head. Her forehead has a hole in it and blood splatters. Her wig moves.
Spx: fut
Spx: spack

Page 12-
1- Big panel. Over the shoulder of Nick Fury looking down to the ground.

Valentina lies dead... but it's not Valentina. It's a Skrull in Valentina's clothes, covered in blue blood.

Valentina wasn't Valentina. Valentina was a Skrull. Her head turned away slightly. Her blood is purple-blue.

Alex- its important that this Skrull be as ugly and real as possible. This is not a goofy alien. This is a serious threat. Horrifying. Terrible.

2- Camera on the floor. She lies on the floor. Silhouette. In the foreground. He gets out of bed and approaches her dead body. Examining it.

3- Same but tighter of Fury. Slight low looking up. He is confused. Sickened. Angry. Embarrassed. All these things at once.

Page 13-
1- Ext. Rooftop- day
Nick Fury is invisible again. We see his outline standing next to a satellite dish on an old dusty, dirty rooftop.

2- Nick Fury's p.o.v. Looking across the street, down to the patio of what was his hotel room. He watches the hotel room.

The man Valentina Skrull was talking to the other day and two women are in his hotel room. They are dealing with the body.

3- Nick Fury, invisible, holds up a cell phone-like device, looking through it with his good eye.

4- Big panel. Nick Fury's p.o.v. through the device. He is zooming in on the conversation.

One of the women is yelling at the man. Not yelling, more like bawling out.

We can see the screen, but everything else about Nick is invisible.

This is a tense moment. The other woman is wrapping up the body and gesturing for the other two to help.

On the screen we see the REC sign in the upper left. We can see the alien font of their dialogue.

On the bottom right reads: LINGUIST IDENTIFICATION. SKRULL, TLIGI DIALECT

MAN
(Skrull font)

WOMAN
(Skrull font)

5- Nick Fury, invisible, Is watching, recording, and steaming.

6- Over Nick Fury's shoulder, the man walks off to the patio and looks around. Taking a moment to himself, as the two women take the wrapped body and head out.

7- Widescreen, Over the man's shoulder, he looks across the rooftop, to where Nick Fury is standing. There's nothing there. Nothing but the hot sun and the satellite dish.

Page 14-
1- Ext. S.H.I.E.L.D. Helicarrier- night
Big panel. A gorgeous establishing shot of the S.H.I.E.L.D. Helicarrier.

Worm's-eye view looking up at the gorgeous blue sky.

The giant silver S.H.I.E.L.D. Helicarrier descends out of the clouds, its bow taking up a mile of the early dawn sky.

U.S. fighter planes flying off and around it in formation. The biggest flying tank in the world keeping watch over all of us.

Reads: S.H.I.E.L.D. Helicarrier.

Floating world headquarters of the U.N.

Peacekeeping task force.

Present location: 1000 feet over San Jose, California

Reads: TWO WEEKS LATER

2- Int. S.H.I.E.L.D. Helicarrier/ private quarters- Same

Tight on Nick Fury's fingers typing away at a thick, metal, hard-core personal laptop.
Spx: tap tap tap tap tap tap tap

3- Tight on Fury, lit by the light of the laptop. Not in disguise or invisible. He is himself. Typing, searching, researching.
Spx: tap tap tap tap tap tap tap

4- Maria Hill is asleep in her bunk in a sports bra and light blanket. Sleeping on her hands.

Spx: tap tap tap tap tap tap tap

5- Same but tighter, Maria wakes from her deep sleep.

Spx: tap tap tap tap tap tap tap

6- Over Maria's shoulder, Nick Fury is at a table across the room. In her room, typing away on the computer. In the dark.

The room is a no-frills quarters. Barely lived in. She hasn't been on board that long. Her clothes are everywhere. She just tosses them wherever she takes them off. One wall of the room is a giant window showing a bit of the Helicarrier underbelly in perspective and the view of the world she is protecting.

7- Maria sits up. Rubbing her face, she can't believe it.

DIRECTOR MARIA HILL
Oh

my

god!

Page 15-
1- Over Maria's shoulder, Nick Fury keeps typing. As if nothing here is out of the ordinary.

NICK FURY
Maria Hill. Director of S.H.I.E.L.D

We've met before, you and I.

2- Maria is awake. Sitting up in her bed, amazed, not sure what to do. Not completely sure if she is dreaming or not.

DIRECTOR MARIA HILL
Once.

NICK FURY
Where?

DIRECTOR MARIA HILL
Madripoor.

3- Nick closes the laptop and removes most of the light from the room as he does. The moonlit sky out the large window lighting the dark room.

NICK FURY
Oh, that's where I know you from?

4- Maria squints her nose She knows this is bull.

DIRECTOR MARIA HILL
Don't pretend that the great Nick Fury who can sneak into the Helicarrier didn't learn every damn thing about me before he broke in.

5- Nick sits forward and smiles.

NICK FURY
Yeah, you're right.

So how's my old job?

6- Maria shrugs. An honest answer.

DIRECTOR MARIA HILL
I've had better.

Oh, and you're under arrest.

7- Same as 5, like he didn't hear her.

NICK FURY
How'd you get the job?

8- Same as 6.

DIRECTOR MARIA HILL
How'd you lose it?

8- Nick leans forward. His hands touching. Serious. This is for real...

NICK FURY
I came here to tell you two things...

Page 16-
Widescreen panels.

1- Nick, profile, right, looks right at her off panel and says it how it is.

NICK FURY
I came here to tell you that you're not safe.
You are surrounded by those who are looking to take you out.

Including people aboard this ship.

2- Nick's p.o.v. Maria, full figure, sitting up on the side of her bed. She's really actually scared of him and this warning.

DIRECTOR MARIA HILL
You think?

NICK FURY
Take my advice and make yourself some of the new design life model decoys.

About a dozen to start.

Start using them.

Send them in when you feel that itch on the back of your neck.

It's not cheating and it's not cowardly.

It's smart thinking.

3- Same as 1. He doesn't budge.

NICK FURY
The other thing is I'll be watching you.
First inkling I get that you ain't what you're supposed to be...

you ain't doin' what's in the best interest of... the planet.

I come in here, while you're sleeping.

You never wake up.

You know plenty of people that know I ain't BSin' you about that.

4- Maria stares at him. Her mouth hanging open.

DIRECTOR MARIA HILL
Got a number I can reach you... in case I need any advice?

5- Over Maria's shoulder, Fury salutes her almost sarcastically as he is about to leave the room.

NICK FURY
Cute.

Remember what I said.

They're right in front of you.

Right under your nose.

Unless you're one of them, then you already knew that,

Page 17-
1- Wide of the room, Maria sits there in shock. Mouth hanging open. In the dark.

2- Maria snaps out of it and dives for the intercom next to her laptop.

DIRECTOR MARIA HILL
Code white!!
Repeat, code white.

3- Ext. S.H.I.E.L.D. Helicarrier- night
Outside the Helicarrier, Nick Fury with James Bond jet pack is falling off the Helicarrier and right for us.

A gorgeous establishing shot of the S.H.I.E.L.D. Helicarrier behind him.

Worm's-eye view looking up at the gorgeous night blue sky.

The giant silver S.H.I.E.L.D. Helicarrier descends out of the clouds. Its bow takes up a mile. U.S. fighter planes flying off and around it in formation.

4- A couple of the jet fighters are circling. They see him. He is being chased.

PILOT
Helicarrier one, we have him. Over.

HELICARRIER
Keep visual. Over.

PILOT
Is that really him? Over.

5- Fury dives right for us. Back to the Helicarrier and heading towards Earth. A couple of agents are following him in similar contraption.

HELICARRIER
Recon two, agents Freda and Cornelius. Report. Over.

AGENT
We are in the air. In pursuit. Over.

AGENT
Should we open fire, over?

6- Over the other agents' heads, hair whipping in the wind. He disappears.

AGENT
Uh, we lost visual.

AGENT
He's cloaked.

Page 18-
1- Int. S.H.I.E.L.D. Helicarrier- day
Wide of the S.H.I.E.L.D. Mission room on high alert. a startled Maria Hill is storming in and putting on her shirt as she is being debriefed as they walk quickly through the room.

Two dozen young S.H.I.E.L.D. agents are running around on high alert. Everyone is taking battle stations. It's a huge glass and metal war room.

The high tech walls are covered with tons of live video screens monitoring just about everything on the planet. Digital world maps are mapping out the complex global political situation.

The screens show a bombardment of information about the Marvel Universe. It shows how wide in scope S.H.I.E.L.D.'s p.o.v. Is. This is the big picture flying by at a blinding speed.

But all the drama has shifted to aerial images of Nick Fury. Everything is about the situation... photos, digital maps, file pictures and downloads of Fury on some of the screens...

This is a very sterile, cold environment.

DIRECTOR MARIA HILL
What?

AGENT
We lost visual,

DIRECTOR MARIA HILL
Are you #@#$%ing kidding me?

AGENT
He's not showing up on infra red or...

2- Maria leans on the console and barks up at the screens. The agents around her hop to.

DIRECTOR MARIA HILL
Are you kidding me? How is he doing that??

AGENT
He has the cloaking devise in his watch. Standard issue.

DIRECTOR MARIA HILL
Standard issue??

AGENT
For level nine and up.

DIRECTOR MARIA HILL
I don't have one.

AGENT
You have to put in a request.

3- Maria thinks. One of the agents leans in and asks her. This is an amazing night.

DIRECTOR MARIA HILL
Then it's not standard issue, is it?

AGENT
We can estimate his departure trajectory but he knows that and probably changed course upon cloaking.

AGENT
He was in your room?

DIRECTOR MARIA HILL
To be fair it used to be his.

AGENT
Did he take anything?

4- Maria thinks. About everything that just happened and everything he just said. The chaos continues around her.

5- Over Maria's head, the photo file of Nick Fury stares down on her from one of the monitor screens over her head. Looking right at her.

Page 19-
1- Ext. San Francisco- day
Big splash of Spider-Woman flying through the caverns of a bright and sunny day San Francisco.

Spider-Woman is back. The city glows like a magical fairy tale land. The air crackles. Her wings wide.

Reads: TWO MONTHS LATER
1- Ext. Rooftop- day
Mid wide, Spider-woman on a dusty dirty rooftop, in profile, full figure. Spider-woman pulls off her mask as she contemplates her life. Lost in thought. Behind her the city glows.

NICK FURY
Jessica Drew.

SPIDER-WOMAN
Wow!

Are you @#$%ing me?

3- From behind Spider-Woman looking at the rooftop entrance of the roof she is standing on. Nick Fury is standing there hands in his long stylish coat. Walls of buildings box in the background.

NICK FURY
You look good, healthy.

SPIDER-WOMAN
I thought you left me hanging out to dry.

NICK FURY
So you're-

SPIDER-WOMAN
You set me up as a double agent reporting to both S.H.I.E.L.D. and Hydra and then you @#$%ed me over because of your stupid secret war.

NICK FURY
So you're angry.

4- From behind Nick, Spider-Woman, maskless approaches, pointing right at him.

SPIDER-WOMAN
They came to me.

Just like you said. S.H.I.E.L.D. Said give you up or they'll put me in prison. Threatened me right to my face, I said, go ahead. The guy bailed on me just like he bailed on you guys.

5- Nick shrugs and looks Spider-Woman in the eyes.

NICK FURY
Are you done?

SPIDER-WOMAN
I trusted you. Completely.

NICK FURY
And I ain't never lied to ya.

SPIDER-WOMAN
S.H.I.E.L.D. told me to go @#$% myself. So you know what that makes me.

A secret agent of Hydra with no way out of it. Thanks to you.

6- Nick knows this is asking a lot. It's almost funny how outlandish it is.

NICK FURY
I need you to go back to S.H.I.E.L.D. And grovel for a reinstatement.

7- Spider-Woman laughs at it, she can't help it.

SPIDER-WOMAN
What?

Page 20-
1- Over spider-Woman's shoulder, her hair whipping in the way of our view of very serious Fury.

NICK FURY
They'll take you back now. It'll be a demotion. Nothing glamorous.

But they need men. They certainly need someone of your skill set.

The whole anti-me thing is settlin' down. They have a business to run.

2- Spider-Woman is amazed he isn't joking.

SPIDER-WOMAN
What would I do that for?

3- Same as 1, but tighter.

NICK FURY
Well, based on my recon of ya the last couple of days, you need the work.

Secondly, I need your eyes in there.

4- Spider-Woman sneers at the invasion of privacy.

SPIDER-WOMAN
Spying on me now? Great.

And- hey- What do you want me there for? What am I looking for?

And wait, You don't work for anyone. So why are you asking me to do this?

5- Same as 3, but tighter.

NICK FURY
For mankind.

6- Spider-Woman sneers at the vagueness.

SPIDER-WOMAN
What am I looking for?

7- Same as 5, but tighter.

NICK FURY
Something... off.

8- Spider-Woman growls right at him.

SPIDER-WOMAN
Wow!

You'll have to do a whole lot better than that at this point in our relationship.

9- Same as 7, but tighter.

NICK FURY
You know what a Skrull is?

Page 21-
1- Profile, two shot. Thin long panel. Spider-Woman's curiosity is piqued. They are in each other's space. Talking quietly.

SPIDER-WOMAN
An alien?

NICK FURY
You ever seen one?

SPIDER-WOMAN
No.

NICK FURY
Thing is you wouldn't know it if you did. They can change shape. They can live among us.

SPIDER-WOMAN
And they're- you think they got into S.H.I.E.L.D.?

NICK FURY
Maybe.

SPIDER-WOMAN
How do we find out?

NICK FURY
Carefully.

SPIDER-WOMAN
Now you got me really creeped. How do I know you're not one?

NICK FURY
You don't. And I really don't know you're not...

2- Over Nick's shoulder Jessica pinches her nose at the intrusion into her life.

NICK FURY
Except that I've been watching you for three days.

SPIDER-WOMAN
I thought it was two.

NICK FURY
It's been a week.

SPIDER-WOMAN
That really creeps me out even more than the other thing.

3- Nick just waits for her to commit to him.

NICK FURY
Hey, what can I tell you. It's the times we live in.

You in?

4- Same as 2, but Jessica rolls her eyes at this even more insane predicament.

SPIDER-WOMAN
So now I'll be a triple agent.

Hydra, S.H.I.E.L.D., And I'm reporting back to you, who works for no one.

5- Spider-Woman squints at him. Nick shrugs, he just wants her to commit.

NICK FURY
Mankind.

SPIDER-WOMAN
Oh yeah, that's right.

NICK FURY
I know this is crappy. I know you've been in limbo. It is what it is.

SPIDER-WOMAN
Was that as close to an apology as I'm going to get out of you?

NICK FURY
You in?

6- Spider-Woman deflates. Of course she is in.

SPIDER-WOMAN
What are you going to do?

7- Int. Basement- night
Same shot of Spider-Woman. But its not her. It's a copied picture of her,

NICK FURY NARRATION
I'll tell you exactly what I'm going to do,

8- Same but wider, Spider-Woman's picture is one of four or five. It's part of what we see, a handful of pictures of the heroes of the Marvel Universe tacked up on a wall.

Spider-Woman is next to Speedball, Captain America, Falcon, Mr. Fantastic, The Sentry. Just hints of the others.

NICK FURY NARRATION
I'm going to figure this out.

I'm going to put all the pieces together.

Page 22-23-
Double page spread
Alex- You're going to curse my name, but this was a pretty easy issue up until now.

The entire spread, bleeding out in every direction. This entire wall of this dark, dank basement hideaway is covered with dozens and hundreds of Poloroid snapshots cut outs of portraits of the icons of the Marvel Universe.

Nick Fury is making a plan. Systematically trying to figure out the Skrull initiative. Everyone he has any association with is up on this wall.

Nick is on the bottom right of the spread. He is working on a laptop. He is working on something, boxes of evidence and clues and research to do. He is diligent. Consumed with his task as the greatest spy on earth, trying to figure out who his enemy is.

What we will reveal next issue is that this is the list of suspects. Not his plan.

He is not looking at the wall he has made that features Ms. Marvel, Iron Man, Wonder Man, Wasp, Black Widow, Sentry, Ares, Luke Cage, Iron Fist, Dr. Strange, Spider-Man, Spider-Woman, Wolverine, Echo, Ronin, Hawkeye, Hulkling, Patriot, Stature, Speed, Vision, Wiccan, Century, Cybermancer, Moonraker, Scarlet Witch, Spider-Woman (Julia Carpenter), U.S.Agent, Darkhawk, Human Torch, Living Lightning, Machine Man, Mantis, Mockingbird, Moon Knight, Henry Pym, Quicksilver, Thing, Tigra, U.S. Agent, War Machine, Hercules, Angel, Iceman, Ghost Rider, Darkstar, The Hulk, Namor, Silver Surfer, Nighthawk, Valkyrie, Hellcat, Clea, Hellstorm, Moondragon, Gargoyle, Andromeda, Doctor Doom, Captain Britain, Dazzler, Nocturne, Sage, Pete Wisdom, Nightcrawler, Phoenix (Rachel Summers), Shadowcat, Lockheed, Widget, Feron, Kylun, Colossus, Black Knight, Warlock, Wolfsbane, Psylocke, Juggernaut, Mister Fantastic, Invisible Woman, Sebastian Shaw, Emma Frost, Phoenix, Sage, Shinobi, Shaw, Donald Pierce, Magneto, Storm, Harry Leland, Trevor Fitzroy, Madelyne Pryor, Selene, Blob, Cyclops, Detonator, Forge, Juggernaut, Longshot, Mastermind, Multiple Man, Mystique, Rogue, Sabretooth, Toad, Unus the Untouchable, Venom, Black Bolt, Medusa, Karnak, Gorgon, Triton, Crystal, Lockjaw, Maximus the Mad, Daredevil, Black Widow 2, Dagger,

Punisher, Shang-Chi, Arachne, Weapon Alpha, Sasquatch, Talisman, Cannonball Danielle Moonstar, Karma, Sunspot, Magik, Magma, Cypher, Doctor Octopus, Shocker, Lizard, Electro, Kraven the Hunter, Mysterio, Sandman, Vulture, Hobgoblin, Hydro-Man, Aurora, Chamber, Copycat, Deadpool, Garrison Kane/Weapon X, Mastodon, Maverick/Agent Zero, Marrow, Sabretooth, Sauron, Silver Fox, Wildchild, X-23.

And many many others. Some are circled in red, some are circled in blue. There are little notes acribbled on some of them. Every idea and motivation he can think of he has jotted down.

This spread is about Fury's loneliness as much as it is about his tactical genius.

NICK FURY NARRATION
And when they show their hand,

I'm going to be ready.

To be continued...